LIBRARY
OWENS COMMUNITY COLLEG.
P.O. Box 10,000
Toledo, Ohio   43699

QP 406 .L53 2002

Lifespan development of
 human memory

DATE DUE

DEC 2 2 2006			
NOV 0 1 2007			
GAYLORD			PRINTED IN U.S.A.

Lifespan Development of Human Memory

Lifespan Development of Human Memory

edited by Peter Graf and Nobuo Ohta

LIBRARY
OWENS COMMUNITY COLLEGE
P.O. Box 10,000
Toledo, Ohio   43699

A Bradford Book
The MIT Press
Cambridge, Massachusetts
London, England

© 2002 Massachusetts Institute of Technology

All rights reserved. No part of this book may be reproduced in any form by any electronic or mechanical means (including photocopying, recording, and information storage and retrieval) without permission in writing from the publisher.

This book was set in Sabon on 3B2 by Asco Typesetters, Hong Kong, and was printed and bound in the United States of America.

First printing, 2002

Library of Congress Cataloging-in-Publication Data

Lifespan development of human memory / edited by Peter Graf, Nobuo Ohta.
     p.   cm.
"A Bradford book."
Includes bibliographical references and index.
ISBN 0-262-07236-X (alk. paper)
1. Memory. 2. Memory in children. 3. Memory in old age. 4. Alzheimer's disease. 5. Development neurobiology. I. Graf, Peter. II. Ohta, Nobuo.
QP406 .L53   2002
612.8'2—dc21   2002016661

Contents

LIBRARY
OWENS COMMUNITY COLLEGE
P.O. Box 10,000
Toledo, Ohio 43699

Preface

This collection of chapters surveys much of the exciting contemporary work on human memory and its development over the lifespan. The scope of the book is broad. It covers the childhood and adulthood development of memory and touches on the breakdown of memory functions in Alzheimer's disease; it includes chapters on working memory, on episodic and autobiographical memory, as well as on prospective memory. By itself, each of these topic areas defines a large, active, and growing field of research. Each has stimulated a host of investigations and resulted in a myriad specialized conferences and books. This book is intended as a counterweight to this proliferation of specialization. It brings together chapters from experts with different research foci, traditions, and methodologies. We hope that this will stimulate a broader perspective and produce a cross-fertilization that results in new investigations.

This book is intended for readers who want a brief introduction, from a cognitive-psychology perspective, to contemporary research on memory and its development across the lifespan. For advanced undergraduate students and graduate students, this book is a convenient gateway to the major theoretical issues that guide contemporary investigations. The book highlights core findings that support prevailing theoretical positions, as well as findings that challenge them. Finally, the book provides a short and accessible summary of the diverse methods and instruments used to investigate different aspects of memory at different stages of its development over the lifespan. We anticipate that this last contribution of the book will yield the greatest long-term benefits and hope that it will motivate and inspire researchers either to develop new methodologies or to adapt current methodologies so that they are suitable for use across the entire lifespan. This development would facilitate the growth of databases that permit more direct comparisons of memory abilities across the entire lifespan.

I

Introduction

1

The Need for a Lifespan Developmental Approach within Memory Research Is More Urgent than Ever

Nobuo Ohta

Reasons for Selecting Lifespan Memory Development as the Conference Theme

The second Tsukuba International Conference on Memory was held in Japan from 18 to 20 December 1999. The theme of the conference was lifespan memory development, and it brought together many researchers concerned with the development of memory from birth to old age with a view to discussing the pressing need for a coherent lifespan-memory approach. There were three main reasons—social, historical, and methodological—behind the selection of this conference theme.

Social reasons

In many societies in the world today the lifespan is increasing, with more and more people living longer and longer than ever before. A serious consequence of this general phenomenon is that the aging populations in these societies are becoming relatively larger. The situation is most acute in Japanese society, which actually has the fastest aging rate in the world. Indeed, according to some estimates, one in every four Japanese will be more than 65 years old by the year 2015. In Japan, there are many new political, financial, medical, and psychological problems associated with this aging population, but the situation is much the same in many countries. Thus, with the emergence of super-aging societies, there is a global need to find acceptable solutions to these problems.

As memory researchers and cognitive psychologists, we must be actively engaged in understanding the memory problems of older people to help make the increasingly longer old-age stages of life as comfortable and happy as possible. We need to conduct more research into the memory mechanisms of older people and into developing cures for memory disorders. Therefore, the first reason for making "lifespan memory development" the theme of our conference is that it is a very timely topic.

Historical reasons

The selection of the "lifespan memory development" theme for the conference was also based on a historical perspective of memory research. Looking back at the advances made in memory research during the last one hundred or so years since Ebbinghaus (1885) first conducted memory experiments, it is possible to identify a number of trends and studies, such as the seminal research by Bartlett (1932), that have been particularly influential in providing the impetus for still further progress. We hope that in the future when we look back at the present time, the lifespan memory development approach will also be seen as a contributing factor behind further advances in memory research. Although I shall trace the historical trends in memory research in more detail below, the lifespan-memory approach represents a natural progression within memory research and was thus felt to be a fitting theme for our conference.

Methodological reasons

Advances in science are often the result of methodological developments. This is also true in the field of memory research, where new methods, techniques, and approaches have led to the discovery of new facts and the formation of new theories. A clear example is the impact that the development of computers has had on cognitive science and a number of models of memory.

Although gerontology has had a long history, the lifespan-development approach has only become popular over the last few decades (Baltes, 1978). The lifespan-development approach regards the lifespan as a continuum, a complete entity, rather than as simply the sum of a series of separate, distinct life periods. Research into child psychology has been conducted for many years. However, much of this research has failed to recognize childhood as a period within the whole lifespan, for the prevailing approach has been to view children merely within childhood.

Although a central concern of memory research is to identify and explain the general mechanisms underlying memory, the vast majority of studies use young adults or university students as subjects. However, to be meaningful at all, these general mechanisms must be understood across the whole lifespan. This research, therefore, should not limit itself to only young adults, but must involve subjects of all ages. Thus, even when researching child memory or adult memory, it is important to approach memory with a lifespan-development perspective, which I shall describe in more detail later.

The Past, Present, and Future of Memory Research

Memory research has made many advances since Ebbinghaus (1885). In particular, I should like to mention five important milestones in the history of memory research.

Gestalt psychology

Although Gestalt psychology is perhaps most strongly associated with the field of perception, where it has been useful in accounting for a number of phenomenon, Gestalt psychologists believed that Gestalt laws are also applicable within the area of memory. Memory research at that time, therefore, was strongly influenced by Gestalt thought, and even today we can recognize Gestalt aspects in some cognitive models of memory.

Bartlett (1932)

This seminal study undoubtedly stands as an important milestone in the history of memory research. In contrast to the nonsense syllables devised by Ebbinghaus, Bartlett employed meaningful materials in his experiments. He firmly believed that experimentation should relate to the real world—a view that was later to find full expression in the work of Neisser (1978), who also stressed the importance of realism. Bartlett developed the notion of a schema to explain the results from a number of experiments that he conducted. Although eclipsed for a while during the heyday of behaviorism, the concept of a schema is still very influential in modern cognitive psychology.

The era of verbal learning

During the era of behaviorism, founded by Watson (1913), the term verbal learning was used instead of memory. Research focused on tasks such as paired associate learning and serial learning, using both words and nonsense syllables. One consequence of the importance behaviorism placed on experimental controls and the properties of stimulus-word items is that many of the norms for word association, image, frequency, and familiarity were standardized during this period and have continued to be used since. The notion of stimuli-response associations is useful in some research areas, where paired associate learning and serial learning are still being used by some researchers even today.

The information-processing approach

The information-processing approach emerged with the advent of computers, and advances were often closely linked with the developments in computing technology. Researchers cast human cognitive activities in terms of computer operations, breaking memory down into encoding, storage, and retrieval components. Shifting attention from the outwardly observable, which had been the prime focus of behaviorism, the information-processing approach focused on inner dimensions of human behavior. As a general cognitive-psychology model, the information-processing approach incorporated aspects of Gestalt psychology, as well as Bartlett's ideas. Compared with the earlier period of verbal learning, the information-processing approach has undoubtedly been more appealing to memory research, and indeed, a number of models concerned with the inner activities of the human mind have developed within this framework. However, this approach is not without its problems, principle among which are the difficulties faced in trying to test the validity of the models within the limitations of current psychological methods.

The start of everyday memory research

Criticizing the laboratory work that was flourishing at the time, Neisser (1978) emphasized the importance of ecological validity within memory research. Although the variables within an experimental design can be manipulated to varying degrees, the value of an experiment can be seriously undermined if the variables themselves are too artificial and un-realistic and the experiment produces results that cannot be explained in human terms. Further research on everyday memory is, therefore, essential to obtain the kind of qualitative data needed to understand the mechanisms underlying real human beings. There has been a general increase in everyday memory research since Neisser, as evidenced by the increased attention to topics such as face memory, flashbulb memory, and eyewitness memory. The more recent active research into prospective memory, autobiographical memory, and false memory, for example, is also partly due to the shift to everyday memory research.

Future milestones
Having identified five important milestones in the history of memory research during this century, it is interesting to speculate about what will be the major milestones in the 21st century. One very real candidate is real-world-problem research, where advances can be expected in the near future.

Recently, false-memory research has attracted a great deal of interest. This research developed originally from concerns about the reliability of testimony given during child-abuse cases. Eyewitness memory, which has been a topic of research for a few decades, is also strongly linked with real-world problems. As various real-world problems, such as pollution of the environment, population problems, international and regional disputes, and welfare, become more acute and strained in the 21st century, science will become increasingly concerned with the real world in the future. Scientists will have to become more involved in these problems, and memory researchers are no exception to this.

Although the formulation and development of new and better theories and models will continue to be important, research in the 21st century will need to be increasingly oriented to solving real-world problems. As the next milestone in the history of memory research, real-world-problem research will need to address a number of issues, one of which is memory in aging. Although aging memory has been researched for a long time, clearly we need to carry out further research into the memory mechanisms of older people and memory disorders. In conducting this research, we must not focus exclusively on older adults, but should rather take a lifespan-development approach to aging memory by also considering other generations, including younger adults as well as children.

The Influence of the Lifespan Approach on Memory Research

In the lifespan-development approach, a given stage of development is viewed in terms of the whole life. Although memory research with children and young adults has a longer history than that of aging memory, this has been an active area over the last couple of decades, and there is now a large body of experimental data for both younger and older people. This is essential for the lifespan approach, which has the potential to bring new insights when the experimental data for young adults are re-evaluated in comparison with data for older adults (and vice versa).

When we start to make these kinds of comparisons, we can start to identify interesting patterns in the lifespan development of memory. In figure 1, for example, 3 patterns for the lifespan development of memory are represented with memory abilities and age plotted along the vertical and horizontal axes, respectively. The first development pattern shows an initial increase in memory abilities with age until a peak is reached, after which there is a gradual decline in abilities with age. This pattern corresponds roughly to explicit memory, such as recall and recognition

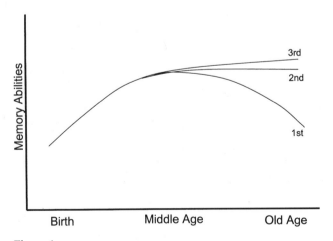

Figure 1
A conceptual representation of the patterns of lifespan memory development.

memory. The second development pattern is the same as the first development pattern up to the peak. However, the memory abilities do not decline even at old ages. Although the contrast between explicit and implicit memory in terms of increasing abilities in childhood is open to debate (Cycowicz, Friedman, Snodgrass & Rothstein, 2000), this development pattern corresponds roughly to implicit memory, such as priming and procedural memory. In the last development pattern, the memory abilities continue to rise throughout the whole lifespan, but what are these abilities? Generally speaking, unlike intelligence, as measured by standard intelligence tests, wisdom increases with age. Wisdom is a kind of intelligence—the practical intelligence of real life, covering, for example, interpersonal skills, ways of living, and problem-solving abilities. Although there has been some research on the characteristics of wisdom, there has been no research on "wisdom memory," which would fall under the third development pattern. Like other kinds of memory, wisdom memory is a product of an individual's experiences and knowledge.

Of the three lifespan development patterns, most research has been devoted to the first pattern. As for the second pattern, although much research has been conducted on implicit memory, there is still a need for further research in this area. However, there has been little research into the third lifespan-development pattern. This is unfortunate, for while it is not clear whether any memory abilities other than wisdom would follow this pattern of development, this direction is well worth exploring to map out the memory abilities of the aged.

The first lifespan development pattern

As just mentioned, there has been a great deal of research concerning the first lifespan-development pattern, in which initial increases in memory abilities continue up to a peak, after which there is a gradual decline in abilities with age. Comparisons of the increases and decreases in memory abilities with age are extremely useful, for they point to potentially very interesting characteristics in memory development. One of these is the symmetry between the increases in childhood and the reverse decreases in later life. Others are the qualitative differences in the nature of the memory abilities of the young and old. Two studies that suggest these kinds of developmental differences are a study of hypermnesia by

Olofsson and Ohta (1999) and a study of metamemory in older adults by Kawano (1999).

Olofsson and Ohta (1999) investigated hypermnesia, the increases in recall performance with successive tests for the same study episode, by comparing different age groups. There are two components in hypermnesia, reminiscence and forgetting, which have been found to be influenced by processing mode, with reminiscence being closely associated with item-specific processing and forgetting with relational processing. Specifically, Olofsson and Ohta investigated the lifespan changes in the balance of these two components and found that older adults had greater forgetting than young adults, although the level of reminiscence was the same for both the younger and older adults. This finding is interesting from the lifespan-development approach, for it seems to contrast with the balance of reminiscence and forgetting that Ohta (2001) found when comparing children of different ages, such as preschool children, who experienced greater forgetting than school children, although the level of reminiscence was similar for both. Such comparative studies into the symmetries between the increases in memory abilities that take place in childhood and the reverse decreases in later life will be an important part of lifespan-memory research in the future.

In a study of metamemory in older adults, Kawano (1999) found a significant negative correlation between memory self-efficacy and memory performance. This is in line with the memory-introspection paradox (Herrmann, 1982), which holds that individuals with poor memory aptitude have more difficulties in remembering just how poor their memories actually are. This finding is also interesting from the lifespan-development perspective, for this would seem to be a characteristic of the older adult's metamemory, which is not likely to be a part of the metamemory in a child. This seems to suggest qualitative differences in the nature of the memory abilities of the young and old.

Theories of lifespan memory development

Memory research taking a lifespan-development approach will, I hope, continue to make advances in the future. One area where more research needs to be conducted is in the formulation of general theories of the lifespan development of memory. The construction of comprehensive theories of lifespan development of memory is essential as a basis for future advances. The multiple-memory-systems theory advocated by Tulving and Schacter (1990) could possibly be extended into a theory of the lifespan development of memory. This theory specifies the multiple systems of episodic memory, semantic memory, a perceptual representation system, and procedural memory, which are arranged in this order from top to bottom in a linear hierarchy, with the higher-level systems being embedded in and supported by the lower-level memory systems. This structural organization is in line with the lifespan-development approach, for higher-level systems develop later than the lower-level systems, but the higher-level systems start to deteriorate earlier in older adults. Although this theory provides a basic framework for understanding the lifespan development of memory, accounts of the functional mechanisms within and between systems need to be developed.

What the lifespan approach promises

In addition to the new findings and theories mentioned above, the lifespan-memory approach will open up new exciting directions for memory research. The first new direction is research into environmental aspects of memory. Memory is not about just what is inside our heads but is also about how we utilize and interact with memory aids, such as notebooks, computers, and other people that exist in the environments around us. The effective use of these memory aids could be extremely beneficial for older adults, and with future technological advances, computers are likely to play an even larger role in daily life and even to help in alleviating some of the burdens on the human memory. Research into this will be a main topic for real-world memory research in the future.

A second direction will be memory research into how memory interacts with other functions, such as perception, thinking, emotional affect, and behavior. In line with the holistic perspective emphasized by the lifespan-memory approach, it is important to recognize that memory can rarely be studied in isolation from other functions. Although there has been little research in this area to date, this kind of research will increase in the future.

In sum, memory takes on different roles during the various stages in the lifespan. In childhood, the prime role is as a basis for intellectual development. In adulthood, memory is important in allowing people to work and function in society. In older adults, memory is important as the repository of the individual's experiences, a source of comfort in fondly recalling pleasant moments and a resource for reflection on life. These are just a few instances of the richness of memory, which we can start to see clearly when we adopt the lifespan-development approach to memory research.

Acknowledgment

I am grateful to Terry Joyce for correcting my English.

References

Baltes, P. B. (1978). *Life-span development and behavior*. Vol. 1. New York: Academic Press.

Bartlett, F. C. (1932). *Remembering*. Cambridge: Cambridge University Press.

Cycowicz, Y. M., Friedman, D., Snodgrass, J. G., & Rothstein, M. (2000). A developmental trajectory in implicit memory is revealed by picture fragment completion. *Memory, 8*, 19–35.

Ebbinghaus, H. (1885). Über das Gedachtnis. Leipzig, Germany: Dunker und Humbolt.

Herrmann, D. J. (1982). Know thy memory: The use of questionnaires to assess and study memory. *Psychological Bulletin, 92*, 434–452.

Kawano, R. (1999). Metamemory in older adults: Characteristics of metamemory and their correlation with memory performance. *Japanese Journal of Educational Psychology, 47*, 421–431. In Japanese.

Neisser, U. (1978). Memory: What are the important questions? In M. M. Gruneberg, P. E. Morris & R. N. Sykes (Eds.). *Practical aspects of memory*. London: Academic Press.

Ohta, N. (2001). Symmetry in the mechanisms of hyperamnesia in younger children and older adults. Poster session presented at the Third International Conference on Memory, July, Valencia, Spain.

Olofsson, U., & Ohta, N. (1999). Lifespan changes in the balance of reminiscence and forgetting in hypermnesia. Poster session presented at the Second Tsukuba International Conference on Memory, December, Tsukuba, Japan.

Tulving, E., & Schacter, D. L. (1990). Priming and human memory systems. *Science, 247*, 301–306.

Watson, J. B. (1913). Psychology as the behaviorist views it. *Psychological Review, 20*, 158–177.

II

The Development of Working Memory

2

Developmental Changes in Working Memory: A Multicomponent View

Graham J. Hitch

Working memory is the part of the human memory system that serves cognition by maintaining temporary information in an active state. Its limited capacity is thought to constrain performance in activities such as reading (Just & Carpenter, 1992), reasoning (Hitch & Baddeley, 1976), and mental calculation (Furst & Hitch, 2000). In view of such a wide-ranging role, it is not surprising that the development of working memory has been seen as playing an important role in cognitive development (Case, 1985; Halford, Wilson & Phillips, 1998). However, while the theoretical concept of working memory is at a stage of maturity where there is agreement on many points, several outstanding issues remain (see, e.g., the recent volume edited by Miyake & Shah, 1999). An important distinction is between working memory as a unitary system (Engle, Tuholski, Laughlin & Conway, 1999) or as multiple subsystems, each with a different capacity and function (Baddeley & Hitch, 1974; Baddeley, 1986). The present chapter describes research suggesting that a multiple subsystems approach is needed to describe the development of working memory. The broader question of how the development of working memory relates to cognitive development is not systematically addressed. However, links between components of working memory and different aspects of cognitive development are emphasized where they illustrate the value of the multicomponent approach.

Components of Working Memory

According to the multicomponent view of working memory proposed by Baddeley and Hitch (1974; see also Baddeley, 1986), working memory consists of a *central executive* closely linked to two modality-specific slave systems, a *phonological loop* and a *visuospatial sketchpad*. The central executive is a general-purpose coordinator that enables ongoing processing to be combined with the storage of temporary information and has access to the peripheral subsystems for support. The phonological loop and the visuospatial sketchpad are specialized for dealing with verbal and visuospatial information, respectively. This tripartite model was originally proposed to account for the interfering effects of performing a short-term memory task while performing a range of other cognitive tasks (Baddeley & Hitch, 1974). Subsequent research has elaborated its components as follows.

The phonological loop is capable of holding small amounts of *inner speech* in serial order over short intervals. It consists of a phonological store and a control process of subvocal rehearsal, which can be used to refresh decaying memory traces in the store (Baddeley, 1986). A major source of evidence about the loop has come from experiments on immediate serial recall of sequences of verbal items. Thus, the disruptive effect of phonemic similarity of items in immediate serial recall (Conrad & Hull, 1964) is explained in terms of the greater difficulty of discriminating partially decayed traces of similar items in the phonological store. The tendency for longer words to be less well recalled than shorter ones, known as the word-length effect (Baddeley, Thomson & Buchanan, 1975) is explained by noting that fewer long words can be refreshed within the time limit set by the rate of trace decay. This time-based interpretation of the loop is supported by the observation of an approximately linear relationship between number of words recalled and the time taken to articulate them as word length varies (Baddeley et al., 1975). A further feature of the phonological loop is that auditory-verbal stimuli are assumed to access the phonological store automatically, whereas visual stimuli have first to be recoded using subvocalization. Consistent with this account, disrupting subvocal rehearsal by requiring articulatory suppression removes the effect of word length for visual and auditory stimuli and removes the effect of phonemic similarity on memory for visual but not auditory stimuli (Baddeley, Lewis & Vallar, 1984).

Although recent data challenge aspects of this simplistic model of the phonological loop (Macken & Jones, 1995; Service, 1998), the general concept has proved remarkably robust and surprisingly fruitful in applications beyond its original remit. For example, the model has been used with some success to analyze selective impairments of auditory-verbal short-term memory in patients with brain lesions (Vallar & Baddeley, 1984a, 1984b). Functional imaging has been used to localize the phonological store and the articulatory rehearsal process in the healthy brain with results that fit with the neuropsychological evidence (Paulesu, Frith & Frackowiack, 1993). In addition, the phonological loop has been implemented as a connectionist network capable of simulating a much wider range of behavioral data than the simplistic conceptual model (Burgess & Hitch, 1999).

Despite ample evidence for dissociating visuospatial and verbal short-term storage systems, the visuospatial sketchpad is less well understood than the phonological loop. Logie (1995) has suggested that the sketchpad has a structure analogous to the loop and consists of a visual store (the "visual cache"), which can be refreshed or transformed by a dedicated control process (the "inner scribe"). However, it is not clear how far this analogy holds. For example, attempts to find a visuospatial analogue of the word-length effect have not proved fruitful (Smyth & Scholey, 1994). For present purposes, it is sufficient to note that there is a visual equivalent of the phonemic similarity effect in immediate memory for visual stimuli. Thus, under conditions that minimize the use of verbal recoding, visually similar stimuli are harder to recall than visually dissimilar stimuli (Walker, Hitch & Duroe, 1993). In Logie's (1995) model, one might assume that memory traces of visually similar items are more difficult to discriminate in the visual cache.

The last and perhaps least well specified component of Baddeley and Hitch's (1974) model is the central executive. Initially, this system was conceptualized as a limited capacity workspace in which resources for storage and processing trade off against each other (Hitch & Baddeley, 1976). This interpretation persists in various forms in models of working memory as a unitary system. Subsequently, however, Baddeley (1986) moved towards the concept of the executive as a purely attentional system, as in Norman and Shallice's Supervisory Attentional System (1986). More recently, due in part to evidence that different executive tasks do not all appear to reflect the same construct, an attempt has been made to fractionate the executive into components serving different functions, such as resource sharing and selective attention (Baddeley, 1996). However, the concept of a fractionated executive has yet to feed through into studies of development. Accordingly, this discussion will focus on the adequacy of developmental accounts that assume the executive behaves as a central workspace where resources for processing and storage trade off against each other.

For the purpose of theoretical clarification, it is useful to regard unitary models of working memory (e.g., Case, 1985; Engle et al., 1999) as mapping onto the executive component in Baddeley and Hitch's model. We also note models assuming that there are different working-memory systems for different domains of cognition, such as language and number (see, e.g., Just & Carpenter, 1992; Daneman & Carpenter, 1980; Daneman & Tardif, 1987). In terms of Baddeley and Hitch's model, these approaches are equivalent to the claim that there are different central executives for different domains.

Developmental Changes in the Phonological Loop

It is well established that the span of immediate memory for verbal items is lower in children than in adults. A range of factors has been proposed to account for this developmental increase, including rehearsal strategies, chunking, and speed of encoding (see, e.g., Dempster, 1981, for a review). More recently, insights have emerged from applying the concept of the phonological loop. The principal findings concern the word-length effect.

As described earlier, studies of adults indicated that immediate serial recall of words of different length can be predicted from the time it takes to articulate the items (Baddeley et al., 1975). This empirical relationship suggested that recall is limited by the rate at which subvocal rehearsal can be used to refresh decaying phonological traces. Consistent with such an interpretation, faster speakers tend to have higher spans (Baddeley et al., 1975). Developmental studies of the word-length effect produced results that conform to the same empirical relationship as in adults (Nicolson, 1981; Hitch & Halliday, 1983; Hitch, Halliday & Littler, 1993; Hulme, Thomson, Muir & Lawrence, 1984). For example, Hulme et al. (1984) found that a single linear function described the relationship between recall of auditorily presented lists and articulation rate from 4 years of age through to adulthood. That is, the improvement in amount recalled during development can be predicted from the increase in speed of articulation. This empirical relationship is consistent with the concept of a time-based phonological loop and suggests continuity in its functional characteristics over a large part of development.

However, developmental data on the word-length effect raise a problem for interpreting the relationship between span and articulation rate in terms of speed of rehearsal. This is because other evidence has established that rehearsal develops around the ages of 6–9, implying that 4-year-olds are unlikely to be rehearsing (Flavell, Beach & Chinsky, 1966; see Kail, 1984, for an overview). Consistent with the late development of rehearsal, the correlation between individual differences in span and speech rate observed in adults is not seen in 4-year-olds (Gathercole, Adams & Hitch, 1994) and articulatory suppression does not disrupt immediate recall in 5-year-olds (Henry, 1991a). However, an ingenious study by Cowan, Day, Saults, Keller, Johnson, and Flores (1992) suggested that differences in rehearsal time are not the only cause of differences in the recall of long and short words. By varying the arrangement of short and long words within lists, Cowan et al. showed that the greater time taken to output long words contributes to their poorer recall. This is consistent with the decay of information in the phonological loop as longer output delays allow more time for forgetting. Indeed, in their connectionist implementation of the phonological loop, Burgess and Hitch (1999) assumed that articulation time has the same effect during recall as in rehearsal.

In a developmental study, Henry (1991b) reported data that point to the importance of output delays for observing the word-length effect in young children. She found that 5-year-olds were sensitive to word length in serial recall but not probed recall. Henry argued that as her probe task involved recalling only a single item, differences in output delays for long and short words were minimal. In contrast, serial recall resulted in large differences in output delays for lists of long and short words. When older children were investigated, Henry found that word length affected performance in both probed and serial recall, as expected from their development of rehearsal strategies. In the light of findings such as these,

Gathercole and Hitch (1993) suggested that the developmental growth of auditory-verbal short-term memory (STM) reflects the increased speed with which information can be read out from the phonological store during rehearsal or recall. Thus, the concept of the phonological loop has helped to describe developmental change in verbal short-term memory, and in turn, developmental data have helped clarify the operation of the phonological loop.

An important further question concerns the function of the phonological loop in development. Much research has focused on its role (or equivalently, that of auditory-verbal STM) in learning to read (see, e.g., Wagner & Torgerson, 1987). As the evidence for such a role is well-established, it will not be summarized here. Other work has found evidence for the involvement of the loop in cognitive skills such as arithmetic calculation (Hitch et al., 1987; see also Logie, Gilhooly & Wynn, 1984). However, it appears that a major function of the phonological loop is in acquiring native vocabulary (Baddeley, Gathercole & Papagno, 1998).

Gathercole and Baddeley (1989a, 1989b; see also Gathercole et al., 1992) reported a longitudinal study of the role of the phonological loop in vocabulary acquisition in children aged from 4 to 8. They took performance on a nonword repetition task as their principal measure of phonological STM. This task measures the ability to repeat individual nonwords containing different numbers of syllables and is simpler for children to comprehend than word or digit span. Cross-lagged correlational analyses in which differences in age and nonverbal intelligence were partialled out showed that nonword repetition at age 4 was a good predictor of vocabulary scores at age 5. Furthermore, this correlation was stronger than the backward association between nonword repetition at age 5 and vocabulary at age 4. These observations suggest that the phonological loop underpins vocabulary learning during this phase of development. When the children were older, similar correlational analyses indicated that nonword repetition is itself influenced by vocabulary skills, which suggests a complex developmental pattern. Research on language-impaired children provides further evidence for a link between the phonological loop and vocabulary. For example, Gathercole and Baddeley (1990) assessed nonword repetition and vocabulary skills in 8-to-9-year-old language-impaired children. As expected, the language-impaired children had poorer vocabulary scores than controls matched on nonverbal intelligence. More interesting, the language-impaired children were significantly poorer at nonword repetition than a group of younger children matched on language ability, which suggests that a deficit in the phonological loop was responsible for their language-learning difficulties. Thus, taken together, evidence from both normal and abnormal development indicates a close relationship between the phonological loop and native-vocabulary acquisition.

It seems that the loop is also involved in acquiring vocabulary in a second language. This has been demonstrated most dramatically in a neuropsychological patient with a selective impairment of auditory-verbal digit span. The patient showed no word-length effect in immediate serial recall and a phonemic-similarity effect only for spoken stimuli, which suggests an impairment of the phonological store (Vallar & Baddeley, 1984a). She showed normal learning of a list of word-word pairs that was repeated several times. However, unlike normal controls, she was unable to learn a list consisting of word-nonword pairs (Baddeley, Papagno & Vallar, 1988). Thus the patient was able to learn new combinations of familiar items, but damage to the phonological store prevented her from learning novel phonological forms.

Because of the obvious importance of vocabulary learning in the development of language and cognition, it is tempting to conclude that this is the primary role of the phonological loop. Interestingly, however, the original concept of the phonological loop made no reference to learning. A step toward rectifying this omission is the inclusion of a learning mechanism in Burgess and Hitch's (1999) network model of the phonological loop, though it remains to be seen whether this model is adequate for simulating vocabulary learning. The loop may also serve other functions besides vocabulary acquisition. We have already mentioned research on reading and arithmetic skills, and we note also evidence that the loop may provide a backup store in comprehension, for example when "first pass" parsing fails (see, e.g., Baddeley & Lewis, 1981; Caplan & Waters, 1999).

Developmental Changes in the Visuospatial Sketchpad

The development of the visuospatial sketchpad has received less attention than the phonological loop. One task used to study it assesses immediate memory for a sequence of spatial locations and is known as Corsi Blocks. The apparatus consists of a set of identical cubes arranged irregularly on a flat horizontal board. On each trial the experimenter touches a random subset of the blocks one at a time and the participant's task is to recall the sequence of locations by pointing. Span is assessed in the normal way by increasing the number of blocks touched until accurate recall is no longer possible. Neuropsychological evidence indicates a double dissociation between Corsi Blocks span and auditory-verbal memory span, consistent with the idea that they reflect different subsystems (De Renzi & Nichelli, 1975). Other evidence is consistent with this interpretation. For example, order of report has a large effect on digit span, such that backward span is lower than forward span, but there is no effect of order of report on Corsi span (Isaacs & Vargha-Khadem, 1989). Another type of evidence is the absence of correlations between individual differences in digit span and Corsi span, as shown in a recent study of 5- and 8-year-olds by Pickering, Gathercole, and Peaker (1998). However, as regards developmental change, Corsi span increases at about the same rate as digit span (Isaacs & Vargha-Khadem, 1989). This similarity is not inconsistent with the hypothesis that the two tasks tap different systems. However, it does suggest that a common factor is involved in developmental change. One proponent of such a view is Kail (1988), who found parallel developmental profiles for speed of processing in a range of tasks and interpreted them in terms of a common, global mechanism.

Another task used to study the development of the visuospatial sketchpad is immediate memory for sequences of pictorial stimuli. Pictures are interesting because they can be encoded visually and verbally. In adults, immediate memory for a series of pictured items is sensitive to word length and phonemic similarity of their names and is disrupted by articulatory suppression (Schiano & Watkins, 1981). This indicates a tendency to recode pictures verbally, using the phonological loop. However, in a similar task Hitch, Halliday, and Littler (1993) found no effect of word length of picture names in 4-year-olds. The word-length effect for pictures emerged progressively with age and became equivalent to its counterpart for verbal materials by age 11. The same developmental pattern was found for effects of phonemic similarity of picture names

(Hitch, Halliday, Schaafstal & Schraagen, 1988). Further studies have shown that young children are sensitive to the visual characteristics of the pictures (Hitch et al., 1988; Hitch, Woodin & Baker, 1989). Thus, Hitch et al. (1989) found that younger children had poorer memory for visually similar pictures, whereas older children were unaffected by visual similarity. Hitch et al. also found that when older children were required to perform articulatory suppression, they became sensitive to visual similarity. Thus, older children make use of the visuospatial sketchpad when their tendency to use verbal recoding is disrupted, which is consistent with adult data described earlier (Walker et al., 1993).

In theoretical terms, therefore, there seems to be a marked developmental change in how subsystems of working memory are used to remember nameable pictures. At around age 5, children primarily rely upon the visuospatial sketchpad, whereas only a few years later, they clearly prefer to use verbal recoding. The reasons for such a major qualitative change are not immediately obvious. One interpretation is that development of the functional capacity of the phonological loop makes verbal recoding of pictures an increasingly effective strategy. However, this explanation seems inadequate on the evidence that adults persist in using verbal recoding even when it impairs their performance. For example, Brandimonte, Hitch, and Bishop (1992) investigated adults' ability to manipulate mental images of recently presented visual stimuli. Performance was critically dependent on memory for the visual appearance of the stimuli. Nevertheless, participants showed a strong tendency to engage in verbal recoding, as evidenced by the improvement in their imagery performance when verbal recoding was disrupted by articulatory suppression. This rare instance of performance improving under dual-task conditions has been replicated on a number of occasions (Brandimonte, Hitch & Bishop, 1992; Hitch, Brandimonte & Walker, 1995). We note that the verbal overshadowing of memory for faces in adults (Schooler & Engstler-Schooler, 1990) may be a related phenomenon. A more plausible reason why verbal recoding becomes pervasive as development proceeds is that it gives access to the vast representational capacity of the language system. Normally, such recoding will be useful, but occasionally, as when memory for detailed visual appearance is required, it is disadvantageous.

However, such an account says nothing about what function the sketchpad serves in cognitive development. Unfortunately, we are far from answering this important question. Useful clues are provided by recent studies of children with Williams's syndrome, a genetic disorder accompanied by deficits in visuospatial and numerical skills but relatively normal language skills. Williams's children are markedly impaired on the Corsi Blocks task but relatively spared on digit span (Wang & Bellugi, 1994; Jarrold, Baddeley & Hewes, 1999). In contrast, children with Down's syndrome show the converse pattern. These observations suggest that the sketchpad may be necessary for the normal development of visuospatial and numerical skills. We note also that genetic dissociation lends further support to the hypothesis that the development of working memory involves separable components.

Developmental Changes in Executive Processes

As stated earlier, this discussion focuses on the concept of a central workspace in which resources for processing and storage trade off against each other. This approach uses tasks devised to measure *working memory span*, the ability to store information while performing processing operations (Daneman & Carpenter, 1980). For example, in a reading-span task, participants were presented with a series of unrelated sentences to read and comprehend, under instructions that they would be asked to recall the last word of each sentence immediately afterwards. By varying the number of sentences, it was possible to find out the span limit on how many sentence-final words could be maintained while reading. Daneman and Carpenter (1980) found that for college students, working memory span was much better at predicting performance on scholastic attainment tests than digit span, a task they viewed as lacking the critical requirement to combine processing with storage. Subsequent research, including variants of Daneman and Carpenter's original tasks, has confirmed working-memory span as a good predictor of cognitive abilities (Daneman & Merikle, 1996). Daneman and Carpenter's interpretation, which has not gone unquestioned, was that cognitive ability depends on the capacity of an individual's workspace. As noted earlier, the concept of a central workspace corresponds to the view of the executive in Baddeley and Hitch's (1974) model. The empirical dissociation between working-memory span and digit span fits their multicomponent model in that these tasks load differentially on the central executive and the phonological loop.

In the context of development, some intriguing findings were obtained using a working-memory span task known as counting span (Case, Kurland & Goldberg, 1982). In the counting span task a series of cards is presented, each containing target shapes among distractors of a different color. The child is required to count the number of target shapes on each card and, at the end of the series, to attempt to recall the count totals for all the cards. The number of cards is increased over trials to determine counting span. Case et al. (1982) measured counting span for children of different ages and, separately, the time it took children to count the target shapes. As expected, older children had higher counting spans, and they counted targets more rapidly than younger children. What was particularly interesting, however, was that when mean counting spans were plotted against mean counting times for different age groups, there was a linear relationship in which counting speed was an excellent predictor of counting span.

Case et al. (1982) interpreted their data in terms of a central workspace. They argued that the size of the workspace remains the same during development but that counting operations become more automatic, as indicated by their increased speed, and so require progressively less workspace for their execution. Thus, for older children, more workspace is available for storing count totals. In this way Case et al. neatly explained the developmental relationship between counting span and counting speed. They went on to investigate the causal basis of the relationship by studying the effect of requiring adults to count using nonsense syllables. This resulted in commensurate reductions in counting speed and counting span, which suggests that counting span is determined by counting speed. Subsequently, Case (1985) built an influential neo-Piagetian theory of cognitive development in which the increase in the amount of workspace available for storage allows progressively more complex tasks to be performed. However, it is interesting to note that the empirical relationship between counting span and counting speed is similar in form to that between word span and articulation rate described earlier. This raises the question of what justifies an interpretation in terms of capacity in one case and decay of stored information in the other.

To address these issues, Towse and Hitch (1995) examined the effect on counting span of varying the amount of attention required for counting operations in children aged from 6 to 11. The workspace model predicts that span will be lower when the counting process requires more attentional capacity. Studies of visual search have shown that distinguishing targets from distractors requires more attention when targets are defined by a feature conjunction than when they can be distinguished on the basis of a single feature (Treisman & Gelade, 1980). Accordingly, in one version of the counting-span task targets were differentiated by a feature conjunction (color and shape) and in another they were distinguished by a single feature (color). To control for the fact that conjunction search takes longer than feature search, a third version of the task was included. This version consisted of feature search with extra targets, such that the total time taken to count was the same as for conjunction search. The results revealed that for all age groups, the critical variable determining span was the time it took to count targets and not the attentional demands of the search process. Thus, counting span was lower when counting took longer, and there was no effect of attentional difficulty. These observations question the appropriateness of the workspace model of counting span. Towse and Hitch proposed instead a *task-switching* model that assumes children alternate between processing and storage in successive phases of the counting-span task rather than sharing resources simultaneously between processing and storage. The task-switching model makes the further assumption that stored information loses activation during intervals when attention is switched away from storage and onto counting operations. Towse and Hitch argued that the developmental relationship between counting span and counting speed reported by Case et al. (1982) may reflect shorter intervals for count totals to lose activation and be forgotten when counting is completed faster, rather than changes in the allocation of resources in a central workspace.

In a further study, Towse and Hitch (1998) looked again to see whether resource-sharing might be a strategy that emerges during development. They evaluated further predictions of the task-switching and resource-sharing models in 6-to-11-year-olds and assessed whether results generalize to other working-memory-span tasks besides counting span. A series of experiments involving reading span, operation span, and counting span compared performance on two versions of each span task. These differed with respect to the time for which temporary information had to be held in store but were equated for the total amount of processing required. According to the workspace model, this manipulation should not affect span. However, task-switching predicts that spans will be lower when temporary information has to be retained over a longer interval.

In the operation-span task, children were shown a series of arithmetic sums one after another. As soon as the child announced the answer to the first sum, the next sum was shown, and so on. At the end of the series the child attempted to recall the answers to each of the sums in turn. The number of sums was increased progressively to determine operation span (see Towse & Hitch, 1998, for further details). The experimental manipulation centered on the order of presenting sums within trials. Thus, in a *short-final* version, each trial started with a sum that took a relatively long time to compute (e.g., $6 + 1 - 0 - 1 =$) and ended with a sum that could be done much more quickly (e.g., $5 + 1 =$). In a *long-final* version the ordering of first and last sums was reversed. Sums at middle positions in the series were equivalent. Thus the two versions of the task were matched for amount of arithmetic processing but differed in that temporary results had to be stored over a longer interval in the long-final version. Analogous short- and long-final versions were constructed for the reading-span and counting-span tasks.

To reiterate, the task-switching model predicts that spans will be lower in the long-final version of each task because there is more time for stored information to lose activation and be forgotten. According to the shared workspace model, span should be unaffected by stimulus order. Note, however, that the storage load increases by one item after processing each stimulus. Thus, according to the workspace model, the capacity available for processing decreases as the trial progresses, which implies that operations should become slower and less accurate. In contrast, the task-switching model generates no expectation about changes in the speed and accuracy of processing within a trial.

The key finding was that for all three tasks, spans were lower in the long-final condition, as predicted by task-switching. Interestingly, this effect of stimulus order did not interact with age, which provides further support for the view that there is no developmental progression from resource-switching to resource-sharing. Changes in the speed and accuracy of processing operations from the beginning to the end of each trial were inconsistent across tasks and experiments. Most comparisons were nonsignificant and significant differences were found on occasion in both directions. Accordingly, Towse et al. (1998) concluded that their data gave no unequivocal support for resource sharing.

The effect of stimulus order is clearly very general in that it occurred in three very different working-memory-span tasks and at all ages at which children were studied. Other work confirms the absence of developmental change in this pattern by showing similar effects of stimulus order in reading span and operation span in adults (Towse, Hitch & Hutton, 2000). However, it would be premature to conclude that span is determined entirely by task switching and decay. For one thing, the experiments may not have provided a sufficiently sensitive test for resource sharing. Furthermore, evidence for task switching is not necessarily evidence against resource sharing. Thus, it is easy to imagine more complex models that combine features of both. Nevertheless, the results pose serious questions for the view that working-memory span is a straightforward way of measuring the capacity of a central workspace and for a capacity-based interpretation of the developmental relationship between working-memory span and processing speed.

More recent work (Hitch, Towse, & Hutton, 2001) has involved a one-year longitudinal follow-up of children who performed the reading- and operation-span tasks reported by Towse and Hitch (1998). The effects of stimulus order on spans were replicated, but this time there was a suggestion that processing became slower and less accurate toward the end of a trial. However, effects were once again small and somewhat marginal. Post hoc considerations suggest that they may have reflected extra rehearsal at the ends of trials, and accordingly, the overall impact of the later study is to reinforce the conclusions drawn by Towse et al. (1998).

Further analyses were made possible by combining data from the two studies. The first of these looked at whether the developmental relationship between counting span and counting speed reported by Case et al. (1982) generalizes to other working-memory-span tasks. To assess this, a plot was made of reading span against reading time (with one data point for each combination of age cohort and test wave) and the same was done for operation span. The two graphs confirmed that there was a linear relationship between span and processing speed for each task. However, the parameters of the two lines were clearly different. If each span task taps a common workspace in which resources for processing and storage trade off against each other, then the two speed/span functions should be the same. Different functions can be accommodated by the shared-workspace model if it is assumed that there are at least two workspaces and that different tasks tap into them differently, consistent with the approach taken by Daneman and Carpenter (1980), Daneman and Tardiff (1987), and Just and Carpenter (1992). However, such a proliferation decreases the theoretical appeal of the workspace model, not to mention its explanatory power. The task-switching model also predicts identical speed/span relationships for different span tasks on the assumption that forgetting is entirely due to time-based decay. Clearly, this version of the task-switching model can be rejected. However, if other time-consuming processes, such as interference, contribute to forgetting, then there is no reason to expect rates of forgetting to be the same in different span tasks. Thus task switching can also accommodate different speed/span functions. However, it is clear that we need to know much more about the dynamics of forgetting in working memory if the task-switching model is to be used predictively.

Children in the longitudinal study were also given standardized tests of reading (The British Abilities Scale Reading Test) and arithmetic (The British Abilities Scale Number Skills Test). The purpose of doing this was to examine relationships with working-memory span. Correlations computed on a total of 79 children showed that operation span was highly correlated with arithmetic attainment ($r = 0.57$) and that reading span was highly correlated with reading attainment ($r = 0.67$). Further analyses used multiple regression techniques to evaluate how well spans predicted scholastic attainment after allowing for variation attributable to age and various measures of processing speed (see Hitch et al., 2001, for details). In the case of arithmetic attainment, reading span and operation spans accounted for significant shared variance. They each explained roughly 10% of the variance in arithmetic attainment when entered in the penultimate step of the regression equation and negligible further variance when entered last. In the case of reading attainment, the picture was interestingly different. Thus, while the two span tasks explained shared variance in reading scores, they also explained a smaller but significant amount of unique variance.

These individual-difference analyses confirm that, like other measures of working-memory span, reading span and operation span are good predictors of children's scholastic abilities. In theoretical terms, the correlations suggest that the tasks tap common as well as different cognitive functions. Leather and Henry (1994) reached a similar conclusion using different span tasks, and there is also evidence linking deficits in different working memory span tasks with different types of learning disability (Siegel & Ryan, 1989; but see also Hitch & McAuley, 1991). In principle, either multiple workspace models or the multicomponent model with a single executive can accommodate shared and unique variance in different span tasks. However, to decide between them it is necessary to know more about the nature of the shared and unique variance.

On a practical note, the Hitch et al. (2001) study provided evidence that working-memory span is a longitudinal predictor of scholastic attainment. Fixed-order multiple regressions were used to predict either reading or arithmetic scores at the second wave of testing. Age was entered first, then working-memory span at the second wave, and finally working-memory span at the first wave. The outcome was that working-memory span at the first wave explained significant unique variance in both reading and arithmetic scores at the second wave. This observation suggests that working memory is crucial for acquiring reading and arithmetic skills. It provides valuable confirmation that working-memory span is a useful measure of individual ability, even though, as we have seen, there are still many unresolved theoretical questions about how it should be interpreted.

Summary and Conclusions

We have briefly considered some of the evidence on the development of working memory in children using the multicomponent model of Baddeley and Hitch (1974) as an organizing framework. In doing so, we have seen that making a distinction between the phonological loop and the visuospatial sketchpad sheds light on the course of development. Although simple memory spans reflecting these components appear to develop at the same rate, there is a marked developmental shift in which older children and adults, unlike younger children, recode visual materials verbally using the phonological loop. We note that this tendency can be so strong as to persist even in tasks where it is highly inappropriate. In contrast, younger children rely on the visuospatial sketchpad to remember visual materials. Further evidence indicates that the development of the two subsystems can be selectively disrupted by different types of genetic disorder. In the light of such evidence it seems difficult to maintain that the development of working memory involves a single, undifferentiated system.

At present, much more is known about the development and functional significance of the phonological loop than of the sketchpad. We know, for example, that the developmental increase in short-term memory for verbal materials is closely related to the developmental increase in articulation speed. A simple interpretation of this relationship is that faster subvocalization offsets effects of the decay of information in the phonological loop. However, recent data have questioned a simple time-based account of the word-length effect, and it remains to be seen what implications this has for accounts of developmental change. There is evidence that the phonological loop serves important functions during development and is particularly strongly associated with vocabulary learning and learning to read. In contrast, the development of the visuo-spatial subsystem is much less well understood in terms of how it changes and what role it plays in cognitive development.

To turn lastly to the important topic of the central executive, we have focused on the assumption that working-memory span reflects the capacity of a central workspace in which resources are shared between storage and processing. Evidence for stimulus-order effects in a variety of working-memory-span tasks casts doubt on the workspace metaphor and favors instead an interpretation in terms of task switching. In this alternative account, working-memory span is limited by the rate of loss of activation of temporary information during ongoing processing. Speed of processing operations is important because it affects the intervals over which temporary information has to be maintained and hence the amount of forgetting. Nevertheless, a simple model of task switching combined with time-based decay of recently stored information cannot account for the observation that developmental functions relating working-memory span to processing speed are different for different tasks. These differences can be accommodated by assuming that forgetting rates vary, but more evidence is needed to justify this assumption. Working-memory span is evidently a useful longitudinal predictor of scholastic attainment. Thus, however one interprets it, the ability to combine temporary information storage with ongoing processing is a clearly an important component in the development of cognitive skills.

We conclude that looking at the development of working memory as a multicomponent system is fruitful. This approach provides a better description of developmental data than the concept of a unitary system. In their turn, developmental data provide useful information about working memory. However, as will by now be obvious, we must acknowledge that we are only just beginning to unfold the larger picture of how working memory develops and how it contributes to cognitive development.

References

Adams, J. W., & Hitch, G. J. (1997). Working memory and children's mental addition. *Journal of Experimental Child Psychology, 67* (1), 21–38.

Ashcraft, M. H. (1995). Cognitive psychology and simple arithmetic: A review and summary of new directions. *Mathematical Cognition, 1,* 3–34.

Baddeley, A. D. (1986). *Working memory.* Oxford: Clarendon Press.

Baddeley, A. D., Lewis, V. J., & Vallar, G. (1984). Exploring the articulatory loop. *Quarterly Journal of Experimental Psychology, 36,* 233–252.

Baddeley, A. D., & Lewis, V. J. (1981). Inner active processes in reading: The inner voice, the inner ear and the inner eye. In A. M. Lesgold & C. A. Perfetti (Eds.), *Interactive processes in reading* (pp. 1107–1129). Hillsdale, N.J.: Lawrence Erlbaum.

Baddeley, A. D., & Hitch, G. J. (1974). Working memory. In G. Bower (Ed.), *The psychology of learning and motivation: Advances in research and theory* (pp. 47–90). New York: Academic Press.

Baddeley, A. D., Papagno, C., & Vallar, G. (1988). When long-term learning depends on short-term storage. *Journal of Memory and Language, 27*, 586–596.

Baddeley, A. D., Thomson, N., & Buchanan, M. (1975). Word length and the structure of short-term memory. *Journal of Verbal Learning and Verbal Behavior, 14*, 575–589.

Brandimonte, M. A., Hitch, G. J., & Bishop, D. V. M. (1992). Influence of short-term memory codes on visual image processing: Evidence from image transformation tasks. *Journal of Experimental Psychology: Learning, Memory, and Cognition, 18*, 157–165.

Brandimonte, M. A., Hitch, G. J., & Bishop, D. V. M. (1992). Verbal recoding of visual stimuli impairs mental image transformations. *Memory and Cognition, 20*, 44–455.

Burgess, N., & Hitch, G. J. (1999). Memory for serial order: A network model of the phonological loop and its timing. *Psychological Review, 106*, 551–581.

Caplan, D., & Waters, G. S. (1999). Verbal working memory and sentence comprehension. *Behavioral & Brain Sciences, 22*, 77–94.

Case, R. (1985). *Intellectual development: Birth to adulthood.* New York: Academic Press.

Case, R., Kurland, M., & Goldberg, J. (1982). Operational efficiency and the growth of short term memory span. *Journal of Experimental Child Psychology, 33*, 386–404.

Conrad, R., & Hull, A. J. (1964). Information, acoustic confusion and memory span. *British Journal of Psychology, 55*, 429–432.

Cowan, N., Day, L., Saults, J. S., Keller, T. A., Johnson, T., & Flores, L. (1992). The role of verbal output time in the effects of word length on immediate memory. *Journal of Memory and Language, 31*, 1–17.

Daneman, M., & Carpenter, P. A. (1980). Individual differences in working memory and reading. *Journal of Verbal Learning and Verbal Behavior, 19*, 450–466.

Daneman, M., & Merikle, P. (1996). Working memory and language comprehension: A meta-analysis. *Psychological Bulletin and Reviews, 3*, 422–433.

Daneman, M., & Tardif, T. (1987). Working memory and reading skill re-examined. In M. Coltheart (Ed.), *Attention and performance* (pp. 491–508). Hillsdale, N.J.: Erlbaum.

De Renzi, E., & Nichelli, P. (1975). Verbal and nonverbal short term memory impairment following hemisphere damage. *Cortex, 11*, 341–353.

Dempster, F. N. (1981). Memory span: Sources of individual and developmental differences. *Psychological Bulletin, 89*, 63–100.

Engle, R. W., Tuholski, S. W., Laughlin, J. E., & Conway, A. R. A. (1999). Working memory, short-term memory, and general fluid intelligence: A latent-variable approach. *Journal of Experimental Psychology: General, 128,* 309–331.

Flavell, J. H., Beach, D. R., & Chinsky, J. M. (1966). Spontaneous verbal rehearsal in a memory task as a function of age. *Child Development, 37,* 283–299.

Furst, A., & Hitch, G. J. (2000). Separate roles for executive and phonological components of working memory in mental arithmetic. *Memory & Cognition, 28,* 774–782.

Gathercole, S. E., Adams, A. M., & Hitch, G. J. (1994). Do young children rehearse? An individual differences analysis. *Memory & Cognition, 22,* 201–207.

Gathercole, S. E., & Baddeley, A. D. (1989a). Evaluation of the role of phonological STM in the development of vocabulary in children: A longitudinal study. *Journal of Memory & Language, 28,* 200–213.

Gathercole, S. E., & Baddeley, A. D. (1989b). The role of phonological memory in normal and disordered language development. In C. von Euler, I. Lundberg & G. Lennenstrand (Eds.), *Brain and reading* (pp. 245–255). Macmillan Press.

Gathercole, S. E., & Baddeley, A. D. (1990). Phonological memory deficits in language disordered children: Is there a causal connection? *Journal of Memory and Language, 29,* 336–360.

Gathercole, S. E., Willis, C., Emslie, H., & Baddeley, A. D. (1992). Phonological memory and vocabulary development during the early school years: A longitudinal study. *Developmental psychology, 28,* 887–898.

Gathercole, S. E., & Hitch, G. J. (1993). Developmental changes in short-term memory: A revised working memory perspective. In A. F. Collins, S. E. Gathercole, M. A. Conway & P. E. Morris (Eds.). *Theories of Memory* (pp. 189–209). Hove: Lawrence Erlbaum Associates.

Halford, G. S., Wilson, W. H., & Phillips, S. (1998). Processing capacity defined by relational complexity: Implications for comparative, developmental, and cognitive psychology. *Behavioral and Brain Sciences, 21,* 803–837.

Henry, L. A. (1991a). The effects of word length and phonemic similarity in young children's short-term memory. *Quarterly Journal of Experimental Psychology, 43* (A), 35–52.

Henry, L. A. (1991b). Development of auditory memory span: The role of rehearsal. *British Journal of Developmental Psychology, 9,* 493–511.

Hitch, G. J., & Baddeley, A. D. (1976). Verbal reasoning and working memory. *Quarterly Journal of Experimental Psychology, 28,* 603–621.

Hitch, G. J., Brandimonte, M. A., & Walker, P. (1995). Two types of representation in visual memory: Evidence from the effects of stimulus contrast on image combination. *Memory & Cognition, 23,* 147–154.

Hitch, G. J., Cundick, J., Haughey, M., Pugh, R. and Wright, H. (1987). Aspects of counting in children's arithmetic. In J. A. Sloboda and D. Rogers (Eds.), *Cognitive processes in mathematics* (pp. 26–41). Oxford: Clarendon Press.

Hitch, G. J., & Halliday, M. S. (1983). Working memory in children. *Philosophical Transactions of the Royal Society London, B 302*, 325–340.

Hitch, G. J., Halliday, M. S., & Littler, J. E. (1993). Development of memory span for spoken words: The role of rehearsal and item identification processes. *British Journal of Developmental Psychology, 11*, 159–169.

Hitch, G. J., Halliday, M. S., Schaafstal, A., & Schraagen, J. M. (1988). Visual working memory in young children. *Memory and Cognition, 16*, 120–132.

Hitch, G. J., & McAuley, E. (1991). Working memory in children with specific arithmetical learning difficulties. *British Journal of Psychology, 82*, 375–386.

Hitch, G. J., & Towse, J. N. (1995). Working memory: What develops? In F. E. Weinert & W. Schneider (Eds.), *Memory performance and competencies: Issues in growth and development* (pp. 3–21). Mahwah, N.J.: Erlbaum.

Hitch, G. J., Towse, J. N., & Hutton, U. (2001). What limits children's working memory span? Theoretical accounts and applications for scholastic development. *Journal of Experimental Psychology: General, 130*, 184–198.

Hitch, G. J., Woodin, M., & Baker, S. L. (1989). Visual and phonological components of working memory in children. *Memory and Cognition, 17*, 175–185.

Hulme, C., Thomson, N., Muir, C., & Lawrence, A. (1984). Speech rate and the development of short-term memory span. *Journal of Experimental Child Psychology, 38*, 241–253.

Isaacs, E. B., & Vargha-Khadem, F. (1989). Differential course of development of spatial and verbal memory span: A normative study. *British Journal of Developmental Psychology, 7*, 377–380.

Jarrold, C., Baddeley, A. D., & Hewes, A. K. (1999). Genetically dissociated components of working memory: Evidence from Down's and Williams's syndrome. *Neuropsychologia, 37*, 637–651.

Just, M. A., & Carpenter, P. A. (1992). A capacity theory of comprehension: Individual differences in working memory. *Psychological Review, 99* (1), 122–149.

Kail, R. (1984). *The development of memory in children*. 2nd Ed. New York: W. H. Freeman & Co.

Kail, R. (1988). Developmental functions for speeds of cognitive processes. *Journal of Experimental Child Psychology, 45*, 339–364.

Leather, C. V., & Henry, L. A. (1994). Working memory and phonological awareness tasks as predictors of early reading ability. *Journal of Experimental Child Psychology, 58*, 88–111.

Logie, R. H. (1995). *Visuo-spatial working memory*. Lawrence Erlbaum.

Logie, R. H., Gilhooly, K. J., & Wynn, V. (1994). Counting on working memory in arithmetic problem solving. *Memory & Cognition, 22*, 395–410.

Macken, W. J., & Jones, D. M. (1995). Functional characteristics of the 'inner voice' and the 'inner ear': Single or double agency? *Journal of Experimental Psychology: Learning, Memory, and Cognition, 21*, 436–448.

Miyake, A., & Shah, P. (1999). *Models of working memory: Mechanisms of active maintenance and executive control.* Cambridge: Cambridge University Press.

Nicolson, R. S. (1981). The relationship between memory span and processing speed. In M. Friedman, J. P. Das & N. O'Connor (Eds.) *Intelligence and learning* (pp. 179–184). Plenum Press.

Norman, D. A., & Shallice, T. (1986). Attention to action: Willed and automatic control of behavior. In R. J. Davidson, G. E. Schwartz & D. E. Shapiro (Eds.), *Consciousness and self-regulation: Advances in research and theory* (vol. 4, pp. 1–18). New York: Plenum.

Paulesu, E., Frith, C. D., & Frackowiack, R. S. J. (1993). The neural correlates of the verbal component of working memory. *Nature, 362,* 342–344.

Pickering, S. J., Gathercole, S. E., & Peaker, S. M. (1998). Verbal and visuo-spatial short-term memory in children: Evidence for common and distinct mechanisms. *Memory & Cognition, 26,* 1117–1130.

Schiano, D. J., & Watkins, M. J. (1981). Speech-like coding of pictures in short-term memory. *Memory & Cognition, 9,* 110–114.

Schooler, J. W., & Engstler-Schooler, T. Y. (1990). Verbal overshadowing of visual memories: Some things are better left unsaid. *Cognitive Psychology, 22,* 36–71.

Service, E. (1998). The effect of word length on immediate serial recall depends on phonological complexity, not articulatory duration. *Quarterly Journal of Experimental Psychology, 51A,* 283–304.

Siegel, L. S., & Ryan, E. B. (1989). The development of working memory in normal achieving and subtypes of learning disabled children. *Child Development, 60,* 973–980.

Schneider, W., & Shiffrin, R. (1977). Controlled and automatic human information processing. I: Detection search and attention. *Psychological Review, 84,* 1–126.

Smyth, M. M., & Scholey, K. A. (1994). Characteristics of spatial memory: Is there an analogy to the word length effect, based on movement time? *Quarterly Journal of Experimental Psychology, 47A,* 91–117.

Towse, J. N., & Hitch, G. J. (1995). Is there a relationship between task demand and storage space in tests of working memory capacity? *Quarterly Journal of Experimental Psychology, 48A* (1), 108–124.

Towse, J. N., Hitch, G. J., & Hutton, U. (1998). A reevaluation of working memory capacity in children. *Journal of Memory and Language, 39,* 195–217.

Towse, J. N., Hitch, G. J., & Hutton, U. (2000). On the interpretation of working memory span in adults. *Memory & Cognition, 28,* 341–348.

Treisman, A., & Gelade, G. (1980). A feature integration theory of attention. *Cognitive Psychology, 12,* 97–136.

Turner, M. L., & Engle, R. W. (1989). Is working memory capacity task dependent? *Journal of Memory and Language, 28,* 127–154.

Vallar, G., & Baddeley, A. D. (1984a). Fractionation of working memory: Neuropsychological evidence for a phonological short-term store. *Journal of Verbal Learning and Verbal Behavior, 23,* 151–161.

Vallar, G., & Baddeley, A. D. (1984b). Phonological short-term store, phonological processing and sentence comprehension: A neuropsychological case-study. *Cognitive Neuropsychology, 1,* 121–141.

Wagner, R. K., & Torgerson, J. K. (1987). The nature of phonological processing and its causal role in the acquisition of reading skills. *Psychological Bulletin, 101,* 192–212.

Walker, P., Hitch, G. J., & Duroe, S. (1993). The effect of visual similarity on short-term memory for spatial location: Implications for the capacity of visual short-term memory. *Acta Psychologica, 83,* 203–224.

Wang, P. P., & Bellugi, U. (1994). Evidence from two genetic syndromes for a dissociation between verbal and visuo-spatial short-term memory. *Journal of Clinical and Experimental Neuropsychology, 16,* 317–322.

Waters, G. S., & Caplan, D. (1996). The measurement of verbal working memory capacity and its relation to reading comprehension. *Quarterly Journal of Experimental Psychology, 49A* (1), 51–70.

3

Childhood Development of Working Memory: An Examination of Two Basic Parameters

Nelson Cowan

Introduction

The two aims of this paper are synergistic. One is a substantive aim: to build an understanding of the development of the elementary processes of working memory in childhood more fully than has been done in the past. By "working memory" I refer to the limited amount of information that can be held temporarily in order to carry out a cognitive task (Cowan, 1988, 1995, 1999a). The second is a methodological aim: to refine a method that can be used to study developmental change in cognitive processes, without the well-known contamination that comes from age differences in the effective level of difficulty of the test materials.

First, I will explain a new methodological approach (Cowan, Saults et al., 1999). It provides a way to obtain what will be termed *difficulty-insensitive* measures of working memory. Then I will briefly explain a set of theoretical working assumptions and, on that foundation, will apply the difficulty-insensitive method to an understanding of two basic parameters of working memory: (1) the rate at which words are retrieved from short-term memory and (2) the capacity of short-term memory for words. The conclusions in both of these areas differ from conventional wisdom that has been put forward by most previous investigators, illustrating the potential of the methods.

Methods of Examining Developmental Change in Cognitive Processes

It is perfectly clear that performance on complex cognitive tasks improves with age in children. The question of interest for cognitive development is what mechanisms account for that improvement. Next I will compare two methods for addressing it.

The traditional differential-deficits approach

The usual method for addressing the question of what distinguishes information processing in different age groups (or, more generally, what distinguishes processing in any two different populations) has been to identify *differential deficits* in performance. In a differential deficit, the groups under study differ in some task A more than they do in some other task B. Therefore, it is said that some process that contributes to task A more than to task B changes with age. However, there are some thorny problems that one faces in assessing the meaning of differential deficits (e.g., Chapman & Chapman, 1978). For example, one must ensure that the differential deficit does not result from different ranges of performance for the different tasks, such that the performance range of task A is more sensitive to condition differences than the performance range of task B.

The existing methods for circumventing these problems are not wholly satisfying. Let me illustrate the problem using a hypothetical example related to working memory. Suppose that one wanted to test the theory that the speed of short-term memory retrieval of abstract words is faster in adults than it is in children. To observe an interpretable differential deficit, one could vary the length of lists of concrete words to identify list lengths that yield equivalent performance levels in the two age groups. A hypothetical data set yielding this pattern of results is shown in figure 1. It indicates that children's reaction times for two-word lists are equivalent to adults' reaction times for four-word lists. One could then use these particular list lengths to examine performance on lists of abstract words. If the expected age difference were obtained, one would conclude that adults are superior to children in dealing with abstract words in this specific short-term memory situation.

This type of result is sometimes difficult to obtain, however. It can also leave unanswered some nagging psychometric questions. In the hypothetical example suppose that when subjects are tested at the adjusted list lengths, there is no age difference in performance on abstract words,

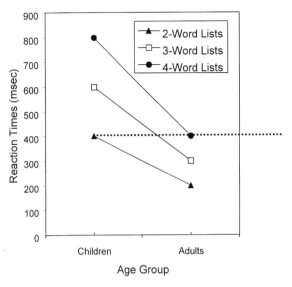

Figure 1
A hypothetical data set displaying response times of two age groups (children and adults) to lists of three difficulty levels (2-, 3-, and 4-word lists). The hypothetical data illustrate an age effect, a difficulty-level effect, and an interaction. The dashed line illustrates a comparison that could be made between the children (using the 2-word lists) and the adults (using the 4-word lists) for which the level of performance is the same. These list lengths, differing for the different age groups, presumably then could be used for an experiment in which some other factor is introduced (e.g., concrete versus abstract words), without the level of difficulty being a confound. This common technique may introduce other theoretical difficulties, however (see text).

either. Should this be taken as evidence that there is no difference in the ability to deal with abstractness? Probably so, but there are alternative possibilities. Perhaps adults had to apply a more effortful strategy to process four concrete words than children had to do to process two concrete words. Perhaps also, abstract words require more effortful processing than concrete words. In that case, four abstract words could be a double demand on effort from the adults. One may reasonably suspect that after all it is not fair to compare the magnitude of the abstract-concrete difference in children using two words with that of adults using four words, despite performance levels being equated across groups for concrete words.

An approach using difficulty-insensitive measures

One can make the case that the potential problem with the differential-deficits approach is that one can make only indirect inferences about the nature of the basic cognitive operations underlying performance. It is the nature of these cognitive operations that one really wants to discover. It seems likely that no single approach will demonstrably allow direct access to them; converging methods may be needed (Garner, Hake & Eriksen, 1956).

One type of measure that could contribute to our understanding is a measure in which the properties of a basic cognitive operation are estimated. The basic operations are difficult to define except within a particular theoretical framework, but operations that I will consider "basic" yield one of the two parameters noted above: (1) the rate at which words are retrieved from short-term memory and (2) the capacity of short-term memory for words. If one can measure a basic operation, one can understand task performance as a combination of such operations. An extension of the previously used hypothetical example is shown in figure 2. In this figure, a reaction time is composed of a number of operations of equal duration. For example, each operation could reflect a search

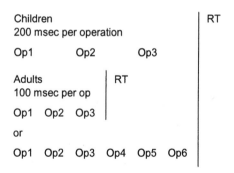

Figure 2
A diagram of hypothetical operation times underlying performance in children and adults. In this example, all operation times are the same. Each operation takes twice as long in the children as in the adults. Therefore, one can equalize the difficulty level for children and adults by making adults go through twice as many operations as children (see bottom row of the figure). The main goal, though, should be to obtain a measure of the basic operation time in each age group, which would be a difficulty-insensitive measure of performance.

through short-term memory to find a particular probed item (Sternberg, 1996). If we hypothetically assume that nothing else influences performance, then the estimate of the basic operation will allow us to predict performance levels. In this hypothetical example, adults are twice as fast at completing each operation as children are. Therefore, reaction times in the two groups are equated when the stimulus difficulty is increased in the adults until it requires twice as many operations as in the children. An alternative model would be one in which the length of operations, rather than the number of operations, increases with stimulus difficulty.

One way to tell if a basic operation is being measured is to examine it at multiple difficulty levels. *A difficulty-insensitive measure* is one in which the same answer is obtained at any level of difficulty. It is an empirical question whether such difficulty-insensitive measures exist. If they do exist, they can be taken as estimates of a basic cognitive operation. In this chapter I will argue that, to an approximation, some difficulty-insensitive measures do exist, and they indicate developmental change during childhood in some basic parameters of information processing related to working memory.

Theoretical Framework

Basic parameters of information processing can be identified only within a specified theoretical framework. Although there are uncertainties within any such framework, I will rely on an "embedded processes" framework (Cowan, 1999a), in which there are two parts to what is meant by "short-term memory." First, there is a limited number of items that can be held at one time in the focus of attention. The information is limited to a particular number of chunks (Miller, 1956). To measure the contents of this focus of attention, it is necessary to seek situations in which the number of chunks is known. One way to do this is to examine situations in which the subject is unable to group items together, so that the number of chunks equals the number of items presented to the subject. Second, there is the set of information that is outside of the focus of attention but nevertheless in a state of activation that makes it more accessible to attention than is the majority of information in long-term memory.

One clear example of information in this activated state is sensory information in an unattended channel (see, e.g., Broadbent, 1958). It seems likely that semantic information also can be activated and yet remain outside the focus of attention (e.g., information that one thought of recently but is no longer the center of one's thoughts). Unlike the focus of attention, there seems to be no capacity limit on activation (Conway & Engle, 1994), though an activated memory presumably is limited by decay over time and by interference from other activated memories. One elementary parameter of information processing, therefore, is the number of chunks that can be held at the same time in the focus of attention. Another is the rate of forgetting of activated information outside the focus of attention, which I will not examine in this chapter because a difficulty-insensitive measure is not yet available (but see Cowan, Nugent, Elliott & Saults, 2000).

The remaining parameter can be viewed as the rate at which the focus of attention can be shifted to encompass information that was previously outside of that focus. These three parameters are illustrated in figure 3, within the theoretical framework of Cowan (1988).

The status of these three parameters of information processing within cognitive development cannot be determined from prior work, but there are clues. The rate at which information can be processed is thought to speed up with development in at least some situations (Baddeley, 1986; Kail & Salthouse, 1994; Keating, Keniston, Manis & Bobbitt, 1980), though different developmental courses seem to apply to different processing rates (Cowan et al., 1998; Cowan, 1999a). There is some evidence from a neo-Piagetian perspective supporting the idea that working-memory capacity increases in childhood (Case, 1995), though it has been controversial in light of the alternative hypothesis that processing simply makes more efficient use of a constant capacity as children mature. These two parameters will be examined here primarily in procedures involving memory for spoken digits.

In the field of cognitive development it is typically held that the rate of decay of automatically activated sensory memory does not change with age in childhood (Bjorklund, 1995; Siegler, 1998). Recent studies, however, suggest that it does (Cowan, Nugent, et al., 2000; Keller & Cowan, 1994; Gomes et al., 1999; Saults & Cowan, 1996).

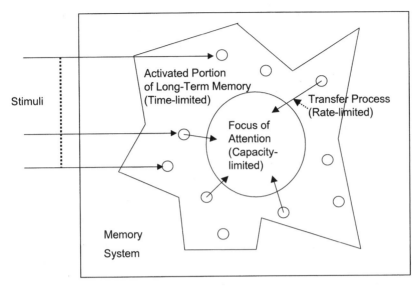

Figure 3
A model of the memory system based on the theoretical framework of Cowan (1988, 1995) and pointing out three parameters that will be discussed: the capacity of the focus of attention (inner circle), the rate of forgetting of information from activated memory outside of that attentional focus (jagged shape surrounding inner circle), and the rate at which information is transferred into the focus of attention (arrows into inner circle).

In taking the present approach, I do not intend to assert that these are the only basic mechanisms of working memory. For example, considerable effort has been devoted to determining the role of controlled attention and/or inhibition in working memory (Engle, Kane & Tuholski, 1999; Gernsbacher, 1993; Hasher, Stoltzfus, Zacks & Rypma, 1991). It is not clear if controlled attention and inhibition depend upon the mechanisms that I will discuss or upon different mechanisms. I believe that we have identified mechanisms that, logically speaking, are very basic building blocks of the processing system, but I do not assume that there are not other, equally important and basic building blocks.

The studies to be described below involved comparisons of three age groups, with 24 subjects per age group. The samples are limited at the low end by the youngest ages at which the tasks can be reliably performed, and yet they traverse a period of marked developmental growth.

Development of a Short-Term Memory Retrieval Rate

We have measured the rate of retrieval of information from short-term memory in situations in which children and adults hear lists of words or digits and are to repeat the list items in the order in which they were presented (Cowan, 1992; Cowan et al., 1994, 1998; Cowan, 1999b; Hulme, Newton, Cowan, Stuart & Brown, 1999). Using only trials in which the recall was completely correct, we have measured the duration of each word and each interword silent interval in the response, using a sound-waveform-editing program to do the timing. These studies have established several findings about the timing of spoken recall, as follows.

1. The duration of silent, interword pauses in the response vary with the difficulty of the list much more than do the durations of words.

2. These interword pauses are longer in the recall of longer lists, which suggests that they involve a mental search through the list to determine which word to recall next.

3. The durations of interword pauses are unaffected by the length of the words, which suggests that they involve not covert phonological rehearsal but rather a search through underlying lexical nodes, similar to what has been found in studies of memory search using a recognition probe (Chase, 1977; Clifton & Tash, 1973).

4. The interword pauses are much longer for lists of nonsense words than for lists of real words, which suggests that lexical knowledge is used to assist in the search for the correct item to be recalled next.

5. The interword pauses for lists of a particular length are longer for older children, and often for children within a particular age group who have higher memory spans.

The first four findings are important for development because of the fifth finding.

These developmental differences in timing also occur for the preparatory interval between the stimulus list and the spoken response. However, unlike the interword pauses, the preparatory intervals are not related to memory span (Cowan et al., 1998).

The interword pauses show considerable promise in assisting our understanding of memory span. Cowan et al. (1998) found that two

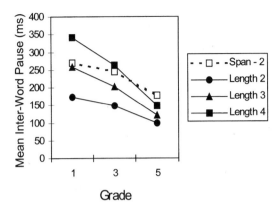

Figure 4
Interword pause times in the spoken recall of digit lists produced by children in the study of Cowan et al. (1998, experiment 1), for three list lengths (solid lines) and for lists two items shorter than span (dashed line), where span was defined as the longest list that the individual could recall. (Reprinted from the left-hand panel of figure 3 of Cowan, Saults, et al., 1999.)

separate types of speed measures both correlated with span at about $r = .4$: the interword pauses in spoken recall and the speed at which children could rehearse aloud when asked to speak quickly (a task discussed at length, for example, by Baddeley, 1986). Yet, these two types of speed measure did not correlate with each other at all, and they picked up different portions of the variance in memory span. Together they accounted for 60% of the total variance in span and 87% of the age-related variance in span. Cowan et al. (1998) suggested that these factors reflected the speed of memory search and phonological rehearsal processes, respectively.

In figure 4, the solid lines depict evidence from Cowan et al. (1998, experiment 1) for the repetition of spoken digit lists, specifically for three list lengths at which the most usable data were available (2-, 3-, and 4-word lists), by children in first grade (7–8 years), third grade (9–10 years), and fifth grade (11–12 years). Clearly, for all list lengths, the durations of interword pauses shortened with age in childhood. However, from that pattern it is not clear how to characterize the amount of change across ages, as it depended on the list length. One could hope to measure the change in a theoretically meaningful manner by examining

each child at the longest list length that he or she could repeat success-
fully. That list length, unfortunately, did not yield enough trials per subject, but one can examine a list length tied to the longest repeatable
length, namely lists two items shorter than span length, which we term
"span − 2." As shown by the dashed line in figure 4, interword pauses
changed across ages even when examined in this manner.

It would be helpful to have a way to identify an elementary operation
underlying the developmental change in interword pauses. One way to
identify an elementary operation would be to derive a measure that displays the same developmental trend regardless of the difficulty level of
the stimulus list (where difficulty level is reflected by the list length). If
such a measure could be found, it would have to be assumed that any
obtained developmental trend results from a developmental change in the
processing parameter and not from the range of difficulty of the stimuli.
Cowan, Saults, et al. (1999) reported on some difficulty-insensitive measures. The reasoning here will become clearer as we proceed.

Let us assume that each interword pause duration involves a mental
search through the memory representation of the entire list to determine
which word to recall next—a theory proposed previously by Sternberg
et al. (1978, 1980) to account for the timing of adults' speeded repetition
of spoken lists. If this and several additional assumptions are met, the
results could present quite a revealing pattern. Assume that each additional item in the list adds a constant amount of time to the search process as in search studies with probed recognition (e.g., Sternberg, 1966);
one need not also assume that the search process proceeds in a serial
manner (Ratcliff, 1978). Finally, assume that the search process is the
main process affecting the interword pauses and that the contributions of
other processes are negligible. Given these assumptions, an individual's
per-item search or retrieval time should be independent of the list length.
This per-item search time could be estimated by *dividing each pause duration by the list length*.

Figure 5 shows the results of this derivation, for the same data shown
in figure 4. One can see from figure 5 that this derived measure (pause
time divided by the list length) changes with age in childhood but nevertheless is almost completely independent of the list length. The difficulty-
insensitive nature of this metric suggests that it reflects an elementary

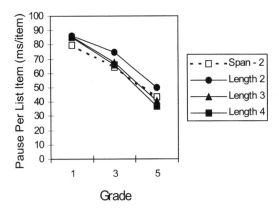

Figure 5
A difficulty-insensitive measure of retrieval rate: pause time divided by list length. (Based on the same data as in figure 4. Reprinted from the right-hand panel of figure 3 of Cowan, Saults, et al., 1999.)

operation, and theoretical considerations suggest that this measure is the per-item search or retrieval time. Helping to validate this assumption, Hulme et al. (1999) found correlations between search measures and interword pauses. The per-item search times shown in figure 5 change across ages in a systematic manner that is similar to what has been observed in developmental studies of memory search using recognition probes (e.g., Keating et al., 1980).

It is also possible to refine the result shown in figure 5 by eliminating any constant amount of time needed to initiate recall of each item. This was done by examining the slope of the interword pauses as a function of the list length. The responses for each age group were nicely linear across list lengths 2, 3, and 4, in close analogy to probed recall (Sternberg, 1966). Fits of the functions indicated that the intercepts (projected back to length 1, which of course includes no pauses) for grades 1, 3, and 5 were rather similar: 89 ms, 90 ms, and 75 ms, respectively. However, these age groups differed much more in the slope of the search functions, which were 84 ms, 57 ms, and 24 ms for the three age groups. It is the small and similar intercepts in the presence of developmentally changing slopes that allows the measure shown in figure 5 to be approximately difficulty-insensitive.

Development of Short-Term Memory Capacity

The measure of memory capacity to be discussed draws upon a logic first developed by Sperling (1960). He presented briefly flashed arrays of printed characters and required that part of the array or the whole array be identified. A tone served as a partial report cue indicating that one particular row was to be recalled. The cue could occur at variable amounts of time after the array. At short partial report-cue delays, most of the information in a particular row of the array could be reported. However, at longer cue delays the number reported decreased, to an asymptotically low level after about 1 sec. The calculated number of items available from the entire array with a long cue delay closely approximated the number actually reported when no cue was presented and the whole array had to be reported. In these situations, about 4 items were available from the array. Importantly, this number available did not depend on the number of characters present in the array. It was interpreted as a capacity limit in the short-term-memory faculty that was needed to hold items as they were retrieved from a large-capacity, but short-lived, sensory memory of the array.

One might wonder why the 4-item limit in short-term memory is smaller than the 7-item limit observed by Miller (1956). One likely answer is that the 7-item limit included chunks of multiple items formed as subjects rehearsed the stimuli. In Sperling's (1960) procedure, so many stimuli were presented quickly and at the same time that it may not have been possible for rehearsal to take place. Therefore, in Sperling's procedure, each character in the array served as a separate chunk in short-term memory. Many different types of study have shown that the basic short-term-memory capacity limit is about 4 chunks (for a review, see Cowan, 1999b). According to the present theoretical framework, as shown in figure 3, the capacity limit is actually a limit in the capacity of the focus of attention at any one moment. Sensory memory information must be drawn into that focus quickly before it decays, if it is to be recalled.

Cowan, Nugent, Elliott, Ponomarev, and Saults (1999) extended the logic of Sperling (1960) and adapted it to spoken lists of digits and to developmental study with first- and fourth-grade children and college students (i.e., adults). Presumably, unlike Sperling's character arrays, the recall of spoken digit lists could benefit from rehearsal and grouping during the reception of the list, since the items were presented slowly, one at a time. However, these processes presumably require attention and could be curtailed if the lists were unattended at the time that they were presented. The assumptions here are that subjects have a sensory memory of sounds that may last up to about 30 sec, and that for a few seconds, at least, some items can be retrieved on the basis of this sensory memory of an unattended list (Cowan, 1984; Darwin, Turvey & Crowder, 1972). The result necessary to show that the memory limit is based on a capacity limit (rather than a sensory-memory limit) is that the *number correct should be independent of the list length,* analogous to Sperling's finding that the whole report limit was independent of the array size.

We followed up on this logic by using a visually attended task first developed by Saults and Cowan (1996). In this task, children first learned standard names for colored pictures to be presented on the computer screen. On each trial, a central picture (e.g., "hair") was surrounded by four peripheral pictures (e.g., "rain," "tail," "chair," "bat"). The task was to use the computer mouse to select the peripheral picture that rhymed with the central picture (in this example, "chair"). The central picture kept changing and the same four peripheral pictures were used throughout an auditory memory trial. The accuracy and speed of performance in this primary task was recorded.

Each subject's memory span was tested using spoken digit lists. Span was defined as the length of the longest list that a subject could repeat correctly at least once, given our need for an integer span estimate. Subsequently, lists were presented at four list lengths: span − 3 (i.e., three items below span for that individual), span − 2, span − 1, and span. Memory for such lists was tested (with stimuli presented through headphones) both with lists that were attended and with lists that were ignored while the rhyming game was played. The rhyming game also was carried out by itself with no auditory stimuli.

When spoken lists were presented during the rhyming game, most lists of spoken digits were to be ignored. Occasionally, though, the rhyming game was interrupted shortly after a spoken list and replaced with a

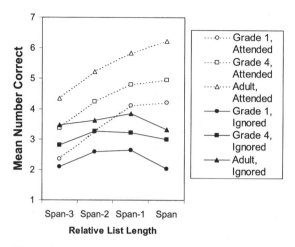

Figure 6
Number correct in the recall of attended speech (dashed lines) and unattended speech (solid lines) in three age groups, for lists of four lengths: span length (i.e., the longest list that could be recalled), span − 1, span − 2, and span − 3. (After Cowan, Nugent, et al., 1999.)

series of response boxes, signaling that the subject was to recall the list of spoken digits that had just ended, by pressing the corresponding keys on the numerical keypad. There was evidence that the use of the keypad as opposed to a spoken response did not increase the age effect. This response mode was used to avoid acoustic interference.

The rhyming task was carried out every bit as well in the presence of ignored speech as it was when carried out in silence—a finding that is helpful in arguing against a suggestion that the auditory-memory results could be attributed to attention wandering into the spoken channel.

Results for the auditory-memory task are shown in figure 6. It is clear that the results were very different for attended lists (dashed lines) versus unattended lists (solid lines). Only the unattended lists show the pattern in which the number correct stays fixed across list lengths, as one would expect if the recall limit is in the capacity of a short-term store or focus of attention. For the attended lists, as the list length grew longer, more items could be recalled, presumably because these items were being rehearsed and grouped together to form larger chunks, requiring less space within the limited-capacity focus of attention.

The results for unattended speech also show that the memory capacity increased across ages. Note how well the estimate for adults agrees with Sperling's (1960) whole-report limit and with other measures of memory capacity when chunking is prevented (Cowan, 1999b).

It is also worth pointing out that the age difference in capacity plays an important role in determining ordinary span. We can tell this because the age differences in memory for attended speech were not much larger than the age differences in unattended speech, which suggests that attention during presentation of the list, though very important in recall at all ages, played little role in the developmental change. Previously, many in the field of cognitive development believed that the development of rehearsal accounts for a large part of the developmental change in memory span— a belief based on evidence that rehearsal does develop markedly (e.g., Flavell, Beach & Chinsky, 1966; Ornstein & Naus, 1978; for an opinion that rehearsal cannot account for much of the developmental change in span, see Dempster, 1981).

When measured in terms of proportions correct, neither memory for attended speech nor memory for unattended speech came close to being difficulty-insensitive. Notice, though, that when measured in terms of the number correct as in figure 6, memory for unattended speech is difficulty-insensitive. This is shown perhaps more clearly in figure 7, which depicts the number correct in unattended speech for several specific list lengths. (These were the list lengths that could be obtained from most subjects' data.) The number correct is independent of list length and yet changes systematically with age in childhood. This reflects what appears to be an increase in the capacity limit for the store that receives information transferred from a sensory form to a categorical form; presumably this store is actually the capacity-limited focus of attention shown in figure 3.

Conclusion

In this chapter I have examined developmental changes in two elementary parameters of information processing taking place during childhood, as observed in memory for spoken stimuli: the short-term-memory search or retrieval rate during spoken recall, and the short-term-memory

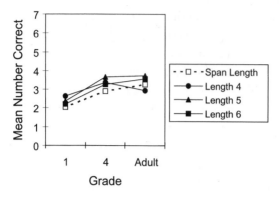

Figure 7
A difficulty-insensitive measure of memory capacity, the number correct, shown here for several list lengths (solid lines) and for span-length lists (dashed line) and based on the same data set as figure 6. (Reprinted from the right-hand panel of figure 2 of Cowan, Saults, et al., 1999.)

capacity limit. These parameter changes can be studied only within the boundaries of a theoretical framework. Within such a framework, they hold the promise of eventually allowing insightful predictions of how children might succeed or fail when confronted with a variety of more complex tasks. The examination of age differences in elementary parameters was possible only after methods were devised to separate the effects of stimulus difficulty from direct effects of the parameters themselves. At least for the retrieval rate and memory capacity parameters, we have found derived measures that show the same developmental course for a range of difficulty levels (i.e., stimulus-list lengths). A similar measure may be possible for sensory-memory decay (Cowan et al., 2000), but we will not know for sure until list lengths and retention intervals are varied within a single unattended-speech experiment. It is hoped that this effort to refine difficulty-insensitive measures of developmental change in the basic parameters of working memory is of use not only in advancing research but also in advancing research methods in cognitive development.

Acknowledgment

This work was supported by NIH grant R01 HD-21338.

References

Baddeley, A. D. (1986). *Working memory.* Oxford Psychology Series, no. 11. Oxford: Clarendon Press.

Bjorklund, D. F. (1995). *Children's thinking: Developmental function and individual differences.* Pacific Grove, Calif.: Brooks/Cole.

Broadbent, D. E. (1958). *Perception and communication.* London: Pergamon Press.

Case, R. (1995). Capacity-based explanations of working memory growth: A brief history and reevaluation. In F. E. Weinert & W. Schneider (Eds.), *Memory performance and competencies: Issues in growth and development* (pp. 23–44). Mahwah, N.J.: Erlbaum.

Chapman, L. J., & Chapman, J. P. (1978). The measurement of differential deficit. *Journal of Psychiatric Research, 14,* 303–311.

Chase, W. G. (1977). Does memory scanning involve implicit speech? In S. Dornic (Ed.), *Attention and performance VI* (pp. 607–628). Hillsdale, N.J.: Erlbaum.

Clifton, C., & Tash, J. (1973). Effect of syllabic word length on memory-search rate. *Journal of Experimental Psychology, 99,* 231–235.

Conway, A. R. A., & Engle, R. W. (1994). Working memory and retrieval: A resource-dependent inhibition model. *Journal of Experimental Psychology: General, 123,* 354–373.

Cowan, N. (1984). On short and long auditory stores. *Psychological Bulletin, 96,* 341–370.

Cowan, N. (1988). Evolving conceptions of memory storage, selective attention, and their mutual constraints within the human information processing system. *Psychological Bulletin, 104,* 163–191.

Cowan, N. (1992). Verbal memory span and the timing of spoken recall. *Journal of Memory and Language, 31,* 668–684.

Cowan, N. (1995). *Attention and memory: An integrated framework.* Oxford Psychology Series, no. 26. New York: Oxford University Press.

Cowan, N. (1999a). An embedded-processes model of working memory. In A. Miyake & P. Shah (Eds.), *Models of working memory: Mechanisms of active maintenance and executive control* (pp. 62–101). Cambridge: Cambridge University Press.

Cowan, N. (1999b). The differential maturation of two processing rates related to digit span. *Journal of Experimental Child Psychology, 72,* 193–209.

Cowan, N., Keller, T., Hulme, C., Roodenrys, S., McDougall, S., & Rack, J. (1994). Verbal memory span in children: Speech timing clues to the mechanisms underlying age and word length effects. *Journal of Memory and Language, 33,* 234–250.

Cowan, N., Nugent, L. D., Elliott, E. M., Ponomarev, I., & Saults, J. S. (1999). The role of attention in the development of short-term memory: Age differences in the verbal span of apprehension. *Child Development, 70,* 1082–1097.

Cowan, N., Nugent, L. D., Elliott, E. M., & Saults, J. S. (2000). Persistence of memory for ignored lists of digits: Areas of developmental constancy and change. *Journal of Experimental Child Psychology, 76,* 151–172.

Cowan, N., Saults, J. S., Nugent, L. D., & Elliott, E. M. (1999). The microanalysis of memory span and its development in childhood. *International Journal of Psychology, 34,* 353–358.

Cowan, N., Wood, N. L., Wood, P. K., Keller, T. A., Nugent, L. D., & Keller, C. V. (1998). Two separate verbal processing rates contributing to short-term memory span. *Journal of Experimental Psychology: General, 127,* 141–160.

Darwin, C. J., Turvey, M. T., & Crowder, R. G. (1972). An auditory analogue of the Sperling partial report procedure: Evidence for brief auditory storage. *Cognitive Psychology, 3,* 255–267.

Dempster, F. N. (1981). Memory span: Sources of individual and developmental differences. *Psychological Bulletin, 89,* 63–100.

Engle, R. W., Kane, M. J., & Tuholski, S. W. (1999). Individual differences in working memory capacity and what they tell us about controlled attention, general fluid intelligence and functions of the prefrontal cortex. In A. Miyake & P. Shah (Eds.), *Models of working memory: Mechanisms of active maintenance and executive control* (pp. 102–134). Cambridge: Cambridge University Press.

Flavell, J. H., Beach, D. H., & Chinsky, J. M. (1966). Spontaneous verbal rehearsal in a memory task as a function of age. *Child Development, 37,* 283–299.

Garner, W. R., Hake, H. W., & Eriksen, C. W. (1956). Operationism and the concept of perception. *Psychological Review, 63,* 149–159.

Gernsbacher, M. A. (1993). Less skilled readers have less efficient suppression mechanisms. *Psychological Science, 4,* 294–298.

Gomes, H., Sussman, E., Ritter, W., Kurtzberg, D., Cowan, N., & Vaughan, H. G., Jr. (1999). Electrophysiological evidence of developmental changes in the duration of auditory sensory memory. *Developmental Psychology, 35,* 294–302.

Hasher, L., Stoltzfus, E. R., Zacks, R. T., & Rypma, B. (1991). Age and inhibition. *Journal of Experimental Psychology: Learning, Memory, and Cognition, 17,* 163–169.

Hulme, C., Newton, P., Cowan, N., Stuart, G., & Brown, G. (1999). Think before you speak: Pause, memory search and trace reintegration processes in verbal memory span. *Journal of Experimental Psychology: Learning, Memory, and Cognition, 25,* 447–463.

Kail, R., & Salthouse, T. A. (1994). Processing speed as a mental capacity. *Acta Psychologica, 86,* 199–255.

Keating, D. P., Keniston, A. H., Manis, F. R., & Bobbitt, B. L. (1980). Development of the search-processing parameter. *Child Development, 51*, 39–44.

Keller, T. A., & Cowan, N. (1994). Developmental increase in the duration of memory for tone pitch. *Developmental Psychology, 30*, 855–863.

Miller, G. A. (1956). The magical number seven, plus or minus two: Some limits on our capacity for processing information. *Psychological Review, 63*, 81–97.

Ornstein, P. A., & Naus, M. J. (1978). Rehearsal processes in children's memory. In P. A. Ornstein (Ed.), *Memory development in children* (pp. 69–99). Hillsdale, N.J.: Erlbaum.

Ratcliff, R. (1978). A theory of memory retrieval. *Psychological Review, 85*, 59–108.

Saults, J. S., & Cowan, N. (1996). The development of memory for ignored speech. *Journal of Experimental Child Psychology, 63*, 239–261.

Siegler, R. S. (1998). *Children's thinking.* 3rd Edition. Upper Saddle River, N.J.: Prentice-Hall.

Sperling, G. (1960). The information available in brief visual presentations. *Psychological Monographs, 74* (498).

Sternberg, S. (1966). High-speed scanning in human memory. *Science, 153*, 652–654.

Sternberg, S., Monsell, S., Knoll, R. L., & Wright, C. E. (1978). The latency and duration of rapid movement sequences: Comparisons of speech and typewriting. In G. E. Stelmach (Ed.), *Information processing in motor control and learning* (pp. 116–152). New York: Academic Press.

Sternberg, S., Wright, C. E., Knoll, R. L., & Monsell, S. (1980). Motor programs in rapid speech: Additional evidence. In R. A. Cole (Ed.), *Perception and production of fluent speech* (pp. 469–505). Hillsdale, N.J.: Erlbaum.

4

Working Memory and Attentional Processes across the Lifespan

Anik de Ribaupierre

Although the definition of working memory (WM) varies among researchers, there is a clear consensus with respect to its function. WM is defined as a system, or as a set of processes, that serves to process and maintain temporary information for use in other cognitive tasks. Thus, in contrast with earlier concepts of primary memory or of short-term memory, WM implies an active mental manipulation in addition to a temporary maintenance of information; that is, it is considered as a process-oriented construct. Moreover, WM is generally considered to be a complex system with a limited capacity, constrained both by limitations in the amount of activation that can be distributed and by limited attentional resources available to activate and maintain task-relevant information while inhibiting task-irrelevant information (e.g., Miyake & Shah, 1999; Richardson, 1996). There is an important controversy with respect to the question of whether WM constitutes a structural entity, i.e., a memory system, such as defined by Schacter and Tulving (1994), with its own, specific processes, or whether it combines a set of processes shared by other psychological functions. Thus, Baddeley (1986, 1992; Baddeley & Hitch, 1974) defines WM as a multicomponent system (in contrast with a unitary view of short-term memory), consisting of three subsystems: two slave systems—the articulatory loop (which is responsible for the maintenance and processing of verbal material) and the visuospatial sketchpad (VSSP, responsible for maintaining and processing visuospatial information)—and the Central Executive (whose main functions are coordination and planning). In contrast, a number of other models suggest that WM designates only an activated subset of long-term memory, and/or call for the same processes as other cognitive tasks.

For instance, Moscovitch (1994) proposes that WM would be more appropriately labeled as "working with memory." Ericsson and Kintsch (1995) also speak of long-term working memory.

However, this controversy around the issue of an underlying (neural) system specific to WM is stronger in the field of adult cognitive psychology or neuropsychology than in developmental psychology. Developmental approaches have generally focused on the capacity of WM more than on its architecture (e.g., Ribaupierre & Bailleux, 1994) and have either simply ignored this controversy and merely considered that WM is complex and calls for a combination of storage and processing processes, or have argued that WM indexes an activated subset of information (e.g., Pascual-Leone, 1987; Pascual-Leone & Baillargeon, 1994). In the latter case, WM appears as a compound of different processes that are also at work in other cognitive tasks, most of which can be considered to be attentional in nature (e.g., Ribaupierre, 1999). Although I adhere to this second perspective, I will not further discuss this controversy here especially because, once again, it does not seem central in developmental psychology, which has essentially focused on changes in capacity with age and on possible factors accounting for this change. However, I would like to argue that it is preferable to speak of performances in WM *tasks* rather than in WM per se, thereby stressing that such tasks call for a number of processes that are also at play in other cognitive tasks.

Age Changes in WM: One or Several Factors?

Most developmentalists insist on changes in WM capacity with age and consider that WM capacity (assessed by performances in WM tasks) serves as an index of general cognitive resources. They also suggest that changes in WM capacity account for more general cognitive changes with age, whether in children or in aging persons. The similarity of hypotheses advanced by researchers in both the cognitive-development field[1] and the cognitive-aging field is striking, as I will try to demonstrate. Thus, in neo-Piagetian models such as Pascual-Leone's (Pascual-Leone, 1970, 1987) and Case's (Case, 1985, 1992a; see also Chapman, 1990), a causal link is assumed between an increase in the quantity of information that can be simultaneously processed and the emergence of stages in cognitive development. Pascual-Leone and Case, for instance, showed that attentional capacity (a) regularly increases until 15 years of age (by one unit every two years in the case of Pascual-Leone's model) and (b) is a good predictor in various developmental tasks. A number of cognitive-aging researchers propose a similar hypothesis, namely that changes in WM capacity account for age differences observed in other memory tasks or in fluid intelligence. Welford (1958, quoted in Salthouse, 1992) already suggested that there is a decrease with age in the joint capacity to maintain information while simultaneously processing the same or other information. It is particularly in the verbal (language and comprehension) and the reasoning domains that a reduction in WM capacity has been considered to account for age differences (for a review, see Salthouse, 1990, 1992). An interpretation of cognitive decrease with age in terms of WM is also compatible with hypotheses brought forward by Craik (Craik & Jennings, 1992) and Light (1991), according to which the more mental and auto-initiated is the activity that a task requires, the larger are the memory difficulties in older subjects.

For a number of cognitive-development and cognitive-aging theorists, WM is a general mechanism, operating across a large range of tasks. However, as Salthouse (1992) noted, WM as a general processing resource is still controversial and cannot be considered to be empirically validated, particularly in older persons. This is in part due to theoretical and methodological weaknesses in many studies. Most often a single indicator of WM has been used, whereas several indicators should be used if the generality of the construct is to be demonstrated; when several tasks were used, sample size was often small. It is therefore difficult to assess whether the relatively weak correlations obtained in some studies were due to lack of reliability or to domain specificity. The theoretical relations between WM and cognitive functioning often remain ill-specified. Furthermore, there is often a confusion between tasks and underlying processes (Ribaupierre, 1993; Ribaupierre & Bailleux, 1994). Even if there are substantial correlations among WM tasks, this does not necessarily imply that WM constitutes one and only one general mechanism; the congruency between WM tasks could merely reflect the fact that a set of common processes are at work.

A number of hypotheses were nevertheless formulated with respect to processes responsible for change in WM capacity with age. Here again, the similarity between the cognitive-development and the cognitive-aging fields is striking. Two processes most often mentioned are activation and inhibition. These two processes are considered as components of *selective attention*[2] in adult cognitive psychology. Processing speed (which is rather vaguely defined in terms of response times in relatively simple cognitive tasks) is also a very highly rated candidate. It can be considered to be an empirical operationalization of the construct of activation, all the more so as activation cannot be directly apprehended except in theoretical task analyses or in connectionist modeling. More rapid processing implies that a larger quantity of information can be processed or activated in a given period of time, which yields an apparently larger processing capacity. Reciprocally, a larger capacity probably allows one to process the same quantity of information in a shorter time. The link between efficiency and rapidity of processing has been explicitly noted by other researchers too (e.g., Case, 1985; for a similar argument, see Kail, 1995).

With respect to cognitive development, increase in WM was first conceptualized in terms of an increase in capacity or activation or processing efficiency (e.g., Case, 1985; Pascual-Leone, 1970). Other authors, however, raised a number of methodological and theoretical problems with this conceptualization (e.g., Dempster & Brainerd, 1995; Dempster, 1985, 1992; Halford, 1993). Dempster, for instance, rejected the hypothesis of an increase in activation with age and suggested, in part on the basis of aging studies, that an increasing resistance to interference (inhibitory capacity) is a major factor in cognitive development. He reviewed a number of empirical studies that back up this hypothesis. Bjorklund and Harnishfeger (1990; Kipp Harnishfeger & Bjorklund, 1993) also favor an interpretation in terms of an increase in inhibitory capacity with age and present some empirical evidence. The argument is that inhibition, which prevents irrelevant information to enter the field of WM, gains in efficiency with age; as a result, there is an increase in the efficiency of processing as well as in the functional capacity of WM.

Processing speed and inhibition are also evoked to account for change in WM capacity in older subjects. For Salthouse (1990, 1992, 1993;

Salthouse & Babcock, 1991), for instance, the speed of execution of elementary operations is an important mediator of age-related performance in a number of cognitive tasks, including WM tasks. Hasher and Zacks propose that inhibitory mechanisms act both at the encoding stage (to influence the content of WM) and at the retrieval stage (Hasher, Stoltzfus, Zacks & Rypma, 1991; Hasher & Zacks, 1988; Stoltzfus, Hasher & Zacks, 1996). Such mechanisms would become less efficient in older person. As a result, more irrelevant information would permeate WM and/or less irrelevant information would be evacuated from WM, leading to a saturation of WM and a larger interference effect.

According to these different models, WM tasks would therefore mediate the influence of age on cognition, while processing speed (or activation power) and inhibition would in turn mediate the influence of age on WM tasks. A third type of mediating variable has also been frequently invoked, namely executive schemes (e.g., Pascual-Leone, 1987) or control processes. They are mentioned here but will not be analyzed further, because their empirical operationalization is rather difficult (see also note 4). Figure 1 shows the paths that are theoretically hypothesized. In this model, processing speed and inhibition should jointly contribute to age changes in WM, whereas, for most authors, they constitute alternative explanations. We argued elsewhere (Ribaupierre, 1993; Rieben, Ribaupierre & Lautrey, 1990; see also Pascual-Leone, 1987) that devel-

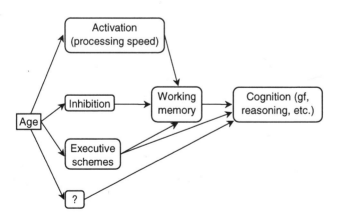

Figure 1
Hypothetical influence of various mechanisms with age.

opmental researchers too often restrict their view of development to a unidimensional one, whereas development should be viewed as depending on several underlying general mechanisms; that is, development should be considered multidimensional and even multidirectional (see, e.g., Baltes, 1987). In the present case, our hypothesis is that change in WM capacity embodies both an increase in the quantity of information that can be processed—whether it is because more information is actually processed or because it is processed more rapidly, or both—and a decrease in the relative amount of "parasite" or irrelevant information that is retained.

The empirical status of these different processes is not equivalent. According to Salthouse's (1992) agenda for developmental psychology, three types of questions are to be addressed to determine whether a given variable is a mediator of the influence of age on another variable. First, does each variable (or group of variables) undergo significant changes with age? Second, does each of these constructs (WM, processing speed, and inhibition) correspond to a general mechanism? Third, do processing speed and inhibition account for age changes in WM?

Only the first question has been submitted to extensive empirical scrutiny, particularly as concerns WM and processing speed. There is abundant empirical evidence according to which performance on WM tasks and on processing-speed tasks changes drastically with age (Case, 1985; Kail, 1988, 1990; Pascual-Leone, 1970, 1987; Salthouse, 1996). Age changes in inhibition or in interference tasks are less well documented.[3] A number of studies have nevertheless shown clear age differences (e.g., Hamm & Hasher, 1992; Hartman & Hasher, 1991; Kipp & Pope, 1997; Tipper, Bourque, Anderson & Brehaut, 1989).

With respect to the issue of generality (the second question), substantial correlations were reported among processing-speed tasks (e.g., Kail & Park, 1992; Salthouse, 1994; Salthouse & Meinz, 1995) and among WM tasks (Case, 1992b; Case, Okamoto, Henderson & McKeough, 1993; Conway & Engle, 1996; Engle, Cantor & Carullo, 1992). In contrast, no authors, to our knowledge, reported significant correlations among inhibition tasks. Moreover, Park et al. (1996), for instance, showed that tasks like the Negative Priming paradigm lack reliability; in their study, neither this task nor the color-word Stroop task could be introduced in a structural-equations model. One explanation for such a divergence in results between WM and processing-speed tasks, on the one hand, and interference tasks, on the other hand, could be that inhibitory processes are domain-specific, and that there is no general inhibitory mechanism. Another reason could be psychometric. Whereas raw performances were used for the first two types of tasks, difference (or ratio) scores were used to assess inhibition. Therefore, scores might be less reliable. More important, scores in this case express probably more "purely" the construct of interest, whereas raw scores in WM or in processing-speed tasks are more likely to reflect the interplay of several underlying processes.

As to the question of whether processing speed or/and inhibition mediate age influence on WM tasks, Salthouse provided some empirical support showing that processing speed accounted for a large part of the age-related variance in WM tasks. However, there is as yet only very scarce evidence of the influence of inhibition on WM, even though theoretical assumptions are usually strong in this respect. Very few studies directly address the relationship between WM and inhibition or among WM, perceptual speed, and inhibition tasks, whether in children or adults. Salthouse and Meinz (1995) argued that inhibition was less powerful than processing speed in predicting age differences between young and older adults. Even regardless of the influence of age, very few studies directly question the relation between WM and inhibition. MacDonald, Just, and Carpenter (1992) presented young adults with ambiguous and unambiguous sentences and observed that the effect of ambiguity was more pronounced in high span subjects (as assessed with reading span). Engle et al. (Engle, Conway, Tuholski & Shisler, 1995; Engle, Kane & Tuholski, 1998) showed that, among young adults, low-span subjects were more sensitive to interference. Yet the field remains largely unexplored.

One objective of the study to be presented below was therefore to assess the generality of the constructs and to question whether not only processing speed but also inhibition act in combination to mediate the influence of age on WM. Another objective was to determine whether their influence was the same during childhood as during older adulthood. Based on Reuchlin's hypothesis of vicarious or equifunctional processes (Reuchlin, 1978), I suggest that the same processes (in the present case inhibition and processing speed) are available in all individuals and at different ages, but that the facility with which they can be triggered as well as their respective weight vary both between individuals and across the lifespan.

An Empirical Study

As mentioned above, this study pursued several objectives: (a) assess whether WM, processing speed and inhibition constitute general mechanisms, by using several tasks supposed to tap each construct; (b) determine whether all three undergo large changes with age throughout the lifespan as assumed in the literature, by using the same tasks with both children and older adults; (c) assess whether processing speed and inhibition account for age differences in WM; and (d) study whether their relative influence on age differences varies in childhood and in older adulthood.

Method

A large battery of tasks was used to address the three constructs of interest here.[4]

Processing speed   This construct was assessed by means of four widely published tasks, three of which were adapted from Salthouse (1992): the *digit-symbol task*, the *letter-comparison task*, and the *pattern-comparison task*. The fourth task is the familiar *crossout task* from the Woodcock-Johnson Educational Battery (Woodcock & Johnson, 1989).

Working memory   I used four tasks to assess working memory, three focusing on visuospatial processing and one on verbal processing.

The localization-span task and the double-color-span task (adapted from Loisy & Roulin (1992)   Each of these tasks involved showing a 36-cell array on a computer screen, with two to five target cells appearing in color on each trial. For the localization-span task, all colored cells were red, and subjects had to remember their location; for the double-color-span task, target cells appeared in distinct colors, and subjects had to remember both the color and position of these cells. The number of recalled positions, or recalled positions and colors, was recorded.

The ghost-peanut task (Ribaupierre & Bailleux, 1994; Ribaupierre, Lecerf & Bailleux, 2000) For this task, an array of sixteen circles was shown on a computer screen. Between two and six circles were displayed in color on each trial and subjects had to remember both their color and position.

The reading span task (adapted from Daneman and Carpenter, 1980) For this task, a set of sentences was presented, and subjects were required to read each sentence (or, in case of the 8-year-olds, to listen to each sentence), to decide whether or not it was semantically correct, and to remember the last words of all sentences.

For all working-memory tasks, trials of different complexity were randomly ordered. This choice was made because of the possibility that older adults are more affected than young adults by presenting items according to their difficulty (Hasher et al., personal communication, July 1999).

Inhibition Four tasks were used to assess inhibition: a Stroop-color task, a Stroop-position task, a proactive interference task, and a negative priming task.

The *Stroop-color task* had three conditions: naming color patches, reading words printed in black ink, and naming words printed in incongruent ink colors. The dependent variable of interest here was Stroop interference, defined as the relative difference between the incongruent and control-naming conditions.

For the *Stroop-position task*, position words ("haut" and "bas," referring to above and below), control words ("bien" and "mal," referring to good and bad), or geometrical figures (a circle and a square) were presented on a computer screen, and subjects had to indicate whether they appeared above or below a star. The task had four conditions defined by the display of neutral words, geometrical figures, position-congruent words and position-incongruent words (e.g., "above" placed below the star). The critical dependent variable was the interference score, that is, the relative difference between the incongruent-word and control-word conditions.

For the *proactive interference task*, subjects were required to learn 3 sets of 4 lists of 10 words. Two sets consisted of semantically related words, and one of phonologically related words. In each set the first three lists belonged to the same category (e.g., animals), and the fourth list belonged to a different category (e.g., vehicles). The number of correctly recalled words was recorded. The number of intrusions from the preceding lists was used as an index of interference.

The fourth task was a familiar *negative-priming task* adapted from Tipper et al. (1989).

All the tasks were administered to all subjects. The sample consisted in 8-, 10-, and 12-year-olds ($N = 47$, 48, and 48, respectively, when considering only the children who had all or nearly all the tasks), 20–30-year-olds ($N = 102$, mean age = 23.2, divided into 2 equivalent subsamples), and older adults, ranging in age from 60 to 84 ($N = 139$, mean age = 69.2). The older adult group was, in some of the analyses, further subdivided into a young-old group (less than 70, $N = 78$, mean age = 65.5) and an old-old group (older than 70, $N = 61$, mean age = 74.2). In the subsequent analyses, the children and young adults (subgroup a) will be referred to as the young sample, and the young adults (subgroup b) and older adults as the adult sample.

Results

Raw performances in each task were first transformed into standard units relative to the young adults sample and then averaged. Figure 2 shows the distribution of these standardized scores, averaged for each of the constructs of interest. The WM and the speed mean scores are based on the standardized scores in the tasks described above (4 WM tasks and 4 speed scores). The inhibition mean score is based on the interference score in the color-Stroop task and on the number of intrusions in the proactive interference task.

Age differences   Results showed clear age differences for all three constructs.[5] However, the age trend was greatest for processing speed and smallest for inhibition. In the latter case, the three children's groups did not differ from each other, while differing from the young adults; in contrast, adults older than 70 differed from both the young and the

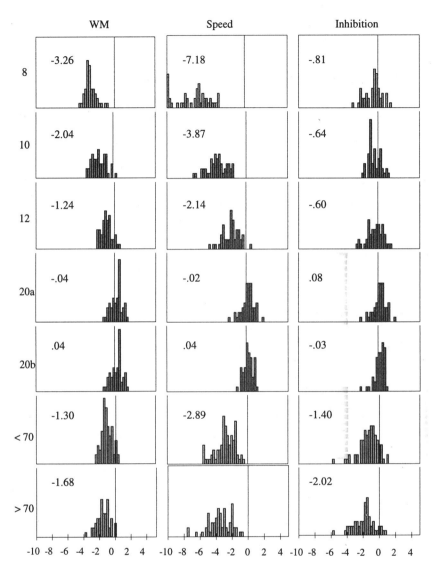

Figure 2
Age differences: standardized units, relative to young adults, by age and construct. Mean scores are indicated. The sample of young adults was randomly split in half (20a and 20b) in most analyses of age differences.

young-old adults. Altogether, the age effects (r^2 for age) were equal to
.64 for WM, .66 for speed, and .12 for inhibition in the young sample
(children and young adults), and .50, .65, and .42, respectively, in the
adult sample (young, young-old, and old-old adults).

**Processing speed and inhibition as mediators of age differences in WM:
regression and commonality analyses**   To assess whether and to what
extent processing speed and inhibition accounted for age differences in
WM tasks, regression and commonality analyses (Pedhazur, 1997) were
run separately for the young sample and for the adult sample. The dependent variable was the mean WM performance; the predictors were
age, age squared (to take into account a possible quadratic trend), speed
and inhibition as previously defined. Although the effect of age, as already mentioned, was important, the role of age alone (unique age) was
small (7% and 3%, in the young and the adult samples, respectively).
Altogether, only 30–40% of the total variance remained unexplained,
and the largest part was explained by a combination of age and speed in
the young sample and by a combination of age, speed, and inhibition
in the adult sample. The age-related variance was partitioned to assess
whether processing speed and inhibition mediated the influence of age on
WM. Together, the two variables accounted for almost all age-related
variance in WM; only 10% (5% in the adult sample) remained unexplained. Speed accounted for a large part in both groups, but particularly so in the young sample (77%); in the older sample, speed alone was
less important, but the largest part of age differences in WM was accounted for by a combination of speed and inhibition. In both groups,
inhibition alone accounted for a negligible part of age differences in WM
(see figure 3).

**Generality of the constructs: confirmatory factor analyses and structural-
equation modeling**   To address the construct-generality issue, confirmatory factor analyses were run for each type of task, again in the two age
samples. The models assumed a single latent variable, defined by the four
WM tasks, by the four speed tasks, or by three inhibition tasks (without
the negative-priming task), respectively. The models were identical for
each of the two age samples, except for slight differences in the parame-

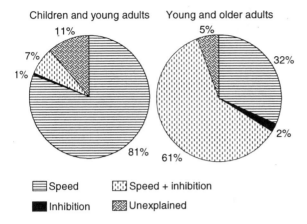

Figure 3
Regression and commonality analyses: age-related variance.

ters. Model fit was good as concerns WM ($\chi^2(3) = 4.12$ for the young sample and $\chi^2(4) = 8.45$ for the adult sample) and speed ($\chi^2(3) = 3.47$ and $\chi^2(4) = 8.42$, respectively). With respect to inhibition, a satisfactory fit was obtained ($\chi^2(1) = .97$ and $\chi^2(1) = 2.26$, respectively); however, the latent variable was almost entirely defined by the color-Stroop task and accounted for almost no variance at all in the other two tasks.

For the question of whether both processing speed and inhibition accounted for age differences in WM tasks, structural-equation modeling was applied using Lisrel (Jöreskog & Sörbom, 1999). Several models were tested, which will not be reported for reasons of space. The model corresponding to our initial hypotheses (figure 4) turned out to be applicable to both age samples and was found to be the best one.

Altogether, this model can be considered to provide a satisfactory fit in both age groups, although the chi-squares were significant (which is often the case with complex models). Among alternative models tested, let me mention two. A model with only one general factor combining speed and inhibition tasks and a model in which speed mediated age differences on both WM and inhibition. Both yielded very poor fits, much worse than the model retained. However, it should be stressed once again that the latent variable inhibition accounted for almost no variance in the observed variables, in either age sample.

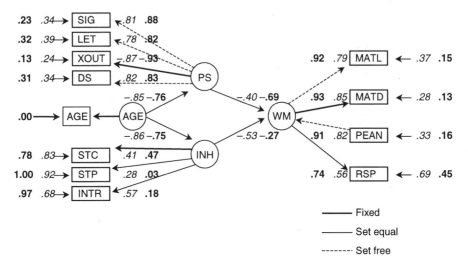

Figure 4
Age, inhibition, processing speed, and working memory: a structural-equations model. SIG, pattern comparison; LET, letter comparison; XOUT, cross-out; DS, digit symbol; MATL, matrices, localization span; MATD, matrices, double color span; PEAN, ghost-peanut; RSP, reading span; STC, Stroop color; STP, Stroop position; INTR, intrusions in proactive interference. Children and young adults: $\chi^2(54) = 125.79$, $p < .01$, RMR (mean square residual) = .075, GFI (goodness of fit index) = .90. Young and older adults: $\chi^2(54) = 126.16$, $p < .01$, RMR = .052, GFI = .90. Parameters are indicated in bold characters for the young sample, and in italics for the adult sample.

It is also remarkable that the same model applied to both age groups. The similarity was restricted, however, to the general architecture (configural invariance and weak factorial invariance) (see, e.g., Schaie, Maitland, Willis & Intrieri, 1998). A multisample analysis (Jöreskog & Sörbom, 1999) showed that it was not possible to constrain all the parameters to be identical in the two groups. The larger numerical differences between the two groups were found in the between-construct relations. Once again, the role of speed seemed more important in the young sample, while inhibition took more importance in the older sample. Combining paths, the "speed way" (i.e., the combination of age to speed and speed to WM) was equal to .52 in the younger sample, while the "inhibition way" was equal to .20; the corresponding values were .34 and .46, respectively, in the older sample.

Conclusion: A Research Agenda

The objectives of this chapter were to provide a coarse review of the literature on age changes in WM across the lifespan and to show how similar were the hypotheses brought forward in cognitive development and in cognitive aging. A long-standing issue in the developmental literature has been to ask whether there are general mechanisms driving cognitive change with age. If such mechanisms are truly general, they should be operational across the lifespan. Even though change in older adulthood is not a full mirror of what happens in childhood, the same processes should be at play, while their respective weight and interplay may vary. A lack of full symmetry between childhood and older adulthood inevitably points to the existence of several underlying processes. It is therefore crucial to adopt a multivariate approach to test both whether the hypothesized processes are general and whether several processes are at work.

The study briefly reported in this chapter was a first attempt on our part to provide preliminary empirical backup to the proposal that both processing speed and inhibition influence age differences in WM across the lifespan. It was not possible to study age in a continuous manner and the study was limited to a comparison of children aged 8 to 12 years of age, young adults, and older adults. The young-adult group was considered as an anchoring group to which compare children on the one hand and older adults on the other hand; the focus was therefore not placed on a comparison of children and older adults. The first question raised was whether all three constructs (or tasks supposed to tap this construct) undergo change with age. The response was clearly affirmative: age differences were significant in all tasks, as well as in the summary scores used in the present chapter. I emphasize, however, that change was steepest for processing speed; the difference between children and young adults, as well as between young and older adults, amounted to several standard deviations, whereas it was much smaller in inhibition tasks. This could, of course, also be due to a greater homogeneity of the young-adult sample in some types of tasks. Nevertheless, the effect of age (variance accounted for by age differences) was much larger for speed and working memory than for inhibition. Note also that the effect of age on inhibition was larger in older adults than in children, relative to young adults.

The second question raised dealt with the generality of each of the three constructs. Correlations among WM tasks, on the one hand, and among processing-speed tasks, on the other hand, were high; a single latent variable for each of these two constructs was easily defined. In contrast, correlations among the inhibition tasks were much lower, and a latent variable accounted for very little variance. It is noteworthy that a model with a single latent variable could nevertheless yield an adequate fit, because other researchers (e.g., Park et al., 1996; Salthouse & Meinz, 1995) encountered difficulties when attempting to include inhibition tasks in confirmatory-factor analyses or in structural-equation models. It should be stressed that inhibition scores reflected only the amount of interference and inhibition, controlling for most other processes that are probably at work in the tasks. In contrast, WM or processing-speed scores were based on raw performances in tasks that certainly also require other processes, such as strategical ones; it is therefore not surprising that they correlated more highly. Nevertheless, the hypothetical generality of inhibition did not receive much empirical support; further studies are obviously necessary before accepting or rejecting a hypothesis according to which inhibition is a general mechanism, all the more so as only two tasks (three in some of the analyses) could be retained.

The third question concerned the possibility that both inhibition and processing speed act as mediating variables between age and WM. Commonality analyses and structural-equation modeling showed that even though processing speed exerted a larger influence, the role of inhibition was not negligible. However, inhibition apparently played a more important role in older adulthood than in childhood. Once again, all conclusions pertaining to inhibition have to be taken with extreme caution and will require replication. Most interesting for our hypotheses was the finding that the same model applied to both the group composed of children and young adults and the group composed of young and older adults, but that the numerical values of the parameters were different. This seems to imply, in line with our hypotheses, that similar processes are at work as far as age changes are concerned, but that their interplay does not remain identical across the lifespan. Moreover, the relative role of inhibition was apparently somewhat stronger in older adulthood.

Because of the complexity of the questions raised, the present study should be considered only as the beginning of a research agenda. A number of issues remain unsolved. First, the meaning and the generality of inhibition need to be clarified by using a greater number of tasks simultaneously. Even though the construct of inhibition is proposed by many researchers as a mediating variable, it is perhaps less general than processing speed or working memory (both of these constructs also requiring further theoretical clarification). A more extensive study is now under way in our laboratory, using more inhibition tasks. Second, other studies using a similar design should be conducted. Third, groups with greater age continuity than the groups studied here should be studied. And last but not least, more detailed theoretical analyses of inhibition tasks should be conducted in order to formulate more precise hypotheses as to which tasks are likely to tap similar processes, and therefore to correlate, and which tasks tap different processes.

Acknowledgment

This paper was made possible by grant no. 1114-040465.94 from the Fonds National Suisse de la Recherche Scientifique. I would like to thank Christine Bailleux, Thierry Lecerf, Joelle Leutwyler, Catherine Ludwig, and Laurence Poget, who worked as collaborators on this project, as well as all the participants, who submitted to a heavy set of tasks.

Notes

1. For the sake of simplicity, and in line with most developmental literature, I will speak of cognitive development as far as changes during childhood are concerned and of cognitive aging when changes in older adults are considered. However, I would like to stress that, in accord with other lifespan researchers (e.g., Baltes, 1987), I consider that development occurs throughout the entire life.

2. Selective attention can be defined in multiple manners. Most definitions refer to the fact that processing is controlled (not automatic) and requires mental effort; there also seems to be a consensus that selective attention implies activation or facilitation and selection (e.g., Posner, 1995). I do not take stand with respect to the level at which selection occurs (e.g., Cowan, 1988); however, given the complexity of the tasks used in the study described in this paper, selective attention is likely to take place at a relatively late stage in information processing.

3. The distinction between inhibition and interference tasks is not always clear. It is not the objective of this paper to clarify the distinction. Therefore, the term

of inhibition task will be used to refer to tasks as diverse as the negative priming task (in which good inhibitors take longer to respond) or the Stroop task (in which good inhibitors are faster). "Inhibition" here refers to some kind of central process that actively suppresses information, and not to peripheral or automatic inhibition (Bjork, 1989).

4. The original design also included the Tower of Hanoi task, supposed to tap executive processes. Because the present chapter focuses on the importance of processing speed and inhibition, and because this task turned out to be particularly unreliable, it is not included in the description. A lexical-categorization task was also administered, the results of which will not be presented here.

5. Analyses of variance showed that all groups differed from all other groups within each of the two age subsamples, except as concerns the inhibition score. In this case, the children groups did not differ from each other, although they all differed from the young adult group. In contrast, the between-group difference remained significant within the adult sample.

References

Baddeley, A. (1986). *Working memory*. Oxford: Oxford University Press.

Baddeley, A., & Hitch, G. J. (1974). Working memory. In G. Bower (Ed.), *Recent advances in learning and motivation* (vol. 8, pp. 47–70). New York: Academic Press.

Baddeley, A. D. (1992). Is working memory working? The fifteenth Bartlett lecture. *Quarterly Journal of Experimental Psychology, 44A*, 1–31.

Baltes, P. B. (1987). Theoretical propositions of life-span developmental psychology: On the dynamics between growth and decline. *Developmental Psychology, 23*, 611–626.

Bjork, R. A. (1989). Retrieval inhibition as an adaptive mechanism in human memory. In H. L. Roediger & F. I. M. Craik (Eds.), *Varieties of memory and consciousness*. (pp. 309–330). Hillsdale, N.J.: Erlbaum.

Bjorklund, D. F., & Harnishfeger, K. K. (1990). The resources construct in cognitive development: Diverse sources of evidence and a theory of inefficient inhibition. *Developmental Review, 10*, 48–71.

Case, R. (1985). *Intellectual development: Birth to adulthood*. New York: Academic Press.

Case, R. (1992a). Neo-Piagetian theories of intellectual development. In H. Beilin & P. B. Pufall (Eds.), *Piaget's theory: Prospects and possibilities* (pp. 61–104). Hillsdale, N.J.: Erlbaum.

Case, R. (1992b). *The mind's staircase: Exploring the conceptual underpinnings of children's thought and knowledge*. Hillsdale, N.J.: Erlbaum.

Case, R., Okamoto, Y., Henderson, B., & McKeough, A. (1993). Individual variability and consistency in cognitive development: New evidence for the existence of central conceptual structures. In R. Case & W. Edelstein (Eds.), *The new structuralism in cognitive development: Theory and research on individual pathways* (pp. 71–100). Basel: Karger.

Chapman, M. (1990). Cognitive development and the growth of capacity: Issues in neo-Piagetian theory. In J. T. Enns (Ed.), *The development of attention: Research and theory* (pp. 263–287). Amsterdam: North Holland.

Conway, A. R. A., & Engle, R. W. (1996). Individual differences in working memory capacity: More evidence for a general capacity theory. *Memory, 4* (6), 577–590.

Cowan, N. (1988). Evolving conceptions of memory storage, selective attention, and their mutual constraints within the human information-processing system. *Psychological Bulletin, 104*, 163–191.

Craik, F. I. M., & Jennings, J. M. (1992). Human memory. In F. I. M. Craik & T. A. Salthouse (Eds.), *The handbook of memory and aging* (pp. 51–110). Hillsdale, N.J.: Erlbaum.

Daneman, M., & Carpenter, P. A. (1980). Individual differences in working memory and reading. *Journal of Verbal Learning and Verbal Behavior, 19*, 450–466.

Dempster, F. N. E., & Brainerd, C. J. E. (Eds.) (1995). *Interference and inhibition in cognition.* San Diego, Calif.: Academic Press.

Dempster, F. N. (1985). Short-term memory development in childhood and adolescence. In C. J. Brainerd & M. Pressley (Eds.), *Basic processes in memory development* (pp. 209–248). New York: Springer Verlag.

Dempster, F. N. (1992). The rise and fall of the inhibitory mechanism: Toward a unified theory of cognitive development and aging. *Developmental Review, 12*, 45–75.

Engle, R. W., Cantor, J., & Carullo, J. J. (1992). Individual differences in working memory and comprehension: A test of four hypotheses. *Journal of Experimental Psychology: Learning, Memory, and Cognition, 18*, 972–992.

Engle, R. W., Conway, A. R. A., Tuholski, S. W., & Shisler, R. J. (1995). A resource account of inhibition. *Psychological Science, 6* (2), 122–125.

Engle, R. W., Kane, M. J., & Tuholski, S. W. (1998). Individual differences in working memory capacity and what they tell us about controlled attention, general fluid intelligence and functions of the prefrontal cortex. In A. Miyake & P. Shah (Eds.), *Models of working memory: Mechanisms of active maintenance and executive control* (pp. 102–134). Cambridge: Cambridge University Press.

Ericsson, K. A., & Kintsch, W. (1995). Long-term working memory. *Psychological Review, 102* (2), 211–245.

Halford, G. S. (1993). *Children's understanding: The development of mental models.* Hillsdale, N.J.: Erlbaum.

Hamm, V. P., & Hasher, L. (1992). Age and the availability of inferences. *Psychology and Aging, 7*, 56–64.

Hartman, M., & Hasher, L. (1991). Aging and suppression: Memory for previously relevant information. *Psychology and Aging*, 6, 587–594.

Hasher, L., Stoltzfus, E. R., Zacks, R. T., & Rypma, B. (1991). Age and inhibition. *Journal of Experimental Psychology: Learning, Memory, and Cognition*, 17, 163–169.

Hasher, L., & Zacks, R. T. (1988). Working memory, comprehension, and aging: A review and a new view. In G. H. Bower (Ed.), *The psychology of learning and motivation* (pp. 193–225). San Diego: Academic Press.

Jöreskog, K., & Sörbom, D. (1999). *Lisrel 8.30*. Chicago: Scientific Software International.

Kail, R. (1988). Developmental functions for speeds of cognitive processes. *Journal of Experimental Child Psychology*, 45, 339–364.

Kail, R. (1990). More evidence for a common, central constraint on speed of processing. In J. T. Enns (Ed.), *The development of attention: Research and theory* (pp. 159–173). Amsterdam: North Holland.

Kail, R. (1995). Processing speed, memory, and cognition. In F. E. Weinert & W. Schneider (Eds.), *Memory performance and competencies: Issues in growth and development* (pp. 71–88). Mahwah, N.J.: Lawrence Erlbaum.

Kail, R., & Park, Y. S. (1992). Global developmental change in processing time. *Merrill-Palmer Quarterly*, 38, 525–541.

Kipp, K. and Pope, S. (1997) The development of cognitive inhibition in streams-of-consciousness and directed speech. *Cognitive Development*, 12, 239–260.

Kipp Harnishfeger, K., & Bjorklund, D. F. (1993). The ontogeny of inhibition mechanisms: A renewed approach to cognitive development. In M. L. Howe & R. Pasnak (Eds.), *Emerging themes in cognitive Development* (pp. 28–49). New York: Springer Verlag.

Light, L. L. (1991). Memory and aging: Four hypotheses in search of data. *Annual Review of Psychology*, 42, 333–376.

Loisy, C., & Roulin, J. L. (1992). Multiple short-term storage in working memory: A new experimental approach. Paper presented at the fifth conference of the European Society for Cognitive Psychology, Paris.

MacDonald, M. C., Just, M. A., & Carpenter, P. A. (1992). Working memory constraints on the processing of syntactic ambiguity. *Cognitive Psychology*, 24, 56–98.

Miyake, A., & Shah, P. (Eds.) (1999). *Models of working memory: Mechanisms of active maintenance and executive control*. Cambridge: Cambridge University Press.

Moscovitch, M. (1994). Memory and working with memory: Evaluation of a component process model and comparisons with other models. In D. L. Schacter & E. Tulving (Eds.), *Memory systems 1994* (pp. 269–310). Cambridge: MIT Press.

Park, D. C., Smith, A. D., Lautenschlager, G., Earles, J. L., Frieske, D., Zwahr, M., & Gaines, C. L. (1996). Mediators of long-term memory performance across the life span. *Psychology and Aging, 11* (4), 621–637.

Pascual-Leone, J. (1970). A mathematical model for the transition rule in Piaget's developmental stages. *Acta Psychologica, 32*, 301–345.

Pascual-Leone, J. (1987). Organismic processes for neo-Piagetian theories: A dialectical causal account of cognitive development. *International Journal of Psychology, 22*, 531–570.

Pascual-Leone, J., & Baillargeon, R. (1994). Developmental measurement of mental attention. *International Journal of Behavioral Development, 17* (1), 161–200.

Pedhazur, E. J. (1997). *Multiple regression in behavioral research: Explanation and prediction.* 3rd Ed. Fort Worth: Harcourt Brace College Publishers.

Posner, M. I. (1995). Attention in cognitive neuroscience: An overview. In M. S. Gazzaniga (Ed.), *The cognitive neurosciences* (pp. 615–624). Cambridge: MIT Press.

Reuchlin, M. (1978). Processus vicariants et différences individuelles. *Journal de Psychologie, 2*, 133–145.

Ribaupierre, Anik de (1993). Structural and individual differences: On the difficulty of dissociating developmental and differential processes. In R. Case & W. Edelstein (Eds.), *The new structuralism in cognitive development: Theory and research on individual pathways* (pp. 11–32). Basel: Karger.

Ribaupierre, Anik de (1999). Working Memory and Attentional Control. In W. Perrig and A. Grob (Eds.), *Control of human behavior, mental processes, and consciousness* (pp. 147–164). Mahwah: Lawrence Erlbaum Associates.

Ribaupierre, Anik de, & Bailleux, C. (1994). Developmental change in a spatial task of attentional capacity: An essay toward an integration of two working memory models. *International Journal of Behavioral Development, 17*, 5–35.

Ribaupierre, Anik de, Lecerf, T., & Bailleux, C. (2000). Is a nonverbal working memory task necessarily nonverbally encoded? *Current Psychology of Cognition/ Cahiers de Psychologie Cognitive, 19*, 135–170.

Richardson, J. T. E. (1996). Evolving issues of working memory. In J. T. E. Richardson, R. W. Engle, L. Hasher, R. H. Logie, E. R. Stoltzfus & R. T. Zacks (Eds.), *Working memory and human cognition* (p. 120–147). New York: Oxford University Press.

Rieben, L., de Ribaupierre, A., & Lautrey, J. (1990). Structural invariants and individual modes of processing: On the necessity of a minimally structuralist approach of development for education. *Archives de Psychologie, 58*, 29–53.

Salthouse, T. A. (1990). Working memory as a processing resource of cognitive aging. *Developmental Review, 10*, 101–124.

Salthouse, T. A. (1992). *Mechanisms of age-cognition relations in adulthood.* Hillsdale, N.J.: Erlbaum.

Salthouse, T. A. (1993). Influence of working memory on adult age differences in matrix reasoning. *British Journal of Psychology, 84,* 171–199.

Salthouse, T. (1994). How many causes are there of age-related decrements in cognitive functioning? *Developmental Review, 14* (4), 413–437.

Salthouse, T. A. (1996). The processing-speed theory of adult age differences in cognition. *Psychological Review, 103* (3), 403–428.

Salthouse, T. A., & Babcock, R. L. (1991). Decomposing adult age differences in working memory. *Developmental Psychology, 27,* 763–776.

Salthouse, T. A., & Meinz, E. J. (1995). Aging, inhibition, working memory, and speed. *Journals of Gerontology. Series B: Psychological Sciences and Social Sciences, 50* (6), P297–P306.

Schacter, D. L., & Tulving, E. (1994). What are the memory systems of 1994? In D. L. Schacter & E. Tulving (Eds.), *Memory systems 1994* (pp. 1–38). Cambridge: MIT Press.

Schaie, K. W., Maitland, S. B., Willis, S. L., & Intrieri, R. C. (1998). Longitudinal invariance of adult psychometric ability factor structures across 7 years. *Psychology and Aging, 13* (1), 8–20.

Stoltzfus, E. R., Hasher, L., & Zacks, R. T. (1996). Working memory and aging: Current status of the inhibitory view. In J. T. E. Richardson, R. W. Engle, L. Hasher, R. H. Logie, E. R. Stoltzfus & R. T. Zacks (Eds.), *Working memory and human cognition* (pp. 66–88). New York: Oxford University Press.

Tipper, S. P., Bourque, T. A., Anderson, S. H., & Brehaut, J. C. (1989). Mechanisms of attention: A developmental study. *Journal of Experimental Child Psychology, 48,* 353–378.

Woodcock, R. W., & Johnson, M. B. (1989). *Woodcock-Johnson psycho-educational battery—Revised.* Allen, Tex.: DLM Teaching Resources.

III

The Development of Episodic and Autobiographical Memory in Children

5

Children's Long-Term Memory of Childhood Events

Robyn Fivush

As adults, we can recall personally significant events over a lifetime. Although forgetting obviously occurs, both for whole events and for details, what is remarkable is the clarity and vividness with which many events are recalled even as the decades pass (see Conway, 1990, and Rubin, 1996, for overviews). Yet, curiously, adults have difficulty recalling events from their early childhood, and most adults cannot recall events that occurred before the age of about 3 to 4 years, a phenomenon labeled childhood amnesia (see Pillemer & White, 1989, for a review). Importantly, childhood amnesia refers to the inability to *consciously* access memories of these early years. Obviously, much information learned in the first few years of life is retained, either implicitly as behavioral tendencies or attitudes or explicitly as semantic knowledge about objects in the world. The claim is that these early experiences are not accessible as episodic memories that might become part of one's autobiographical life history. This paucity of early memories cannot be explained by simple forgetting curves; while it is true that we recall less information as time passes, there remains a significant lack of memories for the first few years of life above and beyond that predicted by normal forgetting functions (Wetzler & Sweeney, 1986).

Explanations of childhood amnesia have ranged from psychodynamic repression of sexual and aggressive content (Freud, 1953/1924) to changes in cognitive schemata and self-organization (Howe & Courage, 1993; Waldvogel, 1982), to neurobiological developments in the ability to store and retrieve information (Spear, 1979). While quite different in theoretical orientation, what these explanations share is an assumption that early memories are qualitatively different from later memories and that memories become accessible for long-term recall when children cross the "childhood amnesia barrier" as the result of a reorganization of the memory system. Thus, even young children should have difficulty recalling the events of their lives before the age of about 3 to 4 years. Yet recent research has demonstrated that even quite young children are able to report accurate details about specific personally experienced events and seem able to retain these memories over extended periods of time. These kinds of findings call into question traditional explanations of childhood amnesia and at the same time raise an even more enigmatic question. If young children are able to recall details of their personal past, why do we become unable to recall these events as we grow older?

In this chapter I first review research demonstrating young children's abilities to recall the past. I then discuss several studies examining long-term retention of these early memories into middle childhood. A consideration of this research leads to a reconceptualization of childhood amnesia that is based on several factors, including distinctiveness, rehearsal, and language development. In the final section I outline a model of childhood amnesia based on the complex interplay of these factors in specific social interactions.

Early Event Memory

Even in the first year of life, infants are able to recognize and recall aspects of specific experiences. For example, in the first 3 months of life, infants can learn a specific contingency between foot kicking and a mobile moving above their crib, and they are able to retain this information over a period of days or weeks, depending on the particulars of training and context of assessment (see Rovee-Collier & Shyi, 1992, for a review). By 6 months of age, children demonstrate recognition of specific pictures seen as much as 2 weeks in the past (Fagan, 1973), and by the end of the first year, infants are able to re-enact a sequence of unusual activities with novel toys even after a delay of several weeks (Bauer, 1996).

While these kinds of findings indicate quite robust memory skills very early in development, there are also significant limitations of early memory. Early memories do not seem to endure as long as later memories;

indeed, Rovee-Collier and her colleagues (Rovee-Collier, 1995) have mapped out the developing ability to retain information over a few days early in the first year, extending to several months by the end of the first year. It is also unclear whether these early memories are implicit or explicit (see Mandler, in press, versus Rovee-Collier & Shyi, 1992, for a full discussion). And perhaps most critical for the issues addressed here, these early memories are quite contextually bound. Infants demonstrate retention of previously experienced events when placed back in the same context and provided with the same objects that were part of the original experience. As aspects of the place and/or the objects change, memory becomes increasingly more variable. Related to this, there is virtually no evidence that these early experiences are recalled verbally as children grow older (see Fivush, 1994a, for a review).

The development of verbal recall heralds a fundamentally new memory ability for several reasons. First, verbal recall is the clearest evidence of a consciously accessible explicit memory of a specific experience. Second, verbal recall is the only way in which past events can be communicated with others in the absence of any other physical cues. Although memories of past events can be demonstrated in action, given the appropriate context and props, verbal memory is completely decontextualized. Third and most important, verbal recall allows the individual to talk about the event with others. The ability to share one's past experiences with others through language provides several new opportunities for memory enhancement, including verbal rehearsal and reorganization of the memory into a more coherent narrative form (see Fivush, Haden & Reese, 1996, and Nelson, 1996, for full theoretical discussions of these points). Thus the ability to verbalize about a personal experience opens up new developmental possibilities for the organization and maintenance of event memories.

Children begin to verbally reference the past soon after they begin talking, at about 18 months of age. At this early developmental period, however, children recall just bits and pieces of a past event, referring almost exclusively to recently completed or routine activities (Eisenberg, 1985; Sachs, 1983). Adults, usually parents, provide a mnemonic scaffold for the child, essentially supporting the child's recall by posing specific questions and giving specific cues. By about age 2.5, children become better able to recall aspects of the past, especially to recall particular episodes over longer periods of time.

For example, Fivush, Gray, and Fromhoff (1987) asked children between the ages of 2.5 and 3 years to recall specific distinctive events that they had experienced either in the previous 3 months or more than 3 months ago. Events to ask each child about were determined in a preinterview with parents and were selected to be distinctive and highly salient. Children were able to recall about half of the events queried and were able to provide many accurate details about these experiences. However, they required many cues and prompts from the interviewer. Perhaps most surprising, children recalled as much information about the more distantly experienced events as about the more recently experienced events and did not need any more cues in order to do so. Similarly, Todd and Perlmutter (1980) asked 3- and 4-year-old children to recall specific events experienced over the previous year and found that children at both ages were able to provide a great deal of accurate information about these events, although older children recalled more than did younger children.

The fact that children this young are able to recall aspects of their past experiences raises the intriguing question of whether they are able to recall these events over more extended periods of time. Fivush and Hamond (1990) reinterviewed children initially interviewed when they were 2.5 to 3 years old again when they were just under 4 years of age. Children were asked to recall only those events that had remained distinctive in their lives, as determined through preinterviews with parents. For example, if at the initial interview children were asked about Halloween, this event was not asked about again, as the children would have experienced this event once or twice more in the interim. But an event that had not recurred, such as a family trip to Seaworld or a relative's wedding, was asked about. Surprisingly, children readily and easily recalled these events. In fact, children recalled more information at the second interview, reporting about 12 units of information as compared to about 9 units of information at the initial interview. Most puzzling, most of the information reported at the second interview was different information from what children reported at the initial interview. Just under 75% of the information children provided at age 4 was different from the information provided at age 2.5 to 3. A closer examination of what information children were providing indicated that in the initial interviews, children focused on what might make this unique event similar to more familiar events. For example, when recalling going on a family camping trip, one young girl reported that they ate dinner, went to sleep, got up, and ate breakfast—exactly what they did at home except that they did it in a tent. At age 4, children were much more likely to focus on the distinctive aspects of the event, what made the event different from other events. Very possibly, when children are first organizing their knowledge about events, they focus on what is routine, what makes the world predictable. But as they get older and begin to have a more established sense of the world and of themselves, they focus more on what makes things different and interesting (see Nelson, 1988, for similar arguments). Thus one reason that very early experiences may be rendered difficult to recall later in development is that the memories are not organized around distinctive memory cues. But these findings also suggest that, even if what is reported early in development focuses on the routine, distinctive aspects must be encoded and stored because they are available for retrieval later in development.

Of course, it is possible that children are simply reporting what they have been told about these events, but this explanation is not likely for several reasons. First, children do not come to report aspects of events that they have heard in parental conversations to any great extent. In interviews following parent-child conversations about specific events, children incorporate less that 10% of information initially provided by parents into their own subsequent recall (Fivush, Hamond, Harsch, Singer & Wolf, 1991; Fivush, 1994b). Further, parents report that, although they talked about these events when they first occurred, they had not talked about these events with their children in the past year. Indeed, this is generally the case with family talk about special occasions. They tend to be talked about a great deal around the time of occurrence, show a sharp decline in family conversations after the first few weeks, and then are talked about rarely if ever unless a related event occurs. This is not to argue that family conversations play no role in enhancing and maintaining early memories. I think they do, as I will argue in more detail later.

But family conversations about past events do not seem to substitute for children's own memories about these experiences.

These results are especially noteworthy because children were recalling events across the so-called "childhood amnesia barrier," which indicates that children are able to verbally recall events of their lives earlier than age 3 and that they are still able to recall these events at age 4. To replicate and extend this finding, Hamond and Fivush (1990) examined children's long-term memories of a family trip to Disneyworld. In this study, all children were asked about a similar event using the same structured interview across children. Further, developmental and retention-interval differences were examined by interviewing, either 6 months or 18 months after the event, children who had been either 37 months or 49 months of age at the time of the family trip. Again, children demonstrated remarkable memory of this experience, recalling an average of about 40 propositions (subject-verb idea units). Moreover, there were no age or retention-interval differences. Even children who had been barely 3 at the time of the experience and who were interviewed after 18 months recalled as much information as older children interviewed after 6 months. However, children who were older at the time of the interview recalled more information in response to open-ended questions than did children younger at the time of the interview, and older children recalled the event in more detail than did younger children (e.g., recalling the "big, flying Dumbo ride" versus recalling just "the Dumbo ride"). Thus while the number of idea units was equal across age, older children recalled more information spontaneously and recalled it in greater detail than did younger children.

Further, parental estimates of how much they had talked about this event with their children (or looked at photos and videos) was not related to how much children recalled at the 6-month retention interval, but it was related at the 18-month retention interval. Those children whose families talked about the event more recalled more after the longer retention interval. However, even though the effect emerged at the later retention interval, most of the family talk occurred close to the time of the experience. This suggests that talking about an event when it occurs may buffer against long-term forgetting.

The pattern of results clearly indicates that early in development children are able to verbally recall details of their personal experiences and remain able to recall these events across the preschool period. Thus childhood amnesia cannot be explained as an inability to encode or retrieve information early in development. Moreover, the fact that at age 4 children are still able to verbally report events that occurred more than a year earlier suggests that childhood amnesia cannot be explained as a reorganization of memory occurring at about age 3.5 to 4 years that renders earlier memories difficult to access or recall. Moreover, the fact that children are able to retain event memories across the preschool years raises the question of the longevity of these memories into childhood and possibly even into adulthood.

Long-Term Retention of Preschool Memories

Only a handful of studies have assessed the retention of memories from the preschool years into childhood. Pillemer, Picariello, and Pruett (1994) had initially interviewed 3- and 4-year-old children about an emergency fire evacuation of their preschool. As it turned out, the emergency was a burning popcorn popper and thus there was no subsequent disaster. Still, most of the children were able to give detailed accounts of what occurred during the evacuation, although older children recalled more information and recalled the information in a more organized fashion than younger children. Seven years later they reinterviewed the children about this early experience. Surprisingly, many of the children still recalled the evacuation, although older children recalled more than did younger children, and all children needed quite specific cues to recall the event at all. Most intriguing, those children who were best able to provide an organized account of what occurred at the time of experience were the children most likely to recall the event seven years later.

In a related study, Fivush and Schwarzmueller (1998) studied children's memories from preschool through school age. Children were initially interviewed as part of a longitudinal study examining autobiographical memory development in social context (see Fivush, Haden & Reese, 1996, for details). In the initial study, children were interviewed four times across the preschool years, when they were 40 months of age, 46 months, 58 months, and 70 months. At each time point, children were interviewed about novel distinctive events that had occurred during the previous year, such as being a flower girl in an aunt's wedding. Different events were asked about at each of these interviews. When the children were 8 years old, we reinterviewed them about many of these events. On the basis of preliminary interviews with parents, we selected only those events that had remained distinctive in the children's lives. Overall, each child was asked about approximately 4 to 6 events from their preschool years. Only general, open-ended questions were asked, such as "Tell me about going to Seaworld." Once the children exhausted their free recall, one cue was given specific to each event and based on the child's previous recall (for example, getting splashed when watching Shamu at Seaworld). Because the vast majority of children's recall was provided in response to the free-recall questions, this distinction will not be further discussed here.

Children recalled just over 85% of all the events queried. More remarkable, children recalled as many idea units (subject-verb propositions) at age 8 as they did when they initially recalled the event years earlier, and virtually all information was accurate according to maternal report. On average, children recalled about 10 idea units in response to an open-ended free-recall question at both the initial interview and again at the age-8 interviews. (Note that this is substantially less then the amount recalled about going to Disneyworld because in that study a full-structured interview was used that included many specific prompts and cues.) Thus 8-year-old children easily recalled a substantial amount of accurate information about events they had experienced 2, 3, 4, and 5 years in the past. Most impressive, 8-year-old children were able to recall events that had occurred when they were barely 3 years old. Yet about 80% of the information they reported at age 8 was different information from what they had reported in the previous interview, although still accurate.

This finding is especially interesting in light of the previous findings of high levels of inconsistency in children's reports during the preschool years. Inconsistency is not simply due to a changing focus of what children deem interesting or important to report. In this study, all the information provided at both interviews was highly detailed and focused on distinctive aspects of the experience. Moreover, these data provide little indication that children are reconstructing "what must have happened" at the age-8 interviews. If this were the case, we would expect the information reported to be general and highly schematic, rather than specific and detailed. To address the question of whether children are reporting what they have been told happened, parents were asked to estimate how much they talked about these events with their children, both at the initial interviews and at the age-8 interviews. Parents reported frequent conversations with their children close to the time of occurrence of the event, followed by a sharp decline. Few of the events had been discussed at all from the time of the initial interview to the final interview at age 8. Because the event had not been talked about in such a long time, it is unlikely that children were recalling what they had been told. Further, the pattern suggests that rehearsal, in the form of talking about the event with others at the time the event actually occurred, may be more important for long-term retention than is talking about the event closer to the time of retrieval after a long duration.

A final study that examined children's long-term retention of early childhood memories focused on children's recall of a natural disaster. Hurricane Andrew was a severe storm that devastated the Florida coast in 1992. Within a few months of the hurricane, we interviewed 3- and 4-year-old children about their experiences (Bahrick, Parker, Merritt & Fivush, 1997). Obviously, this is an event that differs in several important ways from the previous events studied. Most important, it is a highly stressful and emotionally arousing event. Although many of the events asked about in the previous studies were emotionally salient, few were as stressful as the hurricane. Further, children experiencing the worst of the storm also experienced ongoing consequences, including serious damage to house and property requiring extended repairs. A large literature examining relations between stress and memory has documented that in adults, higher arousal leads to better memory (see Christianson, 1992, for a review). Recent reviews examining children's memories of highly stressful and traumatic events concur that traumatic events are recalled at least as well if not better than more mundane experiences (Fivush, 1998; Pezdek & Taylor, 2002). Yet there is also some suggestion that stress may bear a nonlinear relation to memory. In particular, moderate to high stress levels may increase memory by focusing attention and resources, but as levels of stress become extreme, memory may deteriorate as cognitive processing becomes overwhelmed (Easterbrook, 1959).

In this study, we were able to systematically examine the effects of high levels of stress on children's memories of a natural disaster. Three groups of children were interviewed. While all children had prepared for the hurricane, children in the low-stress group experienced only a mild storm. Children in the moderate-stress group were hit by the hurricane but sustained damage only to the exterior of the house. In contrast, children in the high-stress group weathered the fury of the storm. These children experienced flying glass, falling roofs, and water flooding into the home, often having to move from room to room to avoid personal injury during the storm. Thus we were able to compare children's memories for preparing for the storm, for the storm itself, and for its aftermath under three levels of stress: low, moderate, and severe. Children were interviewed using a structured series of questions moving from open-ended free recall to heavily cued prompts.

Not surprisingly, all children were able to report a great deal of information about their hurricane experience, although, as found previously, older children recalled more information than younger children and recalled more information in response to more open-ended questions. Most intriguing, children in the moderate-stress group recalled more information than did children in the high-stress group, which suggests that extremely high levels of stress may have had a deleterious effect on these young children's memories. However, it must be emphasized that even the children in the high-stress group recalled a surprisingly large amount of information.

More pertinent to the issues addressed here, we were able to re-interview these children six years later, when they were 9 and 10 years old (McDermott, Goldberg, Park, Fivush, Bahrick & Parker, 1999). Importantly, none of these children had experienced another hurricane, nor had they prepared for the possibility of a hurricane in the interim. All of the children were easily able to recall this event; in fact, children recalled twice as many propositions (subject-verb units) at age 9–10 than they did when they were younger, averaging about 50 propositions at the first interview and just over 100 at the second interview. More interesting, stress still had an effect on recall. Children in the highest-stress group recalled less about preparing for the storm than did children in the moderate- or low-stress group but just as much information about the storm itself and its aftermath. But children in the highest-stress group needed more questions and prompts to recall as much information as children in the moderate- and low-stress groups, which suggests that they have more difficulty accessing or talking about this very stressful event.

While final conclusions about the role of stress on long-term memory must await completion of analyses, several conclusions can be drawn from the data examined thus far. First of all, young children remember more information in verbal recall, as evidenced by the doubling of information provided when children were older and had more sophisticated language skills. Moreover, whereas one might expect recall to become more difficult over time, with children needing more specific cues and prompts, the obtained pattern is just the reverse. Although more time has passed, it is also the case that children are more linguistically and mnemonically competent at the second interview, and thus are able to provide more information in response to open-ended questions. Most important, it is clear that children have enduring clear and vivid memories of a stressful experience from their early childhood.

Overall, these studies demonstrate that children are able to recall events from age 3 well into middle childhood. However, it must also be noted that the events studied are highly distinctive and often highly rehearsed at time of occurrence. Certainly, everything we know about human memory would indicate that distinctiveness and rehearsal would lead to better recall (see Schwartz & Reisberg, 1991, for an overview). But how might these factors interact, and more important, how might they contribute to the phenomenon of childhood amnesia?

Explaining Childhood Amnesia

The research findings are paradoxical. Adults have difficulty recalling events that occurred before the age of 3.5 to 4 years, yet children are able to recall events that occurred as early as 2.5 years of age. Moreover, although different methods are used to assess early memories with adults and children, this is not simply a methodological artifact. Even when asked about specific distinctive events that occurred in the first 3 years of life, adults have difficulty recalling them. For example, Sheingold and Tenney (1982) asked participants ranging in age from 4 years to college about the birth of a sibling that had occurred when they were 4 years of age. Thus retention intervals varied from a few months to 20 years. All respondents recalled accurate details of this event. However, another group of participants who were 3 years of age when their sibling was born showed almost no memory of this event. Following up on this methodology, Usher and Neisser (1993) asked college students to recall specific events they had experienced when they were 2, 3, 4, or 5 years of age. Events targeted were birth of a sibling, an overnight hospitalization, moving to a new house, and death of a family member. They found that different events displayed different retention functions. Specifically, overnight hospitalization was recalled even if it occurred at age 2, but the other events were not recalled if they occurred before age 3 or 4. They argue that the saliency and distinctiveness of a given event will contribute to whether it will be recalled into adulthood.

This pattern conforms to Pillemer and White's (1989) description of the findings on childhood amnesia. Upon reviewing research on both children and adults recalling childhood events, they concluded that there are virtually no memories for events that occurred before the age of 2, a few memories survive from the ages of 3–4 years, and from age 5 on we see normal retention and forgetting functions. Thus, to account for childhood amnesia we need to account for both the early emergence of a few memories that survive from very early childhood and the burst of memories that survive from about age 4 or 5 on.

Certainly, distinctiveness must play a role in why some very early events remain memorable. Those memories that survive seem to be those that remain distinctive in one's life. As similar events recur, memories for these experiences become fused into more generic scriptlike structures, rather than remaining singular memories, for both adults (Graesser, Woll, Kowalski & Smith, 1980) and children (Hudson, Fivush & Kuebli, 1992). These events form the background of our life story; they are the familiar and routine events that define our everyday existence. But it is unlikely that we recall each episode in detail, or are even able to differentiate one episode from another. For an event to maintain its episodic quality, it must remain discriminable from other life events. Distinctive events are well recalled both because they have unique memory cues associated with them and because they are not confusable with other similar events that we have experienced. But distinctiveness cannot be the entire explanation. First, distinctive events occur even before the age of 2 or 3, and these events are not remembered. Second, distinctiveness cannot explain the steplike nature of childhood amnesia, with few memories from ages 2–3 and burgeoning memories thereafter.

An obvious factor that must be considered is language. It may very well be more than a coincidence that the earliest memories recalled into childhood and adulthood occur just as children are becoming mature language users. Language allows for a fundamentally new way of organizing memories, that is, the narrative form. Although events unfold in time and memories consist of a multiplicity of images and sensations, linguistically based narrative forms provide a coherent organizational framework for understanding the past (Bruner, 1987; Fivush & Haden, 1997). In particular, narratives go beyond representing a sequence of actions, to provide ways of understanding how events are related together and an evaluative stance, or subjective perspective, on what occurred. When we narrate the past, we do not simply tell what happened, we tell why it was interesting or important or funny. Essentially, we tell why it was personally meaningful (Labov, 1982).

Critically, what matters is not language per se but the ability to organize an event into a story that will remain memorable. As children learn conventionalized narrative forms for reporting the past, they begin to organize their memories coherently and thus are able to retain them over extended periods of time. Although 2-year-old children can reference the past, they cannot yet organize this information into a coherent narrative. Beginning at about age 3, children start developing simple narrative skills, placing reported events in context, and especially providing evaluative information (Umiker-Seboek, 1979). However, these skills are still quite rudimentary. Over the course of the preschool years, children become more competent narrators of their personal experiences (Fivush, Haden & Adam, 1995), and by age 5 they are able to give a clear, well-organized personal narrative, although, of course, these skills continue to develop through childhood (Hudson & Shapiro, 1991).

Moreover, children learn narrative skills in social contexts. When children first begin referencing the past, they do so in social interactions, usually with parents. In fact, it is often the parent who initiates the conversation (Eisenberg, 1985). Talking about the past with adults facilitates memory in two ways. First, it provides a form of rehearsal. Each time an event is talked about, each time it is accessed, it strengthens the event memory. But just as important, by participating in discussions about past experiences with adults, children learn the conventionalized forms for organizing and reporting the past.

Several studies have documented that children are learning specific narrative skills in social interaction. Both McCabe and Peterson (1991) and Fivush (1991) found that mothers who use a great deal of orienting information in conversations with their 2-year-old children, placing the event in spatial and temporal context, have children who, a year later, include more orienting information in their independent narratives. Further, mothers who use a great deal of evaluative information, and especially emotional information, while reminiscing with their young children, have children who subsequently use more evaluative information in their own personal narratives (Fivush, 1991). In the most comprehensive study of this type, Haden, Haine, and Fivush (1997) examined parent-child conversations about the past across the preschool period. Mothers who used more orienting and evaluative information when reminiscing with their children had children who included more of this type of information in their own narratives. Importantly, this effect held even when controlling for children's language skills and previous narrative abilities. Thus, how mothers narratively structure conversations about past events with their young children has a decided effect on children's developing narrative skills. Children are not learning *what* to remember in parent-child conversations; they are learning *how* to remember, *how* to organize and report a personally experienced event in narrative form.

Thus the offset of childhood amnesia can be explained in two phases. When children first become able to verbally reference the past, at about

2 years of age, they also become able to engage in conversations with adults about those events. These early conversations help strengthen specific memories through a form of rehearsal, but children still have difficulty verbally organizing these memories, even with adult help. Logically more distinctive and meaningful events are more likely to be discussed, and thus children may retain a few such memories from this early verbal period. As children grow older, they are better able to participate in reminiscing with adults and are better able to take advantage of narrative forms to help them organize their memories. By about age 4, children are able to provide a coherent narrative without substantial adult guidance. At this point, children become able to organize their memories for themselves, and thus are able to retain these memories over long durations.

Thus, childhood amnesia should not be conceptualized as a "barrier" before which no memories are available and after which a flood of memories are accessible. Rather, as with virtually all other developmental phenomenon, childhood amnesia is better conceptualized as a process. As children engage in conversations about past events with adults, they develop narrative skills. In turn, as these skills develop, children become better able to share their memories with others and to reflect on these memories themselves in more coherently organized ways. It is not simply rehearsal, but the creation of an organized story accessible over time, that leads to enduring personal memories. Thus the formation of autobiographical memories is a dialectical process in which children's skills develop in and through social interaction. Highly distinctive and rehearsed events even from very early in development may become a part of one's autobiographical story as they are discussed and organized in social reminiscing. But only when children are able to engage in such conversations, even in rudimentary forms, can these early memories become enduring. Thus, we see virtually no memories before about age 2, when children are first able to engage in adult-guided reminiscing, a few distinctive memories from age 2 to 4, when children still highly rely on adults to help them organize their memories into coherent narratives, and a burst of memories at about age 4–5, when children become able to organize personally experienced events into coherent, memorable stories for themselves.

References

Bahrick, L., Parker, J., Merritt, K., & Fivush, R. (1997). Children's memory for Hurricane Andrew. *Journal of Experimental Psychology: Applied, 4,* 308–331.

Bauer, P. (1996). Recalling past events: From infancy to early childhood. *Annals of Child Development, 11,* 25–71.

Bruner, J. (1987). Life as narrative. *Social Research, 54,* 11–32.

Conway, M. (1990). *Autobiographical memory: An introduction.* Buckingham: Open University Press.

Christianson, S. A. (1992). Emotional stress and eyewitness memory: A critical review. *Psychological Bulletin, 112,* 284–309.

Easterbrook, J. A. (1959). The effect of emotion on utilization and organization of behavior. *Psychological Review, 66,* 183–201.

Eisenberg, A. (1985). Learning to describe past experience in conversation. *Discourse Processes, 8,* 177–204.

Fagan, J. F., III (1973). Infants' delayed recognition memory and forgetting. *Journal of Experimental Child Psychology, 16,* 424–450.

Fivush, R. (1991). The social construction of personal narratives. *Merrill-Palmer Quarterly, 37,* 59–82.

Fivush, R. (Ed.) (1994a). *Long-term retention of infant memories: A special issue of Memory.* Hillsdale, N.J.: Erlbaum.

Fivush, R. (1994b). Young children's event recall: Are memories constructed through discourse? *Consciousness and Cognition, 3,* 356–373.

Fivush, R. (1998). Children's recollections of traumatic and nontraumatic events. *Development and psychopathology, 10,* 699–716.

Fivush, R., Gray, J. T., & Fromhoff, F. A. (1987). Two year olds' talk about the past. *Cognitive Development, 2,* 393–409.

Fivush, R., & Haden, C. (1997). Narrating and representing experience: Preschoolers' developing autobiographical recounts. In P. van den Broek, P. A. Bauer & T. Bourg (Eds.), *Developmental spans in event comprehension and representation: Bridging fictional and actual events.* Hillsdale, N.J.: Erlbaum.

Fivush, R., Haden, C., & Adam, S. (1995). Structure and coherence of preschoolers' personal narratives over time: Implications for childhood amnesia. *Journal of Experimental Child Psychology, 60,* 32–56.

Fivush, R., Haden, C., & Reese, E. (1996). Remembering, recounting and reminiscing: The development of autobiographical memory in social context. In D. Rubin (Ed.), *Remembering our past: An overview of autobiographical memory* (pp. 341–359). New York: Cambridge University Press.

Fivush, R., & Hamond, N. (1990). Autobiographical memory across the preschool years: Towards reconceptualizing childhood amnesia. In R. Fivush & J. A.

Hudson (Eds.), *Knowing and remembering in young children* (pp. 223–248). New York: Cambridge University Press.

Fivush, R., Hamond, N. R., Harsch, N., Singer, N., & Wolf, A. (1991). Content and consistency of young children's autobiographical recall. *Discourse Processes, 14*, 373–388.

Fivush, R., & Schwarzmueller, A. (1998). Children remember childhood: Implications for childhood amnesia. *Applied Cognitive Psychology, 12*, 455–473.

Freud, S. (1953/1924). *A general introduction to psychoanalysis.* New York: Pocket Books.

Graesser, A. C., Woll, S. B., Kowalski, D. J., & Smith, D. A. (1980). Memory for typical and atypical actions in scripted activities. *Journal of Experimental Psychology: Human Learning and Memory, 6*, 503–515.

Haden, C., Haine, R., & Fivush, R. (1997). Developing narrative structure in parent-child conversations about the past. *Developmental Psychology, 33*, 295–307.

Hamond, N. R., & Fivush, R. (1990). Memories of Mickey Mouse: Young children recount their trip to Disneyworld. *Cognitive Development, 6*, 433–448.

Howe, M., & Courage, M. (1993). On resolving the enigma of childhood amnesia. *Psychological Bulletin, 113*, 305–326.

Hudson, J. A., Fivush, R., & Kuebli, J. (1992). Scripts and episodes: The development of event memory. *Applied Cognitive Psychology, 6*, 483–505.

Hudson, J. A., & Shapiro, L. (1991). Effects of task and topic on children's narratives. In A. McCabe & C. Peterson (Eds.), *New directions in developing narrative structure* (pp. 89–136). Hillsdale, N.J.: Lawrence Erlbaum Associates.

Labov, W. (1982). Speech actions and reaction in personal narrative. In D. Tannen (Ed.), *Analyzing discourse: Text and talk.* Washington, D.C.: Georgetown University Press.

Mandler, J. (in press). Journal of Cognition and Development.

McCabe, A., & Peterson, C. (1991). Getting the story: A longitudinal study of parental styles in eliciting narratives and developing narrative skill. In A. McCabe & C. Peterson (Eds.), *Developing narrative structure* (pp. 217–253). Hillsdale, N.J.: Lawrence Erlbaum Associates.

McDermott, J., Goldberg, A., Park, S., Fivush, R., Bahrick, L., & Parker, J. (1999). Children's long-term memory of a stressful event. Poster presented at the meetings of the Cognitive Development Society, October, Chapel Hill, N.C.

Nelson, K. (1988). The ontogeny of memory for real events. In U. Neisser & E. Winograd (Eds.), *Remembering reconsidered: Ecological and traditional approaches to the study of memory* (pp. 244–276). New York: Cambridge.

Nelson, K. (1996). *Language in cognitive development.* New York: Cambridge University press.

Pezdek, K., & Taylor, J. (2002). Memories of traumatic events. In M. L. Eisen, J. S. Quas & G. S. Goodman (Eds.), *Memory and suggestibility in the forensic interview* (pp. 165–184). Hillsdale, N.J.: Erlbaum.

Pillemer, D. B., Picariello, M. L., & Pruett, J. C. (1994). Very long term memories of a salient preschool event. *Journal of Applied Cognitive Psychology, 8,* 95–106.

Pillemer, D., & White, S. H. (1989). Childhood events recalled by children and adults. In H. W. Reese (Ed.), *Advances in child development and behavior* (vol. 22). New York: Academic.

Rovee-Collier, C. (1995). Time windows in cognitive development. *Developmental Psychology, 31,* 147–169.

Rovee-Collier, C., & Shyi, C. W. G. (1992). A functional and cognitive analysis of infant long-term memory retention. In M. L. Howe, C. J. Brainerd & V. F. Reyna (Eds.), *Development of long-term retention.* New York: Springer-Verlag.

Rubin, D. (Ed.) (1996). *Remembering our past: An overview of autobiographical memory.* New York: Cambridge University Press.

Sachs, J. (1983). Talking about the there and then: The emergence of displaced reference in parent-child discourse. In K. Nelson (Ed.), *Children's language* (vol. 4, pp. 1–28). Hillsdale, N.J.: Lawrence Erlbaum Associates.

Schwartz, B., & Reisberg, D. (1991). *Learning and memory.* New York: Norton.

Sheingold, K., & Tenney, Y. J. (1982). Memory for a salient childhood event. In U. Neisser (Ed.), *Memory observed* (pp. 201–212). San Francisco: W. H. Freeman.

Spear, N. (1979). Experimental analysis of infantile amnesia. In J. F. Kihlstrom & F. J. Evans (Eds.) *Functional disorders of memory* (pp. 75–102). Hillside, N.J.: Erlbaum.

Todd, C., & Perlmutter, M. (1980). Reality recalled by preschool children. In M. Perlmutter (Ed.), *Children's memory* (pp. 69–86). San Francisco: Jossey-Bass.

Umiker-Seboek, D. J. (1979). Preschool children's intraconversational narratives. *Journal of Child Language, 6,* 91–109.

Usher, J., & Neisser, U. (1993). Childhood amnesia and the beginnings of memory for four early life events. *Journal of Experimental Psychology: General, 122,* 155–165.

Waldvogel, S. (1982). Childhood memories. In U. Neisser (Ed.), *Memory observed* (pp. 73–76). San Francisco: W. H. Freeman

Wetzler, S. E., & Sweeney, J. A. (1986). Childhood amnesia: An empirical demonstration. In D. Rubin (Ed.), *Autobiographical memory* (pp. 202–221). New York: Cambridge University Press.

6

Children's Eyewitness Memory: Changing Reports and Changing Representations

David F. Bjorklund, Rhonda Douglas Brown, and Barbara R. Bjorklund

At its modern onset in the 1960s, research in memory development focused on strategic processes relevant for children in schooled societies (see Schneider & Bjorklund, 1998, in press, for reviews). In the 1980s this focus began to shift away from the study of children's deliberate efforts to remember lists of pictures or words to investigations of their recollections of everyday life. In particular, modern memory researchers have focused on children's *event*, or *autobiographical*, memory, which involves forming narratives to recount personally experienced events (see Fivush, 1997; Nelson, 1996, for reviews).

Recently, sociocultural forces have steered research in children's event memory towards applied issues, particularly concerning the accuracy of children as eyewitnesses. Much of this interest has stemmed from the increase in children testifying in courts, both as victims and witnesses. According to Ceci and Bruck's (1998) conservative estimate concerning the situation in the United States, about 100,000 children testify annually in criminal and civil cases. Whitcomb (1992) reported that children often participate in multiple interviews, up to 12, often across several years, by police officers, social workers, and attorneys. During the late 1980s through the early 1990s, there were a number of high-profile cases in which preschool personnel were accused of sexually abusing their wards (see Brown, Goldstein & Bjorklund, 2000; Ceci & Bruck, 1995, for reviews). During this time, it was estimated that 13,000 children testified in sexual abuse cases each year (Ceci & Bruck, 1998). Many cases led to conviction and jail time for the accused abusers (e.g., State v. Francisco Fuster, 1985). However, some of these cases were later overturned because of evidence that the children were inappropriately interviewed (e.g., State v. Michaels, 1988). For example, suggestive interviewing techniques, such as the use of anatomical dolls and leading questions, were an integral component to what became referred to as "The Miami Method," used to prosecute accused sexual offenders in the Old Cutler (State v. Fijnje, 1991) and Country Walk (State v. Francisco Fuster, 1985) day-care cases. The use of such techniques raised the question of whether children's reports reflected their true memories, acquiescence to social-demand characteristics inherent in forensic interviews, or false memories (i.e., changes in memory representations) planted by suggestive interviewing techniques.

Particularly important were issues related to age differences in suggestibility. Adults, of course, are not immune to the effects of suggestion or misinformation (see, e.g., Loftus & Pickrell, 1995), but are children especially susceptible to suggestion? Given the realities of forensic interviews, how do children respond to repeated questioning, both within and between interviews? How durable are their memories? When faced with misinformation and the demands of an authoritative interviewer, will they succumb to the pressure and change their answers? And if they do, will such questioning actually serve to change their memory representations of events?

These and related questions were posed by memory development researchers across the past two decades. We have accrued a substantial knowledge base about the many factors that affect children's eyewitness memory (see Ceci & Bruck, 1998; Goodman, Emery & Haugaard, 1998, for reviews). In this chapter, we will review some of this research, focusing on work we have done over the past decade, particularly as it relates to children's suggestibility. Although our research addressed a number of issues pertinent to children's eyewitness memory, our central concern revolved around the extent to which suggestion and misinformation changes children's answers (i.e., the responses they give to interviewers) versus their minds (i.e., their actual memory representations).

Theoretical Perspectives on Changing Answers and Changing Representations

Within the context of forensic interviews that use suggestive questioning techniques, do children's concurrences with suggested answers indicate that they actually believe their misstatements, or alternatively, are they just succumbing to social pressures by agreeing with an authoritative interviewer? Before presenting the series of experiments we have conducted on this issue, several theoretical perspectives are presented. Some explanations of these effects are non-memory-based, which suggests that *social-demand characteristics* present within the interviewing context contribute to children's acquiescence to leading questions. Other explanations are based on *cognitive mechanisms*, such as integration and source-misattribution hypotheses. Below, we outline each of these explanations of children's responses to leading questions.

Social-demand characteristics

Several social-demand characteristics are present in forensic interviewing contexts that likely contribute to children's acquiescence (Zaragoza, 1991). First, *interviewer characteristics* contribute to social pressures experienced by child witnesses. For example, in the Old Cutler and Country Walk cases, two renowned therapists, Drs. Joseph and Laurie Braga, served as the primary interviewers. Children view such high-status adults as trustworthy authority figures, a perspective that may inhibit skepticism of the interviewers' questions and orient children towards pleasing these adults by telling them what they want to hear (see, e.g., Dodd & Bradshaw, 1980; Greene, Flynn & Loftus, 1982). Second, *interview characteristics*, such as the use of misleading and repeated questioning, may heighten social pressures experienced by child witnesses. Consider the situation of child witnesses who have incomplete or no memories for the events or details that are the subject of the interviewers' questions. The use of misleading rather than open-ended questions provides children with information to fill in the gaps in their memories (see, e.g., Ceci & Bruck, 1995). Children may assent to misleading questions because they do not know the answer and do not want to confess ignorance. Furthermore, repeated questioning could suggest to child witnesses that the answers they are providing are incorrect and that the suggested response is actually the correct one. Alternatively, children may assent to repeated suggestive questions in order to get the interviewer to cease the line of questioning. It is likely that these and other social-demand characteristics influence children's acquiescence to misleading questions. Importantly, this perspective allows for the possibility that children may assent to misleading questions while maintaining unaltered memories for the original event. Furthermore, some researchers propose that children may be consciously aware of the dissonance between their reports and their memories (Ceci & Bruck, 1995).

Cognitive mechanisms

In contrast to the social perspective, many researchers believe that suggestive interviewing techniques do more than superficially change children's answers to questions. Researchers invoking cognitive mechanisms as explanations for children's suggestibility believe that children's acquiescence to misleading questions reflects changes in their beliefs and memory representations of experienced events. That is, because of exposure to misleading questions, children come to *believe* misinformation suggested by the questions either because the misinformation becomes integrated with other information or because they confuse the source of the misinformation.

Integration   Researchers dating back to Binet (1900) have hypothesized that misinformation becomes incorporated into memory either through an "overwriting" process, where misinformation replaces original information, or through integration, where old information is combined with suggested information (e.g., Hyman, Husband & Billings, 1995; Loftus, 1979). In discussing the results of their false-memory investigations, Hyman et al. (1995) suggested that a form of schematic reconstruction, in which individuals access some relevant background information, might contribute to the creation of false memories. More specifically, they hypothesized that when individuals first encounter the false event, they may retrieve schematic knowledge closely related to it. When asked to recall the false event during subsequent interviews, they may recall the false information and the underlying schema, which supports the false event by providing true background information and generic scenes. Hyman and his colleagues further hypothesized that the more similar the false event is to true events or to an individual's personal knowledge, the more likely he or she will be to accept the event as true.

Source misattribution   Hyman and colleagues (1995) also acknowledged the role of source confusions in false-memory creation. The source-misattribution explanation has its roots in a broader literature that investigates children's source and reality monitoring (for a review, see Johnson, Hashtroudi & Lindsay, 1993). *Source monitoring* is the process of distinguishing among sources of true events, such as remembering the location and time of an event's occurrence and accurately assigning actions and dialogue to players. An example of one type of source misattribution relevant to eyewitness memory is when a child confuses what an interviewer suggested to him or her with what really happened. *Reality monitoring* is the process of distinguishing memories for true events from memories of imagined events. Some forensic-interviewing techniques rely on guided imagery as a procedure for helping children recall additional information about a witnessed event. When such techniques are used, children may confuse imagined events with events that really happened.

Many researchers have attributed misinformation effects and false-memory creation to source confusions (e.g., Ceci, Crotteau-Huffman, Smith & Loftus, 1994; Ceci, Loftus, Leichtman & Bruck, 1994; Johnson, Foley, Poole & Lindsay, 1995). Ceci and his colleagues (1994a, 1994b) demonstrated that even when an unfamiliar interviewer informed preschoolers in the final session that the previous interviewer had mistakenly told them that they experienced events that had not actually happened, most continued to confuse fictitious events for true ones. They interpreted this finding as evidence for the source-misattribution hypothesis and suggested that preschoolers' false-memory creation may result from confusion among multiple inputs into the memory system.

It is important to note here that most researchers concede that suggestibility effects are complex phenomena that cannot be explained by a single mechanism. Thus, it is likely that social pressures and cognitive mechanisms interact within and between interviews to produce suggestibility effects and false-memory creation. For example, a child may initially comply with misinformation, yet in reconstructing the event, he or she may begin to question the experience, which may lead to changes in memory representation. For example, in one study, Leichtman and Ceci (1995) provided preschoolers with stereotypical knowledge about the clumsiness of a character named "Sam Stone." When exposed to repeated questioning about Sam Stone's behavior, children often became increasingly convinced that suggested clumsy events had truly occurred.

This result provides evidence that children's beliefs about experiences can become modified due to repeated questioning. Furthermore, Ceci and Bruck (1995, p. 268) raised concerns regarding possible age differences in interactions between social and cognitive factors, stating, "Although cognitive as well as social factors may play a role in suggestibility effects, the important question, for which we have no empirical data, is whether there are age-related differences in the interaction of these factors. Specifically, do younger children differ from older children and adults in terms of how quickly false reports, which may have initially been motivated by social factors, come to be believed (i.e., a cognitive factor)?"

Below we present research from our laboratory that specifically addresses the issue of age-related differences in social and cognitive factors contributing to suggestibility effects.

Age Differences in Children's Eyewitness Memory

In most studies of eyewitness memory, children are shown a video, witness an event in their schools, or are personally involved in some activity, and are later asked to recall the event. In most investigations, children are first questioned using general prompts (requests for free recall), which are then followed by more specific prompts, some of which may suggest a particular interpretation (i.e., leading questions) (e.g., Binet, 1900; Cassel & Bjorklund, 1995). Children may be interviewed over repeated sessions, with changes in their answers being of particular interest to investigators (as they are to attorneys, judges, and juries).

In one study that attempted to simulate aspects of a realistic witness experience, Cassel and Bjorklund (1995) showed a brief video of a boy and a girl in a park, with the boy eventually taking the girl's bike without permission. Six- and 8-year-old children and college adults were interviewed 15 minutes after viewing the video and again one week and one month later. At each interview, participants were first asked for free recall. During the initial interview, participants were then asked unbiased follow-up questions for information they had not mentioned in free recall (e.g., "Tell me what the girl was wearing"). At the one-week interview, after free recall, some children were asked sets of *misleading questions*, suggesting events that did not happen (e.g., "The girl said it was okay for the boy to take her bike, didn't she?"), whereas others were asked sets of *positive leading questions*, suggesting events that were actually depicted in the video (e.g., "The girl told the boy not to take the bike, didn't she?"). At the one-month interview, following free recall, children were questioned by two interviewers: one who had interviewed them previously and who posed the same type of questions as at the one-week interview (i.e., either misleading or positive-leading questions), and then by a second interviewer, asking similar questions but with the opposite valence (i.e., asking misleading questions if the other interviewer had asked positive-leading questions and vice versa).

Consistent with other research (e.g., Baker-Ward, Gordon, Ornstein, Larus & Clubb, 1993; Poole & Lindsay, 1995), initial free recall was absolutely low for the youngest children (7%) and increased with age (13% for the 8-year-olds and 20% for the adults). Not all items were recalled with equal frequency, however. Items that were forensically central (i.e., central to the issue of whether a crime had been committed) were also psychologically central. For all groups of participants, central items were recalled at a significantly higher rate (47%, 70%, and 87% of total correct free recall for the 6-year-olds, 8-year-olds, and adult participants, respectively) than noncentral items (4%, 8%, and 22% of total correct free recall for the 6-year-olds, 8-year-olds, and adult participants, respectively)—a finding that has been consistently reported in the literature (e.g., Baker-Ward et al., 1993, Poole & White, 1995). Also, levels of correct recall increased comparably for all groups of participants when the unbiased cues were provided (increases of 27%, 31%, and 39% for the 6-year-olds, 8-year-olds, and adult subjects, respectively), indicating that all participants remembered more information than they had spontaneously offered during free recall.

In eyewitness memory research, what is remembered incorrectly is as important as what is remembered correctly. There was virtually no incorrect free recall during the initial session for any age group (0%, 0%, and 1.2% for the 6-year-olds, 8-year-olds, and adult participants, respectively), a finding we have replicated repeatedly (Bjorklund, Bjorklund, Brown & Cassel, 1998; Bjorklund, Cassel, Bjorklund, Brown, Park, Ernst & Owen, 2000; Cassel, Roebers & Bjorklund, 1996; Owen,

Kennedy, Alonza, Galliano, Bjorklund & Cassel, 1998). The pattern was different for the unbiased cued questions, however. Levels of incorrect recall to these seemingly innocuous questions (e.g., "Tell me what the bike looked like") produced elevated levels of incorrect recall for all groups of participants ($M = 17\%$). Thus, these unbiased questions are a double-edged sword, being necessary for levels of recall to exceed floor levels for the youngest children, but inducing relatively high rates of incorrect recall with correct recall.

Not surprisingly, the children, particularly the 6-year-olds, tended to follow the lead of the examiner during the one-week and one-month interviews, which produced high levels of correct responses when they were asked positive leading questions and high levels of incorrect responses when they were asked misleading questions (see also Ackil & Zaragoza, 1995; Poole & White, 1995, among others). Furthermore, when children were asked both sets of positive leading and misleading questions by different people within the same interview, the children frequently changed their answers. For example, when asked about the color of the bike, 71% of the 6-year-olds who had agreed with the suggestion of the first interviewer later modified their answer to comply with the suggestion of the second interviewer. The corresponding percentages for the 8-year-old children and adults were 53% and 35%, respectively. For the more critical central question of whether the girl had given the boy permission to take her bike, 42% of the 6-year-old children changed their answers in response to the second interviewer, whereas only 7% of the 8-year-olds and 12% of the adults did so. These data make it clear that younger children are highly susceptible to the suggestions of an adult interviewer, modifying their answers, it seems, to suit the desires of the person who is interviewing them.

But does such questioning actually change children's memories, or does it only serve to change their answers? To assess this, Cassel and Bjorklund (1995) compared levels of free recall at the one-week and one-month interviews. Children made many incorrect responses to the unbiased questions in the initial interview and also to the misleading questions some of them received during the second interview (62%, 57%, and 20% for 6-year-olds, 8-year-olds, and adults, respectively). Would these errors find their way into subsequent free recall, which would suggest a

Table 1
Ratio of correct responses to correct + incorrect responses during free recall for immediate, 1-week, and 1-month interviews

	6-year-olds	8-year-olds	Adults
Initial interview	1.0	1.0	0.96
One-week	0.96	0.97	0.93
One-month	0.85	0.93	0.93

Based on data from Cassel & Bjorklund, 1995.

change of mind as well as a change of response? The answer was no. Levels of incorrect free recall never exceeded 2.4% at any interview. Table 1 presents the accuracy ratios (correct responses/[correct + incorrect responses]) for free recall at each interview for each age group. A ratio of 1.0 reflects perfect accuracy and a ratio of .5 reflects comparable recall of correct and incorrect information. As can be seen, ratios of all cells were absolutely high, with all but one exceeding .90. In other words, although absolute levels of correct free recall vary with age, accuracy does not (see also Howe, Courage & Peterson, 1995; Rudy & Goodman, 1991). This reflects the fact that the suggestions and misinformation we provided children were sufficient to alter their answers but not sufficient to change their minds (i.e., memory representations of the witnessed event).

Cassel and Bjorklund's (1995) study produced mixed results concerning the effects of repeated questioning. On the one hand, asking participants for free recall several times affected neither their absolute level of performance nor their accuracy, even for children who had been asked sets of misleading questions. On the other hand, being asked repeated leading questions in the final interview produced substantial answer changes, even for central items, at least for the 6-year-old children.

Possible explanations for the lack of influence of misleading questions on children's memory representations, as reflected by their subsequent free recall, are that they did not receive enough repeated exposures to the questions (recall that court witnesses are interviewed up to 12 times [Whitcomb, 1992]) or that the questions were not asked with appropriate authority. When social workers, police, and even lawyers interview children about an event, they rarely take the first response as the last one, especially if it is a response they do not like or believe. An initial question is often followed up by a second or third question, frequently phrased more forcefully or more suggestively than the first.

In an experiment designed to assess the effects of such repeated, increasingly suggestive questioning, Cassel, Roebers, and Bjorklund (1996) showed a brief video to 6-, 8-, and 10-year-old children and college adults. One week later, participants were asked for their free recall of the events in the video. After free recall, participants were asked a set of misleading questions that required a yes/no response (e.g., "The mother owned the bike, didn't she?").[1] If participants failed to follow the misleading question (i.e., rejected the suggestion of the interviewer) or said they didn't know the answer, they were asked a second, more strongly worded follow-up question (e.g., "The girl said the mother owned the bike, didn't she?"). Regardless of their response to this second-level question, children were immediately asked a three-choice recognition-memory question for that item (e.g., "Did the bike belong to (a) the mother, (b) the boy, or (c) the girl?"). We reasoned that recognition-memory performance would serve as a better indicator of children's actual memory representation. If the repeated questioning caused children to alter their memory for the event as well as their answers, this should be reflected in their recognition-memory performance.

Results for the first-level leading questions produced the expected age differences, with correct answers generally increasing with age and incorrect answers generally decreasing with age. Age differences for the most critical central items were limited, however, to the 6-year-old children. These youngest children accepted the false suggestion of the interviewer for these few critical items (e.g., "The mother owned the bike, didn't she?") 31% of the time. The corresponding percentages for the 8-year-olds, 10-year-olds, and adults were 14%, 3%, and 7%, respectively. Thus, even central items (the most critical for establishing evidence in a legal case) were subject to the effects of suggestion for the 6-year-old children.

More telling, however, were the effects of the second-level questions, which are shown by age in figure 1. As can be seen, all but the youngest children continued to reject the more strongly worded follow-up ques-

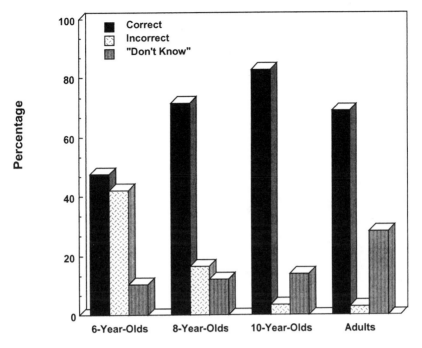

Figure 1
Percentages of correct and incorrect responses to the follow-up questions for participants in the misleading condition by age. (Based on data from Cassel, Roebers & Bjorklund, 1996.)

tions. Yet the 6-year-olds made nearly as many incorrect responses as correct ones, changing their answers in compliance with the questions posed by the interviewer. Moreover, this effect was found for both central and noncentral items. Table 2 presents the percentage correct, incorrect, and "don't know" responses to the second-level questions by age, separately for the central and noncentral items. As can be seen, the 6-year-olds were as likely to accept the false suggestions for the central items as they were for the noncentral items. These data clearly indicate the greater suggestibility of 6-year-olds in comparison with children only two years their senior.

Most critical to this investigation was participants' performance on the recognition questions, asked immediately after they had responded to the corresponding leading questions. Overall performance on the recognition

Table 2
Percentage of correct, incorrect, and "don't know" responses to follow-up central and noncentral questions for participants in the misleading condition by age

	6-year-olds	8-year-olds	10-year-olds	Adults
Central questions				
Correct	50.0	75.8	90.5	88.2
Incorrect	45.8	17.8	2.4	5.9
"Don't know"	4.2	6.4	7.1	5.9
Noncentral questions				
Correct	46.8	71.1	80.8	66.8
Incorrect	43.5	17.5	5.7	2.3
"Don't know"	9.8	11.5	13.5	31.0

Based on data from Cassel, Roebers & Bjorklund, 1996.

questions for participants in the misleading condition is shown in figure 2, which again reveals substantial differences between the 6-year-olds and all other participants. These youngest children actually made slightly more incorrect than correct responses on the recognition items. Most critical, however, were these young children's responses to the central items. Would they respond to these items as they had earlier, which would indicate a modification of their memory representation? Or would they show a change of response to these critical questions, which would show that, despite their immediately earlier compliance, they had not, in fact, misremembered these central aspects of the event? The answer appears to be the latter. Levels of incorrect recognition responses for the central items did not vary with age (9%, 0%, 0%, and 2% for 6-, 8-, and 10-year-olds, and adults, respectively).

These results indicate that repeated questioning of the type used in this study does indeed adversely affect the performance of young children, even for central items. However, the findings also illustrate that such questions serve to change children's answers and not their memories, at least for the central items. Their high levels of recognition performance for the central items suggest that these young children's high rate of errors to the leading questions can be attributed to the social-demand characteristics of the situation, and that repeated questioning with mis-

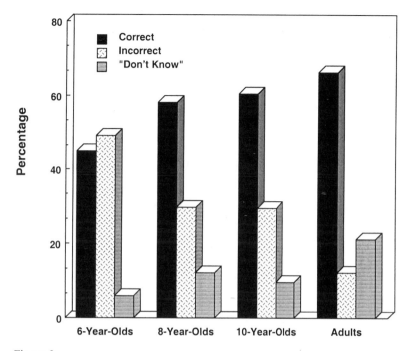

Figure 2
Percentages of correct and incorrect responses to the recognition questions for participants in the misleading condition by age. (Based on data from Cassel, Roebers & Bjorklund, 1996.)

leading questions, although possibly affecting their memory representations of the noncentral items, did not adversely affect their memory for the central items.

Changing Children's Memories as Well as Their Answers

The findings of Cassel and his colleagues (1996) are quite encouraging. They suggest that although it is easy to get young children to change their answers, it is relatively difficult to actually change their memory representations about important aspects of witnessed events. We have great confidence in these findings, which have been replicated in part in samples from the United States (Bjorklund et al., 2000; Owen et al., 1998) and Germany (Roebers, Rieber & Schneider, 1995).

However, our findings are somewhat perplexing in light of evidence that young children can be led relatively easily to create false memories of events that they had never experienced merely by participating in multiple interviews using repeated, suggestive questioning (e.g., Ceci et al., 1994a; Ceci et al., 1994b). In one study, Ceci, Loftus, and their colleagues (1994b) interviewed children over an 11-week period about events that might have happened to them. For example, children were asked if they ever remembered getting their finger caught in a mousetrap. Although a few children claimed to experience these false events in the initial interviews, by the conclusion of the study, nearly 60% of the pre-school children and 45% of 5- to 6-year-olds assented that these events did indeed happen, and they often provided substantial detail in their descriptions of them. Moreover, many children continued to believe that these events actually occurred even after being told by the interviewers and their parents that they never really happened. It seems that, under some conditions, false memories of plausible but extraordinary events are relatively easy to implant into young children's minds (see Ceci, Bruck & Battin, 2000).

Why, then, were the youngest children in our studies so resistant to actual change in their memories of the event? One possibility is that the questioning we used was not sufficiently subtle. Our suggestions were obvious, and perhaps, although causing children to change their answers, they were too obviously incorrect to cause them to change their memory representations. We doubt that this is the case, however. Real-world cases of false-memory creation often involve hard-hitting suggestion by a parent, a detective, or a therapist (see Ceci & Bruck, 1998), which suggests that our questions were too subtle, if anything. Rather, we believe that our questions were of the proper level of suggestion, and that we would see changes in children's memory representations if we questioned them more frequently (i.e., increased the number of interviews).

Bjorklund, Bjorklund, Brown, and Cassel (1998) investigated this possibility by interviewing 6- and 8-year-old children repeatedly over a 6-week period. After viewing a brief video about a boy stealing a Gameboy video game from a girl, children were asked sets of either unbiased or misleading questions. Free recall and responses to leading questions were again assessed 2 weeks, 4 weeks, and 6 weeks after the immediate interview. Children were asked an initial set of three-choice recognition questions (*initial recognition*) either two days after the 2-week interview, two days after the 4-week interview, or two days after the 6-week interview. Recognition and free recall were assessed for all children two days after the 6-week interview (*final recognition*). Thus, free recall was assessed for all children at five sessions (immediate, week 2, week 4, week 6, and final); responses to leading questions (either misleading or unbiased) were assessed at four sessions (immediate, week 2, week 4, and week 6); initial recognition was assessed two days after week 2, week 4, and week 6; and final recognition was assessed for all children two days after the week 6 interview. (For children in the 6-week initial-recognition condition, initial and final recognition were the same.) We hypothesized that if leading questions are influencing children's memory representations, free recall and recognition performance should be more hindered the farther away the assessments are from the original "witnessing" of the event.

Before discussing the effects of repeated leading questions on subsequent recall and recognition, we briefly describe the results of the leading questions. First, levels of incorrect responses for both the unbiased and misleading questions were relatively high, ranging from a low of 18% for central questions for the 8-year-olds to a high of 35% for noncentral items for the 6-year-olds. Thus, as in prior research, the children in this study made many incorrect responses to both the misleading and unbiased questions (e.g., Bjorklund et al., 2000; Cassel et al., 1996). Second, 8-year-olds made more correct and fewer incorrect responses than the 6-year-olds. Finally, children who answered misleading questions provided more correct responses and fewer incorrect responses than children who answered unbiased questions. This finding may at first appear anomalous, but we have found similar patterns in previous research (e.g., Bjorklund et al., 2000; Cassel et al., 1996; Owen et al., 1998; Roebers et al., 1995). We believe that the explanation of this effect is related to inherent differences between the characteristics of misleading and unbiased questions. More specifically, misleading questions required only a yes/no response from children, whereas in their answers to unbiased questions, children were required to generate a response. This more demanding recall requirement understandably produced lower levels of

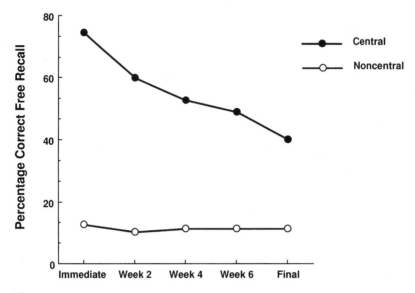

Figure 3
Percentages of correct free recall for central and noncentral items by week of testing. (Based on data from Bjorklund, Bjorklund, Brown & Cassel, 1998.)

correct responses for children participating in the unbiased condition, but also yielded higher levels of incorrect responses.

The most critical data for addressing the relationship between changes in children's answers and changes in their memories were patterns of change in children's free recall and recognition over weeks of testing. Figure 3 presents the results for percentage of correct free recall for central and noncentral items by week of testing. As can be seen, there was no change in the correct recall of the noncentral items over weeks, which hovered around 15% at each testing. In contrast, correct recall declined over weeks for the central items. An inverse pattern was observed for the noncentral items (see figure 4). Although levels of incorrect free recall never exceeded 5%, they did increase significantly over weeks for the noncentral items while never exceeding 1% for the central items.

Why should children show a steady decline in recall of correct central information and a small but significant increase in recall of incorrect noncentral information? The latter effect can be attributed to the intrusion of incorrect information brought about by the leading questions.

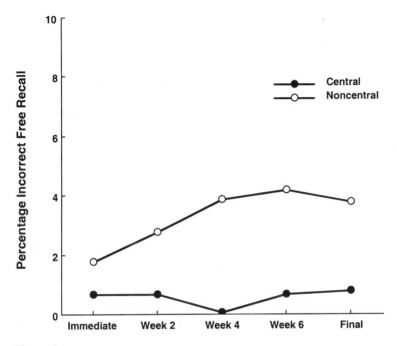

Figure 4
Percentages of incorrect free recall for central and noncentral items by week of testing. (Based on data from Bjorklund, Bjorklund, Brown & Cassel, 1998.)

That the absolute levels of such errors were low attests to the accuracy of children's free recall, even after repeated misstatements (Bjorklund et al., 2000; Cassel & Bjorklund, 1995). However, the decline in correct central recall is puzzling. Why should children show a steady decline in correct recall of central information over repeated sessions? In another study (Bjorklund et al., 2000), we have found such a decrease in the recall of central information over two testing sessions, following sets of misleading or unbiased questions, which suggests that the result is not due to chance. A similar effect was not found for the noncentral items. One possibility is that children's erroneous retrieval to the misleading questions caused them to question their interpretation of the event ("Did the girl actually give the boy permission to take her Gameboy?"). This uncertainty may have caused children occasionally to recall a false memory for *noncentral* items (figure 4), but not for central items. The uncertainty produced by the repeated misleading questions may have caused children to take a more conservative approach to the central items. Instead of retrieving misinformation associated with the central items, the uncertainty may have caused them simply *not* to recall what they believed to have happened ("The boy stole the Gameboy"), which resulted in a steady decrease in correct recall over weeks of testing (figure 3). In other words, the repeated misleading questions resulted in increased errors of commission for noncentral items, but only increased errors of omission for the central items.

To further explore changes in children's memory representations, we examined the effects of repeated misinformation on recognition memory in two ways. First, we predicted that recognition performance would be hindered the later the *initial* recognition test was given. This prediction was based on the premise that children who are asked recognition questions after only a few interviews would experience less misinformation than children who were interviewed more frequently before first being questioned. Figure 5 presents the percentage of correct initial responses to the three-choice recognition questions by week of testing for the noncentral items. Although only marginally significant, correct initial recognition decreased and incorrect recognition increased for the children in the week-6 group relative to those who had received their initial recognition test earlier. There were no differences in performance as a function of when children were first administered a recognition test for the central items. Second, we proposed that children who were administered two recognition tests (e.g., at 2 weeks and again at 6 weeks) would display higher levels of performance for the initial recognition test than for the final recognition test. This pattern was confirmed, but only for the 6-year-olds in the misleading condition for noncentral items, who made more incorrect responses on the final interview (47%) than during the initial interview (37%). This finding suggests that repeated testing did cause some children to change their memory representations and is consistent with our hypothesis that repeated interviews adversely affect recognition performance for noncentral information.

Levels of incorrect recognition for central items were absolutely low, which is consistent with past findings that central items resist the influence of misleading information when assessed via recognition tests (Bjorklund

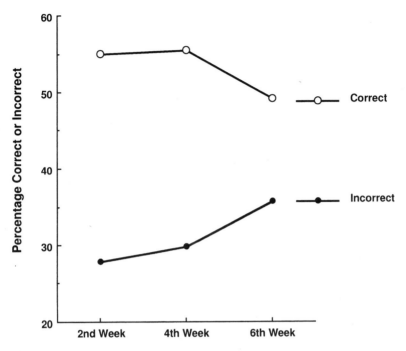

Figure 5
Percentages of noncentral correct and incorrect initial responses to the three-choice recognition questions for children at weeks 2, 4, and 6. (From Bjorklund, Bjorklund, Brown & Cassel, 1998.)

et al., 2000; Cassel et al., 1996; Roebers et al., 1995). However, about 5% of the 6-year-olds in this experiment did show elevated levels of erroneous recognition for central items during the final interview. This suggests that repeated exposure to misinformation can affect young children's memory representations, even for central information, although apparently only for a minority of children.

Some Differences between Studies of Suggestibility and Studies of False-Memory Creation

Despite our "success" of seemingly implanting false memories into the minds of children through repeated questioning, the levels of incorrect responses, especially for the central items, were substantially less than the erroneous statements that children and adults make in studies using the "false-memory creation" paradigm (e.g., Ceci et al., 1994a, 1994b; Hyman et al., 1995; Loftus & Pickrell, 1995). Many differences in methodology between the suggestibility studies we have conducted and false-memory-creation studies can account for the difference in results, but we would like to focus briefly on two that deserve greater research attention: the nature of the initial representation and the involvement of the self.

With respect to differences in the initial representation, fuzzy trace theory (Brainerd & Poole, 1997; Brainerd, Reyna & Poole, 2000) provides a framework for interpreting the differences between the two types of studies. In suggestibility studies, children witness an event, in our studies, a brief video. There is a perceptual experience, and presumably this experience is encoded using both verbatim (i.e., literal) and fuzzy (gistlike) traces. In false-memory-creation experiments, there is no event that children actually experience. Rather, they are told to think about an event that might have happened to them at some time in the past. There are no literal traces for an actual event. Rather, the verbal presentation of the scenario provides the only perceptual traces for this "event." Thus, participants in suggestibility experiments have true verbatim and gist traces available to them, whereas participants in false-memory-creation experiments have only false verbatim traces, those suggested by the interviewer. In suggestibility experiments, participants can always return to their literal representations to assess the validity of a suggestion. When participants in false-memory-creation experiments check their literal representations for the supposed event, they have only the experience of the interviewer's suggestion.

Research has shown that in some situations, false memories are actually more resistant to forgetting than true memories (Brainerd, Reyna & Brandse, 1995; Brainerd & Mojardin, in press; Poole, 1995). According to fuzzy trace theory, *true* memories are based on verbatim memory traces, which are more susceptible to forgetting than the less-exact gist traces. In contrast, *false* memories must be based on gist traces because there are no verbatim traces for false memories. Gist traces are more resistant to forgetting than verbatim traces, and thus gist-based false memories become more likely to be remembered over long delays than the more easily forgettable verbatim-based true memories. This pattern may be especially robust when participants have no immediate perceptual experience on which to base their recollections, as is the case in false-memory-creation studies.

A second major difference between most suggestibility studies and false-memory-creation studies concerns the involvement of the self. In suggestibility studies, children are sometimes participants (e.g., Leichtman & Ceci, 1995), but often are only witnesses. In false-memory-creation studies, participants are always centrally involved. They imagine an event that supposedly happened to them some time in the past. The events are plausible, consistent with experiences children have actually had, and supposedly supported by an authority figure (usually a parent). The consequences of *not* remembering some significant event that allegedly happened to one's self may be greater than the conquences of not remembering events that allegedly happened to someone else. The event *may* have happened, and a desire to construct an integrated self, one who remembers important past events that are remembered by significant others, may provide the motivation to construct scenarios that match the suggestion. If this is so, children and adults should be less likely to create false memories when there is no external validation of the memory (i.e., when no one else has a recollection of the event, or when participants are explicitly told that their parents have no recollection of these events). They should also be less likely to create false memories for less plausible events.

The role of plausibility in false-memory creation has recently been demonstrated for high-school students (Pezdek, Finger & Hodge, 1997) and children (Pezdek & Hodge, 1999; see Pezdek & Taylor, 2000, for a review). For example, in the study by Pezdek and Hodge (1999), about one-third of the 5- to 7-year-old children "remembered" being lost in a mall (which they had not been), whereas only one of 19 children "remembered" being given an enema. Although most of these children knew what an enema was, the event was implausible. If such an embarrassing and invasive event had happened to them, they certainly would have remembered. Pezdek and Hodge (1999) also found that children reported more details for true memories than for false ones.

Similarly, a series of studies from our lab investigated whether it is more difficult to implant false memories in children for events that involve physical harm than for events that do not. In one study (Brown, Delrocco & Renteria, 1998), 44% of 7-year-old children provided full or partial reports of fictitious events that involved physical harm (e.g., sticking a jellybean in their ear and going to a hospital to have it removed). In contrast, for events that did not involve physical harm (e.g., losing mom after getting off the teacups ride at Disney World), 68% of the 7-year-olds provided full or partial reports. These findings provided preliminary evidence that it is relatively more difficult to implant false memories for events that involve physical harm than for events that do not, yet it is still possible. Furthermore, children in this experiment mentioned fewer details in their narrative accounts of fictitious events that involved physical harm in comparison to events that did not involve physical harm.

In a second study (Brown, Chalson, Liss, Abramson, Zorn & Barman, 1999), event descriptions were controlled so that they varied only in terms of physical harm. Stories with similar premises but different outcomes in terms of physical harm were presented to 6- and 7-year-old children in a between-subjects design, rather than the within-subjects design used in the previous study (e.g., physical-harm condition: "Remember when you were with your mom/dad at McDonald's Playland and while you were going down the slide you fell off sideways *and hit your head on a rock?*"; no-physical-harm condition: "Remember when you were with your mom/dad at McDonald's Playland and while you were going down the slide you fell off sideways *but your mom/dad reached out and caught you?*"). Contrary to the results of the earlier study, children reported full reports for both types of fictitious events nearly 70% of the time. The seemingly contradictory results between these two studies may be due to differences in the plausibility of the fictitious events used, with the first study using more bizarre fictitious events than the second (see Pezdek & Taylor, 2000). Nevertheless, such findings indicate that under certain conditions, young children are highly likely to create false memories for events never happening to them, and that the likelihood of such false-memory creation may depend on the plausibility of the event.

The findings from both suggestibility and false-memory-creation studies indicate that young children will change their answers when confronted with misleading questions. When exposed to multiple interviews using increasingly suggestive leading questions or repeating the possibility that they may have experienced some event, young children, especially children 6 years of age and younger, will change not only their answers but also their memory representations of events. Yet it is far easier to change children's answers than it is to change their minds, at least within the suggestibility paradigm. Future research needs to investigate further the child and situation factors associated with false-memory creation, in a variety of paradigms. We also need to learn more about the duration of true and false memories, the type of false events that children and adults are more likely to accept as potentially real, the effect of individual differences on suggestibility and false-memory creation, and how to differentiate true and false memories with reasonable accuracy. In the process, we hope that we will thereby develop a unified theoretical framework for understanding event memory and suggestibility in children.

Acknowledgment

This research was supported by NSF grant SBR-9422177 to David F. Bjorklund.

Note

1. Other participants were asked unbiased questions that merely directed participants' attention to a particular aspect of the video they had watched ("Can you tell me who owned the bike?"), or sets of positive-leading questions that suggested the correct answer. However, because of space considerations, we will discuss here only the results for the misleading condition.

References

Ackil, J. K., & Zaragoza, M. S. (1995). Developmental differences in eyewitness suggestibility and memory for source. *Journal of Experimental Child Psychology*, *60*, 57–83.

Baker-Ward, L., Gordon, B. N., Ornstein, P. A., Larus, D. M., & Clubb, P. A. (1993). Young children's long-term retention of a pediatric examination. *Child Development*, *64*, 1519–1533.

Binet, A. (1900). *La suggestibilité*. Paris: Schleicher Freres.

Bjorklund, D. F., Bjorklund, B. R., Brown, R. D., & Cassel, W. S. (1998). Children's susceptibility to repeated questions: How misinformation changes children's answers and their minds. *Applied Developmental Science*, *2*, 99–111.

Bjorklund, D. F., Cassel, W. S., Bjorklund, B. R., Brown, R. D., Park, C. L., Ernst, K., & Owen, F. A. (2000). Social demand characteristics in children's and adults' eyewitness memory and suggestibility: The effect of different interviewers on free recall and recognition. *Applied Cognitive Psychology, 14,* 421–433.

Brainerd, C. J., & Mojardin, A. H. (in press). Children's and adults' spontaneous false memories for sentences: Long-term persistence and mere-testing effects. *Child Development.*

Brainerd, C. J., & Poole, D. A. (1997). Long-term survival of children's false memories: A review. *Learning and Individual Differences, 9,* 125–152.

Brainerd, C. J., Reyna, V. F., & Brandse, E. (1995). Are children's false memories more persistent than their true memories? *Psychological Science, 6,* 359–364.

Brainerd, C. J., Reyna, V. F., & Poole, D. A. (2000). Fuzzy-trace theory and false memory: Memory theory in the courtroom. In D. F. Bjorklund (Ed.), *False memory creation in children: Theory, research, and implications* (pp. 93–127). Mahwah, N.J.: Erlbaum.

Brown, R. D., Chalson, R., Liss, B., Abramson, P., Zorn, S., & Barman, N. (1999). Children's false memory creation: The roles of physical harm and infantile amnesia. Poster presented at the meeting of the Society for Research in Child Development, April, Albuquerque, N.M.

Brown, R. D., Delrocco, N., & Renteria, E. (1998). Individual differences in children's false memory creation for emotional and physical events. Poster presented at the meeting of the Conference on Human Development, March, Mobile, Ala.

Brown, R. D., Goldstein, E., & Bjorklund, D. F. (2000). The history and zeitgeist of the repressed/false memory debate: Scientific and sociological perspectives on suggestibility and childhood memory. In D. F. Bjorklund (Ed.), *False memory creation in children: Theory, research, and implications* (pp. 1–30). Mahwah, N.J.: Erlbaum.

Cassel, W. S., & Bjorklund, D. F. (1995). Developmental patterns of eyewitness memory and suggestibility: An ecologically based short-term longitudinal study. *Law and Human Behavior, 19,* 507–32.

Cassel, W. S., Roebers, C., & Bjorklund, D. F. (1996). Developmental patterns of eyewitness responses to repeated and increasingly suggestive questions. *Journal of Experimental Child Psychology, 61,* 116–133.

Ceci, S. J., & Bruck, M. (1995). *Jeopardy in the courtroom: A scientific analysis of children's testimony.* Washington, D.C.: American Psychological Association.

Ceci, S. J., & Bruck, M. (1998). Children's testimony: Applied and basic issues. In I. E. Sigel & K. A. Renninger (Eds.), *Child psychology in practice* (pp. 713–774), vol. 4 of *Handbook of child psychology.* New York: Wiley.

Ceci, S. J., Bruck, M., & Battin, D. (2000). The suggestibility of children's testimony. In D. F. Bjorklund (Ed.), *Research and theory in false-memory creation in children and adults* (pp. 169–201). Mahwah, N.J.: Erlbaum.

Ceci, S. J., Crotteau-Huffman, M., Smith, E., & Loftus, E. F. (1994a). Repeatedly thinking about nonevents. *Consciousness and Cognition, 3*, 388–407.

Ceci, S. J., Loftus, E. F., Leichtman, M. D., & Bruck, M. (1994b). The role of source misattributions in the creation of false beliefs among preschoolers. *International Journal of Clinical and Experimental Hypnosis, 62*, 304–320.

Dodd, D. H., & Bradshaw, J. M. (1980). Leading questions and memory: Some pragmatic constraints. *Journal of Verbal Learning and Verbal Memory, 19*, 695–704.

Fivush, R. (1997). Event memory in early childhood. In N. Cowan (Ed.), *The development of memory in childhood* (pp. 139–161). Hove, East Sussex, U.K.: Psychology Press.

Goodman, G. S., Emery, R. E., & Haugaard, J. J. (1998). Developmental psychology and law: Divorce, child maltreatment, foster care, and adoption. In I. E. Sigel & K. A. Renninger (Eds.), *Child psychology in practice* (pp. 775–874), vol. 4 of *Handbook of child psychology*. New York: Wiley.

Greene, E., Flynn, M. S., & Loftus, E. F. (1982). Inducing resistance to misleading information. *Journal of Verbal Learning and Verbal Behavior, 21*, 207–219.

Howe, M. L., Courage, M. L., & Peterson, C. (1995). Intrusions in preschoolers' recall of traumatic childhood events. *Psychonomic Bulletin and Review, 2*, 130–134.

Hyman, I. E., Husband, T. H., & Billings, F. J. (1995). False memories of childhood experiences. *Applied Cognitive Psychology, 9*, 181–197.

Johnson, M. K., Foley, M. A., Suengas, A. G., & Raye, C. L. (1988). Phenomenal characteristics of memories for perceived and imagined autobiographical events. *Journal of Experimental Psychology: General, 117*, 371–376.

Johnson, M. K., Hashtroudi, S., & Lindsay, D. S. (1993). Source monitoring. *Psychological Bulletin, 114*, 3–28.

Leichtman, M. D., & Ceci, S. J. (1995). The effect of stereotypes and suggestion on preschoolers reports. *Developmental Psychology, 31*, 568–578.

Loftus, E. F. (1979). The malleability of memory. *American Scientist, 67*, 312–320.

Loftus, E. F., & Pickrell, J. E. (1995). The formation of false memories. *Psychiatric Annals, 25*, 720–725.

Nelson, K. (1996). *Language in cognitive development: The emergence of the mediated mind*. New York: Cambridge University Press.

Owen, F., Kennedy, E., Alonza, A., Galliano, M., Bjorklund, D. F., & Cassel, W. S. (1998). Effects of hierarchical levels of suggestive leading questions on children's and adults' free recall: A longitudinal-sequential study. Poster presented at Conference on Human Development, March, Mobile, Ala.

Pezdek, K., Finger, K., & Hodge, D. (1997). Planting false childhood memories: The role of event plausibility. *Psychological Science, 8*, 437–441.

Pezdek, K., & Hodge, D. (1999). Planting false childhood memories in children: The role of event plausibility. *Child Development, 70,* 887–895.

Pezdek, K., & Taylor, J. (2000). Discriminating between accounts of true and false events. In D. F. Bjorklund (Ed.), *Research and theory in false-memory creation in children and adults* (pp. 69–91). Mahwah, N.J.: Erlbaum.

Poole, D. A. (1995). Strolling fuzzy-trace theory through eyewitness testimony (or vice versa). *Learning and Individual Differences, 7,* 87–93.

Poole, D. A., & Lindsay, D. S. (1995). Interviewing preschoolers: Effects of non-suggestive techniques, parental coaching, and leading questions on reports of nonexperienced events. *Journal of Experimental Child Psychology, 60,* 129–154.

Poole, D. A., & White, L. T. (1995). Tell me again and again: Stability and change in the repeated testimonies of children and adults. In M. S. Zaragoza, J. R. Graham, G. C. N. Hall, R. Hirschman & Y. S. Ben-Porath (Eds.), *Memory and testimony in the child witness* (pp. 24–43). Thousand Oaks, Calif.: Sage.

Roebers, C., Rieber, F., & Schneider, W. (1995). Eyewitness testimony and suggestibility as a function of recall accuracy: A developmental study. *Zeitschrift für Entwicklungspsychologie und Paedagogische Psychologie, 27,* 210–225.

Rudy, L., & Goodman, G. S. (1991). Effects of participation on children's reports: Implications for children's testimony. *Developmental Psychology, 27,* 527–538.

Schacter, D. L. (1996). *Searching for memory: The brain, the mind, and the past.* New York: Basic Books.

Schneider, W., & Bjorklund, D. F. (1998). Memory. In D. Kuhn & R. S. Siegler (Eds.), *Cognitive, language, and perceptual development* (pp. 467–521), vol. 2 of *Handbook of child psychology* (5th Ed.). New York: Wiley.

Schneider, W., & Bjorklund, D. F. (in press). Memory and knowledge development. In J. Valsiner & K. Connolly (Eds.), *Handbook of developmental psychology.* London: Sage.

State v. Fijnje, 11th Judicial Circuit Court, Dade County, Florida, no. 89–43952 (1991).

State v. Francisco Fuster, 11th Judicial Circuit Court, Dade County, Florida, no. 84–19728 (1985).

State v. Michaels, Superior Court, Essex County, New Jersey (1988).

Suengas, A. G., & Johnson, M. K. (1988). Qualitative effects of rehearsal on memories for perceived and imagined events. *Journal of Experimental Psychology: General, 103,* 377–389.

Whitcomb, D. (1992). *When the child is a victim.* 2nd ed. Washington, D.C.: National Institute of Justice.

Zaragoza, M. (1991). Preschool children's susceptibility to memory impairment. In. J. L. Doris (Ed.), *The suggestibility of children's recollections* (pp. 27–39). Washington, D.C.: American Psychological Association.

7

The Role of Knowledge in Children's Memory

Hidetsugu Tajika

Lifespan memory development deals with research on memory development from infants to old age. In this chapter, however, I examine the role of prior knowledge only in elementary-school children's memory.

It is well known that prior knowledge generates constructive memory (see, e.g., Bartlett, 1932; Bransford & Franks, 1971; Schacter, Norman & Koutstaal, 1998). Constructive memory emphasizes active processes of filling out the meaning of information during encoding and retrieving, with errors frequently occurring. So prior knowledge not only facilitates memory but also hinders memory because of its constructive nature. A variety of research on memory (Bartlett, 1932; Bransford & Franks, 1971; Roediger & McDermott, 1995) shows that people may generate errors, distortions, and inferences from prior knowledge in a way that depends on the constructive nature of memory processes. The constructive nature of memory processes is revealed in false memories (Bartlett, 1932; Bransford & Franks, 1971; Bruck & Ceci, 1999; Roediger & McDermott, 1995) and inferences (e.g., Paris & Lindauer, 1976, 1977; Paris, Lindauer & Cox, 1977).

People often draw inferences that go beyond the information given on the basis of their prior knowledge (see Graesser & Bower, 1990). Inference may be defined as the generation of new information from old. Human cognitive processes, such as sentence understanding, effective social interaction, and so on, usually involve inferences that go beyond what is explicit. Children also draw inferences when they understand and memorize text. Recent research on inferences has turned toward analyses of the constructive nature of memory, namely analyses of the elaborative operations and strategies employed by children to encode and retrieve target sentences (Graesser & Bower, 1990; van Meter & Pressley, 1994).

Two types of inferences may be found in sentence processing: necessary inferences and elaborative inferences (Sanford, 1990). Necessary inferences, including bridging inferences, are made to construct a coherent representation of the text. On the other hand, elaborative inferences (e.g., instrumental inferences) are made to process each sentence and fill out its meaning. When necessary and elaborative inferences are made in the course of reading and memorizing sentences, we find evidence of the constructive nature of memory.

There are several reasons why I refer here to children's instrumental inferences (e.g., inferring that a spoon is used in stirring coffee) as a type of elaborative inference. First, children and adults generally construct memories by elaborating given information on the basis of their prior knowledge. They use instrumental inferences to understand and memorize sentences. To investigate how the ability to draw instrumental inferences from sentences changes developmentally is important for learning about children's understanding and memory of sentences.

Second, many studies using the usual paradigm of instrumental inferences (e.g., Paris & Lindauer, 1976; Paris, Lindauer & Cox, 1977; van Meter & Pressley, 1994) showed that younger children do not use implicit instruments as effective retrieval cues, because they do not make instrumental inferences at encoding (i.e., on-line inferences). However, our studies (Suzuki, 2000; Tajika, Collins & Taniguchi, 1996; Tajika & Taniguchi, 1995), using an implicit memory test, have shown that even younger children make instrumental inferences during encoding, as stated below. The results of our studies will be shown later. Clarifying the gap in the results between making on-line and off-line instrumental inferences may help us understand developmental changes in the constructive nature of memory.

Previous studies seem to suggest that implicit memory does not show any developmental change (e.g., Graf, 1990; Tajika, 1999). Students in implicit memory experiments are not asked to consciously retrieve target items. Word completion tests are frequently used to assess implicit memory. Some researchers have suggested that implicit-memory-test performance largely reflects automatic encoding processes (e.g., Graf &

Mandler, 1984; Jacoby, Toth & Yonelinas, 1993). The results of our studies using a word completion test suggest that younger students have automatically activated their knowledge to make on-line instrumental inferences.

If implicit memory test performance mainly reflects automatic and nonstrategic processing and explicit memory test performance reflects strategic processing, the gap in the results between on-line and off-line instrumental inferences may have arisen from the difference between strategic and nonstrategic processing. It is necessary to distinguish between strategic and nonstrategic processing when the role of knowledge in children's memory is examined. I predict that younger students automatically activate their knowledge to make on-line instrumental inferences, but they cannot elaborately use them as retrieval cues.

Younger Students Do Not Make Instrumental Inferences Using Their Knowledge

Paris and Lindauer (1976) conducted research on the role of instrumental inferences in children's comprehension and memory for sentences. The results showed that younger students (7- and 9-year-olds) recalled explicitly cued sentences more than implicitly cued sentences and that older students (11 years old) recalled the implicitly and explicitly cued sentences equally well (see also Paris, Lindauer & Cox, 1977).

Van Meter and Pressley (1994) reexamined whether spontaneous encoding of instruments occurs when 10- to 14-year-olds read target sentences. They used a word-fragment completion test. However, it was not an implicit memory test. They instructed students that the fragments were from words in the sentences that students had just read. Implicit memory tests are operationally defined as memory tests for which the participant is given no instructions to consciously retrieve information from a prior study list, even though performance on the test may be affected by previous exposure to the list (e.g., Roediger & McDermott, 1993). The results showed that the instrument-fragment completion rates of the students who were instructed to read instrument-implicit sentences were much lower than the rates of students who were instructed to generate instruments and of students who read instrument-explicit sentences.

Even Younger Students Make Instrumental Inferences Using Their Knowledge

Judging from the results of the studies mentioned above, can we conclude that younger students never automatically make instrumental inferences while reading and memorizing sentences (i.e., on-line)?

We used an implicit memory test to examine confidence in the above conclusions of prior studies. In the experiments from our three studies (Suzuki, 2000; Tajika et al., 1996; Tajika & Taniguchi, 1995), our goal was to examine the occurrence of younger students' instrumental inferences while reading and memorizing sentences. The logic of the experiments was that even younger students could automatically generate instrumental inferences while memorizing sentences, but that they could not use instruments as retrieval cues.

In the study phase of our experiments (Tajika et al., 1996; Tajika & Taniguchi, 1995), the participants were 80 students in grades 3 (mean age = 9 years, 7 months; N = 40), 6 (mean age = 12 years, 8 months; N = 40) from two elementary schools and 102 university students (mean age = 19 years, 8 months). A 2 × 3 × 2 factorial analysis was carried out. The first factor was learning instruction, with two levels: generation and control. The second factor was grade, with three levels: third grade, sixth grade, and university students. The third factor was word type on the implicit memory test, with two levels: target words and nonstudied words. The first and second factors were manipulated between subjects. The third factor was manipulated within subjects. Students were instructed that they would have a memory test and that they would have to read and memorize each sentence written on the booklet. Students in the generation group were also instructed to generate an instrument for each sentence when they memorized it. Most of the target sentences had the form subject, verb, object, similar to those of Paris and Lindauer (1976). Fourteen target sentences were used for the elementary school children, and sixteen were used for the university students. Target sentences and their instruments generated by children of the third grade, who did not participate in the experiment, showed an 80% or better agreement rate. Here are three examples of the target sentences used in the experiments.

Yasuko stirred the coffee (with a spoon).

Hanako took a picture of the scene (with a camera).

The workman dug a hole in the ground (with a shovel).

The noun words in parentheses are the instruments.

In the test phase, students were instructed that they would first have a word-stem-completion test, which was a word-completion game, and then they would have a recall test. For the word-stem-completion test, a set of 28 concrete nouns was selected (32 for university students). Half of the words were instruments of the target sentences. The remaining half were referred to as nonstudied words.

Strictly speaking, the word-stem-completion test we used was not an implicit memory test, to judge from our definition of an implicit memory test stated earlier, as each instrument was not included in the prior-study list along with the nonstudied words. However, I do examine the constructive nature of memory, especially inferential processes in sentence memory. So I regard the word-stem-completion test we used as an implicit memory test.

The number of letters used in the word-stem-completion test was from two to five for each Japanese word. The average rate of instruments of target sentences generated in the word-stem-completion test was a little less than 5%, very similar to that of nonstudied words (4%) in a pilot study. University students (5%) generated a few more instruments of target sentences than third graders (3%). On a word-stem-completion test, only the first letter printed in hiragana characters was presented at random (e.g., "su___" in Japanese to "spoon" in English and "ka___" in Japanese to "camera" in English). Students were instructed to fill in each blank with the remaining letters of each word that first came to mind. They understood the number of letters of each word from the number of blanks.

After the word-stem completion test, each student received one of the recall tests. Students who received the free recall test were instructed to write target sentences in any order they remembered. Students who received the cued recall test were instructed to write target sentences they remembered. They were also instructed that each instrument would serve as a cue to help them recall target sentences.

The results showed that students of each group generated target words more frequently than nonstudied words. Even third-graders generated target words (6%) more frequently than nonstudied words (3%). However, there was an interaction between grade and learning instruction. Namely, the amount of priming was the same between university students and third-graders in the control groups but was greater in university students than in third-graders in the generation-instruction groups. The results of the sentence-recall tests in the three groups were similar to those of Paris and Lindauer (1976).

In Suzuki's (2000) study, she replicated our experiments in her first experiment and extended our experiments in her second experiment. The logic of her experiments was similar to ours. The pattern of the results of her first experiment was very similar to ours.

In the study phase of her second experiment, she used 409 students in grades 2 (mean age = 8 years, 7 months; $N = 131$), 4 (mean age = 10 years, 7 months; $N = 138$), and 6 (mean age = 12 years, 8 months; $N = 140$) from an elementary school. She carried out a $2 \times 3 \times 2$ factorial analysis. The first factor was the recall material, with two levels: one sentence and three sentences. The second factor was grade, with three levels: second grade, fourth grade, and sixth grade. The third factor was word type on the implicit memory test, with two levels: target words and nonstudied words. The first and second factors were manipulated between subjects. The third factor was manipulated within subjects. One group of recall materials was a three-sentence group, in which the number of learning sentences in a set was three. The other group of recall materials was a one-sentence group, in which the number of learning sentences in a set was one. Eleven sets of learning sentences were chosen from a pilot study. One set of the three-sentence group used in the experiment was as follows:

We went to the Nagoya Dome.

The baseball player hit the ball (with a bat).

He swung fast and ran to first base.

The second sentence was the target sentence in the three-sentence group and in the one-sentence group. Students in the one-sentence group were given only the second sentence in each set. These sentences were the same as the target sentences of our experiments. The noun word in parentheses was the instrument in each set of learning sentences. When students were asked to read each set of learning sentences and generate an instrument for each second sentence in a pilot study, even second-graders generated each instrument at an agreement rate of 80% or better.

In the test phase, recall materials used in a word-stem-completion test were also selected from a pilot study and were similar to ours. A set of 22 concrete nouns was selected for the word-stem-completion test. Half of the words denoted the instruments of the target sentences. The remaining half were nonstudied words. The average rate that students generated instruments of the target sentences in the word-stem-completion test was a little less than 5%, similar to that of nonstudied words (5%) in a pilot study. Students in the three-sentence group who received the free-recall test were instructed that to write each second target sentence in any order they remembered. In addition to the instruction, students in the three-sentence group who received the cued-recall test were also instructed that each instrument would help them recall target sentences.

The results showed that students in both the one-sentence and three-sentence groups generated target words more frequently than nonstudied words. Students in each grade group also generated target words more frequently than nonstudied words. Even second-graders in the one-sentence group generated target words (9%) more frequently than nonstudied words (4%). The amount of priming was the same among the three grade groups. The results of the sentence-recall tests in the three grade groups were similar to ours.

Conclusions

The results of our studies showed that when students' prior knowledge was equalized for each grade and an implicit memory test was used, even such young students as second-graders (8-year-olds) and third-graders (9-year-olds) made instrumental inferences while reading or memorizing target sentences. According to the literature on verbal perceptual implicit memory tests (e.g., Roediger & McDermott, 1993), a reliable amount of priming of implicitly introduced instrument words on an implicit memory test predicts that instrumental inferences have occurred during encoding sentences. However, the results of van Meter and Pressley (1994) showed that priming of implicitly introduced instrument words did not produce recall in children equivalent to that of explicitly presented instrument words. These results seem to mean that even younger students automatically activate their knowledge to make on-line instrumental inferences, but they cannot use it to retrieve instrument words as effectively as when instrument words are explicitly presented.

There are some explanations for the gap in the results between the implicit memory test and the explicit memory test. One possible explanation is that metacognitive processes in younger students do not work well. Younger students automatically activate their prior knowledge about relations between target sentences and their instruments. However, they did not understand well how instrumental cues might help them consciously retrieve target sentences encoded during reading and memorizing.

Another possible explanation refers to off-line results. Younger students are more likely to recall verbatim information than older students. As Brainerd and Reyna (1990) have stated, memory representations are on a continuum from literal and verbatim to fuzzy and gistlike. People extract gist and verbatim information from information they receive, although there is in general a bias toward extracting gist information rather than verbatim information and relying on gist in thinking about verbatim information. According to Brainerd and Reyna's theory, the developmental increase in reliance on gist is sensible and adaptive, because fuzzy traces have more accesses and uses and are less susceptible to interference and forgetting than verbatim traces. Older students encode and rely on gist more than younger students do. Even though younger students generate instruments while reading and memorizing target sentences, they encode target sentences less often in the gist form in which instruments are embedded.

There is little doubt that to construct meaning meaningfully while processing words, sentences, and longer texts involves interactions between prior knowledge and externally presented information. In particular, on the basis of prior knowledge, even younger students often construct inferences that go beyond the information encoded while memorizing sentences. However, it seems that it is in some ways more difficult for younger students to consciously remember target sentences even though they appear to encode them automatically using their knowledge.

Acknowledgment

I would like to thank Professor Ewald Neumann of the University of Canterbury, New Zealand, for his suggestions on English style and his helpful comments on this chapter.

References

Bartlett, F. C. (1932). *Remembering: A study in experimental and social psychology*. Cambridge: Cambridge University Press.

Brainerd, C. J., & Reyna, V. F. (1990). Gist is the grist: Fuzzy-trace theory and the new intuitionism. *Developmental Review, 10*, 3–47.

Bransford, J. D., & Franks, J. J. (1971). The abstraction of linguistic ideas. *Cognitive Psychology, 2*, 331–350.

Bruck, M., & Ceci, S. J. (1999). The suggestibility of children's memory. *Annual Review of Psychology, 50*, 419–439.

Graesser, A. A., & Bower, G. H. (Eds.) (1990). *Inferences and text comprehension*. San Diego: Academic Press.

Graf, P. (1990). Life-span changes in implicit and explicit memory. *Bulletin of the Psychonomic Society, 28*, 353–358.

Graf, P., & Mandler, G. (1984). Activation makes words more accessible, but not necessarily more retrievable. *Journal of Verbal Learning and Verbal Behavior, 23*, 553–568.

Jacoby, L. L., Toth, J. P., & Yonelinas, A. P. (1993). Separating conscious and unconscious influences of memory: Measuring recollection. *Journal of Experimental Psychology: General, 122*, 1–16.

Paris, S. G., & Lindauer, B. K. (1976). The role of inference in children's comprehension and memory for sentences. *Cognitive Psychology, 8*, 217–227.

Paris, S. G., & Lindauer, B. K. (1977). Constructive aspects of children's comprehension and memory. In R. V. Kail Jr. & J. W. Hagen (Eds.), *Perspectives on the development of memory and cognition* (pp. 35–60). Hillsdale, N.J.: Erlbaum.

Paris, S. G., Lindauer, B. K., & Cox, G. L. (1977). The development of inferential comprehension. *Child Development, 48*, 1728–1733.

Roediger, H. L., III & McDermott, K. B. (1993). Implicit memory in normal human subjects. In F. Boller & J. Grafman (Eds.), *Handbook of neuropsychology* (vol. 8, pp. 63–131). Amsterdam: Elsevier.

Roediger, H. L., III & McDermott, K. B. (1995). Creating false memories: Remembering words not presented in lists. *Journal of Experimental Psychology: Learning, Memory, and Cognition, 21,* 803–814.

Sanford, A. J. (1990). Language comprehension. In M. W. Eysenck (Ed.), *The Blackwell dictionary of cognitive psychology* (pp. 203–208). Oxford: Blackwell.

Schacter, D. L., Norman, K. A., & Koutstaal, W. (1998). The cognitive neuroscience of constructive memory. *Annual Review of Psychology, 49,* 289–318.

Suzuki, Y. (2000). Do elementary school children make on-line instrumental inferences in reading? *Japanese Journal of Educational Psychology, 48,* 1–11. Japanese with English summary.

Tajika, H. (1999). The development of children's implicit memory. *Japanese Psychological Review, 42,* 172–184. Japanese with English abstract.

Tajika, H., Collins, S. F., & Taniguchi, A. (1996). Children's instrumental inferences using an implicit memory test. *Psychologia, 39,* 135–143.

Tajika, H., & Taniguchi, A. (1995). Instrumental inferences using an implicit memory test. *Japanese Psychological Research, 37,* 21–28.

Van Meter, P., & Pressley, M. (1994). Encoding of instruments when 10- to 14-year-olds process isolated instrument-implicit sentences: More evidence of improved encoding during childhood resulting from elaborative instructions. *Journal of Educational Psychology, 86,* 402–412.

IV

The Normal and Abnormal Development of Episodic and Autobiographical Memory in Adulthood

8

Age-Related Effects on Memory in the Context of Age-Related Effects on Cognition

Timothy A. Salthouse

Negative age relations on measures of episodic memory are well-established because they have been found in literally hundreds of studies involving a wide variety of samples. Perhaps the most convincing illustration of this phenomenon is apparent in the results from the large nationally representative samples used to establish the norms for standardized tests of memory. For example, figure 1 portrays results from tests of immediate and delayed recall or recognition of stories, words, paired associates, and faces from the normative sample for the Wechsler Memory Scale III (Wechsler, 1997a). Notice that there is a performance difference of about 1 to 1.5 standard score units between age 20 and age 80. If this difference can be interpreted as reflecting changes occurring within an individual, then someone who at age 20 is at the 85th to 90th percentile of the population on a variable would be at the 50th percentile at age 70, and someone who is at the 50th percentile at age 20 would be between the 10th and 15th percentile at age 70. Expressed somewhat differently, because the range from −3 to +3 standard deviations encompasses over 99.7% of a normal distribution, a difference of 1 to 1.5 standard deviation units corresponds to between 1/6 and 1/4 of the effective range of scores in the population. Differences of this magnitude are likely to have a substantial impact on an individual's quality of life.

Most attempts to explain these types of age-related memory differences have focused on processes or components presumed to be involved in particular tasks. That is, because almost all memory and cognitive variables are hypothesized to reflect a mixture of different processes, many researchers have attempted to refine or purify the assessment to identify which specific processes are contributing to the age differences

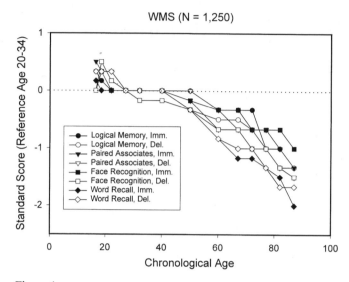

Figure 1
Performance in various episodic memory tasks (intermediate and delayed) as a function of age. (Data from Wechsler, 1997a.)

observed in a particular task. A primary motivation underlying this search for individual processes is the assumption that it is difficult, if not impossible, to understand the nature of age-related effects on a given task until the specific aspects responsible for the age differences in performance of the task can be identified and isolated. The decomposition or fractionation approach has had some success, as differential aging patterns have been observed on certain variables. For example, age-related effects are typically greater on conscious controlled processes than on automatic processes, and on processes related to encoding and retrieval than on processes related to storage.

However, large negative age relations are also evident on other types of cognitive variables besides those reflecting episodic memory. To illustrate, figure 2 portrays results on measures of working memory, perceptual speed, spatial visualization, and reasoning from the normative sample for the Wechsler Adult Intelligence Scale III (Wechsler, 1997b). Once again, it can be seen that the performance difference between age 20 and 80 is about 1 to 1.5 standard score units.

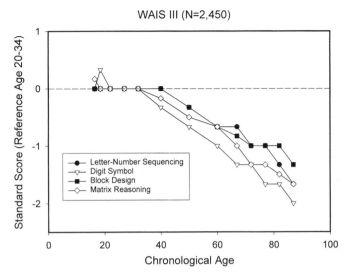

Figure 2
Performance in various cognitive tasks as a function of age. (Data from Wechsler, 1997b.)

The presence of age-related effects on so many different variables raises questions about the extent to which the age-related effects on memory variables are independent of the age-related effects on other types of variables. That is, regardless of the specific process suspected to be most age-sensitive in a particular task, the wide variety of variables exhibiting age-related differences suggests that it is meaningful to ask whether the age-related effects on a given variable are unique or are shared with the age-related effects found on other variables.

An implicit assumption among many cognitive researchers is that distinct causal factors are responsible for the age-related effects on different types of cognitive variables. That is, memory functioning might be impaired by age-related effects on processes such as encoding, on structures such as secondary memory, or on strategies such as organization that are specific to memory tasks, though qualitatively different mechanisms are presumed to be responsible for the age differences on variables reflecting other types of functioning.

If the age-related effects on memory are attributable to influences on processes, structures, or strategies specifically associated with the performance of memory tasks, then one might expect most of the age-related effects on memory variables to be independent of the age-related effects apparent on other types of cognitive variables. As a crude analogy to illustrate this point, consider the functioning of an automobile. A large number of distinct components are involved in the optimal functioning of an automobile, and the various components are often associated with separate and independent problems. For example, the failures that occur in the brake system are usually attributable to quite different factors than those that occur in the transmission system, the fuel system, or the steering system. It is possible that cognitive functioning is also somewhat modular with respect to age-related influences, so that age-related effects on memory are largely independent of age-related effects on reasoning, which in turn are independent of age-related effects on spatial abilities, etc.

However, an alternative possibility is that age-related effects on memory and other cognitive variables are not independent of one another but instead are shared to varying degrees. In terms of the automobile analogy, nonindependent influences might occur if there are cascading effects, as when weak steering leads to an increase in wear and tear on the brakes and the transmission, or if there are systemic effects, as when the materials in all components are subject to the same type of corrosive deterioration.

Distinguishing between these alternatives is important, because if only a small proportion of the age-related variance in memory variables is unique and independent of the age-related influences on other types of variables, then broad and general types of interpretations would presumably be needed to explain the shared age-related effects. Process interpretations restricted to specific tasks could still be viable for explaining how age-related effects are manifested in a particular task, but more inclusive explanations would also be necessary to account for the existence of age-related effects that are shared across different types of tasks.

How can the independence of age-related influences on different cognitive variables be investigated? Patrick Rabbitt (1993), in the title of an article published several years ago, asked, "Does it all go together when it goes?" The independence issue essentially concerns this question. Either cross-sectional or longitudinal data can be used to investigate the question, but it is important to recognize that the two types of data do not necessarily address the same issues. Longitudinal data are concerned with within-individual change, and thus are inherently developmental. Cross-sectional data can also be viewed as developmental if the between-individual differences are considered approximations to within-individual changes. However, it is also possible to consider the age variable in cross-sectional data as a static individual difference, such as sex, ethnic group, or socioeconomic status, in which case it is of interest to describe the nature and pattern of the observed differences, regardless of any relation those differences might have to longitudinal changes. It is important to emphasize that the issue of the independence of age-related effects on different variables is relevant to either conceptualization of cross-sectional comparisons, as well as to longitudinal contrasts.

If longitudinal data are available, then independence of age-related influences might be investigated by simply examining the correlations among change scores. That is, the magnitude of the correlations among the change scores can be interpreted as the degree to which the age-related effects on the variables are shared, or "go together."

Although conceptually straightforward, several complications have limited the investigation of correlations among change scores. First, the longitudinal retest interval needs to be large enough to allow moderate age-related effects to be manifested in each variable, because if there is little change in the variables, then the correlations among them may be low or nonexistent. For many variables, this may require intervals of 10 to 20 years, unless the individuals are in the period of very late adulthood, where more pronounced age-related effects might be expected.

And second, change or difference scores often have low levels of reliability that severely restrict the magnitude of possible correlations with other variables. That is, because only the reliable or systematic variance in a variable is available to be associated with other variables, correlations among difference scores may not be interpretable if their reliabilities are unknown.

At the current time, therefore, only weak conclusions regarding the degree of independence of age-related influences on memory and other cognitive variables are possible from longitudinal data. Only a few studies have reported relevant correlations, and in each case the variety of variables was limited, and the retest interval was relatively short compared to the age range typically studied in cross-sectional comparisons.

Investigation of the independence of age-related influences is somewhat more complicated with cross-sectional data and is most easily accomplished with various types of statistical-control methods. For example, we can use mediation analysis if data from each individual are available on age, V_x (target variable), and V_1 (some other variable). That is, given information on these variables, it is possible to determine the relations between age and V_x, between age and V_1, and between V_x and V_1, and then the effects of V_1 (the hypothesized mediator) on V_x can be controlled when examining the age-related effects on V_x. The relation of age to V_x indicates the total age-related effects on that variable. Because control of V_1 removes all effects shared between V_1 and V_x, the effects of age on the residual V_x measure can be inferred to be unique and independent of any age-related effects on V_1. By comparing the age-related variance before and after statistical control of another variable, this analytical method provides estimates of the amount of age-related variance that is unique (i.e., of age-related effects on the residual of V_x after control of V_1), and of the amount of age-related variance that is shared (i.e., total minus unique).

This type of statistical-control analysis can be illustrated with measures of performance on free-recall and matrix-reasoning tasks as the V_x and V_1 variables, respectively. The free-recall variable was the average number of items correctly recalled across three trials of a list of 15 unrelated words, and the matrix-reasoning variable was the score in an abbreviated version of the Raven Progressive Matrices Test. To express performance in each task in a common metric, all variables were converted to standard-score units. Participants in this study (Salthouse, 2001) consisted of 206 healthy adults ranging from 18 to 84 years of age.

Figures 3 to 5 contain scatterplots of the relations between pairs of variables, and figure 6 the scatter plot of the relation between age and the residual measure of free recall created by partialling out the linear effect of matrix reasoning from the free-recall variable. Comparison of figures 3 and 6 reveals that the age relation to free recall is much weaker after controlling for the influence of matrix reasoning. Expressing the two relations in terms of proportions of variance indicates that only a

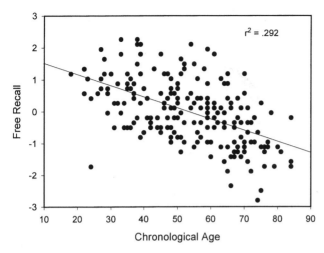

Figure 3
The relation between age and free recall in a sample of 206 adults. (Data from Salthouse, 2001.)

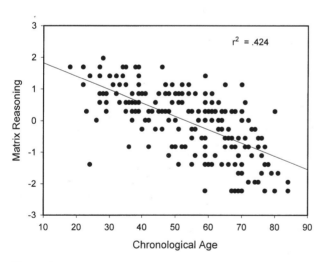

Figure 4
The relation between age and matrix reasoning in a sample of 206 adults. (Data from Salthouse, 2001.)

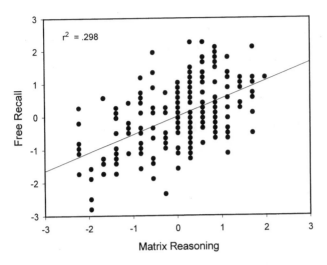

Figure 5
The relation between free recall and matrix reasoning in a sample of 206 adults.
(Data from Salthouse, 2001.)

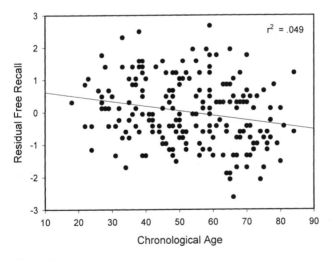

Figure 6
The relation between age and residual free recall after partialling out the linear
effect of matrix reasoning on free recall. (Data from Salthouse, 2001.)

small proportion (i.e., .049/.292 = 17%) of the total age-related variance in the free recall variable was unique to that variable and independent of the variance in the matrix reasoning variable. Age-related effects on memory-specific mechanisms can therefore be inferred to be responsible for only a fraction of the total age-related effects observed in these particular free-recall measures.

Results with control of a single variable are informative about the relation between that particular variable and the target variable, but selection of the variable to function as the controlled or mediator variable is somewhat arbitrary. Certain variables or constructs are sometimes assumed to have a special status because they have been hypothesized to be causal mediators of the age-related effects on other variables. For example, a number of researchers have postulated that working memory and speed of processing function as mediators of age differences in other cognitive variables. However, many different types of variables could be hypothesized to serve in this role, and a large number of variables could be effective statistical mediators even if they are not plausible as causal mediators. To illustrate, the results summarized above indicate that matrix reasoning functions as an effective statistical mediator of age differences in free recall, but because matrix reasoning does not appear to be more fundamental or primitive than free recall, it is unlikely to be meaningful as a causal mediator. Unfortunately, distinguishing between mere statistical mediators and true causal mediators is difficult, if not impossible, with correlational analyses.

In part because of the ambiguity about the status of mediators, an alternative statistical control procedure has recently been used in which no variable is assumed to have causal priority, but instead all variables are viewed as sharing something negatively influenced by age. This perspective distinguishes two types of age-related effects on variables: one that is shared with other variables and a second that is unique to a particular variable. Shared age-related influences are those operating through a factor that accounts for the variance common to all variables, whereas unique influences on the variable in question are the independent effects associated with age that remain after control of the common effects.

This shared-influence analytical procedure can be implemented as follows. First, obtain an estimate of the variance the variables have in common by computing either the first principal component or the first principal factor that represents variance shared among all variables. Next, control the age-related effects on this estimate of what is common to all variables before examining the effects associated with age on individual variables. Any residual age-related effects on the target variable observed under these conditions can be inferred to be unique and independent of the age-related effects on other variables. When applied to variables reflecting memory functioning, the shared-influence analytical procedure provides a means of estimating the degree to which memory-specific factors contribute to the age differences observed in episodic memory variables. That is, by including variables from a variety of other cognitive tasks in this type of analysis, any unique age-related effects on memory variables can be inferred to be attributable to memory-specific mechanisms, whereas age-related influences shared with other types of cognitive variables would presumably require broader or more general explanatory mechanisms.

The shared-influence analytical procedure can be illustrated with results from my laboratory in which the target variables consisted of episodic-memory measures from free-recall and paired-associates tasks. The free-recall variable was the average number of words correctly recalled across two to six trials with either the same or different lists of 12 to 15 unrelated or categorized words, and the paired-associates variable was the average number of response terms recalled across two trials with six pairs of unrelated words. In addition to measures of episodic memory, each of the studies involved a mixture of other types of cognitive variables, primarily representing speed, reasoning, and spatial abilities. The samples of participants consisted of between 121 and 305 healthy adults who ranged from 18 to 95 years of age.

Figure 7 portrays the estimates of the total and unique age-related variance in the episodic-memory measures derived from the shared-influence analyses. It can be seen that only a very small proportion of the age-related effects on these episodic-memory variables was unique and independent of the age-related effects on other types of variables. Expressed in terms of shared influences, the percentage of age-related variance in the free-recall variables that was shared with other variables ranged from 94.0% to 99.9%, and from 95.1% to 99.9% for the per-

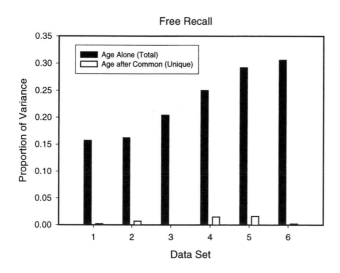

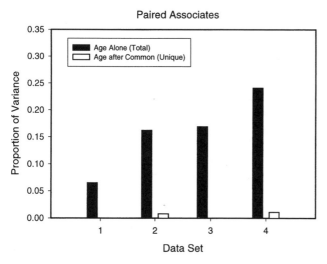

Figure 7

Proportions of variance in episodic memory variables associated with age. (Data sets for the free-recall analyses are as follows: 1—Salthouse, Hambrick & McGuthry, 1998; 2—Salthouse, 1993; 3—Salthouse, Toth, Hancock & Woodard, 1997; 4—Salthouse, Fristoe & Rhee, 1996; 5—Salthouse, 2001; and 6—Salthouse, 1996. Data sets for the paired-associates analyses are the following: 1—Salthouse, Toth, Daniels, Parks, Pak, Wolbrette & Hocking, 2000; 2—Salthouse, 1996; 3—Salthouse, 2001; and 4—Salthouse, Fristoe & Rhee, 1996.)

centage of age-related variance in the paired associates variables. These findings suggest that very little of the age-related effects on measures of episodic memory can be attributed to influences on processes that are specific to memory, as opposed to processes involved in other types of cognitive variables.

The shared-influence analytical procedure is relatively crude because it assumes no structure among the variables except that based on the relation each variable has with age. However, the assumption of no structure is unrealistic because most variables have small to moderate correlations with one another. Therefore, although the shared-influence method is informative about the nature of age-related effects on variables, it is incomplete, because it ignores interrelations that clearly exist among the variables.

Patterns of correlations among variables are often interpreted in terms of structural models. The currently most-accepted model of the structure of cognitive abilities is a hierarchical model in which there are from two to four levels intervening between the observed variables and the highest-order construct (e.g., Carroll, 1993; Cattell, 1987; Gustafson, 1984; Horn & Hofer, 1992). Variables representing episodic memory are not often included within hierarchical models, but when they have been included, they have been found to exhibit a coherent relation to other types of cognitive variables.

A major advantage of a hierarchical-structure representation is that it is possible to determine the level in the structure at which most of the age-related influences are operating. Age-related effects could be at the level of individual variables, such as the score in a particular task, at the level of first-order cognitive abilities or constructs, such as episodic memory, or at the level of the highest-order constructs representing variance common to all variables, such as Spearman's g. If the age-related influences on memory variables are specific to those variables, then many of the age-related effects would be expected to operate at low levels in the hierarchical structure. For example, if it is hypothesized that aging impairs the use of imagery in associating to-be-remembered items, then direct or independent age-related effects would be predicted on variables assessing paired-associates performance. Alternatively, direct or independent age-related effects on free-recall variables would be expected if it is postulated that increased age is associated with specific deficits in the effectiveness of organization-based retrieval. In contrast, any age-related effects found to operate at higher levels in the hierarchy are necessarily broader and more general because the influences are not restricted to particular variables.

The implications for understanding the nature of age-related effects on memory and other variables are therefore quite different depending on the level at which age-related influences operate. On the one hand, if the age-related influences operate at relatively low levels in the hierarchy, then this would indicate that at least some of the age-related influences on memory variables are independent of age-related influences on other types of variables, and explanations would be needed to account for the unique age-related influences on memory-specific processes. On the other hand, if most of the age-related influences operate at high levels in the hierarchy, then there would be little evidence for distinct age-related effects on memory variables when those variables are considered in the context of age-related effects on other variables. If this turned out to be the case, then explanations would be needed both for why aging has broad effects and for how those effects influence particular variables, such as those reflecting memory functioning.

Hierarchical models of the organization of memory and cognitive variables can be examined with structural-equation modeling procedures, first by specifying a model with hierarchical structure among the variables, and then by determining the levels at which age-related effects operate within that structure. Examination of the age-related influences in this type of analysis should start at the highest level, because it is the most general, and hence any effects at this level need to be controlled before considering effects at more specific levels (Carroll, 1993, p. 623).

Results of hierarchical analyses of age-related influences involving episodic memory and cognitive variables are available for three separate data sets. The first data set is from a study by Salthouse, Fristoe, and Rhee (1996) involving 259 adults between 18 and 94 years of age. The episodic-memory variables in this study were recall performance on the second and sixth trials of the Rey Auditory Verbal Learning Test, and paired-associates performance in terms of the number of associates recalled in each of two lists. The second data set is from a recent study

(Salthouse, 2001) involving 206 adults between 18 and 84 years of age. Memory was represented by recall on three successive lists of words and paired-associates recall on each of two lists. The third data set is based on the normative sample of 1,580 adults between 20 and 95 years of age for the Woodcock-Johnson Psycho-educational Battery, Revised (see Salthouse, 1998). Episodic memory in this data set was represented by four variables: (a) learning associations between unfamiliar names and pictures of novel creatures, (b) learning associations between unfamiliar visual symbols and familiar words, (c) immediate reproduction of auditorily presented words, phrases, or sentences, and (d) immediate reproduction of unrelated words in correct sequence.

Figures 8 to 10 illustrate the models with each data set, and tables 1 to 3 contain two types of information relevant to evaluating the accuracy of the models. One type of evaluative information consists of conventional fit statistics for structural-equation models. The other type of information consists of the observed and predicted age correlations for the memory variables. The predicted values were derived from the product of the coefficients for all paths in the model from age to the variable. Inspection of tables 1 to 3 reveals that the overall fits of the models were good, and that the age correlations were accurately predicted with the single age-related influence at the highest level in the hierarchy.

Within each data set, relations were also examined from age to the lower-level memory constructs or variables. None of these were significant except with the Woodcock-Johnson data in data set 3. In that case there was a positive relation from age to episodic memory because the negative age effects were overestimated on the basis of the age effects on the highest-level factor. Examination of table 3 indicates that this overestimation stemmed primarily from the memory-for-sentences variable, for which the predicted age correlation was $-.41$ but the actual correlation was $-.29$.

Conclusion

The results described above reveal a consistent pattern across the mediation, shared influences, and hierarchical analyses. In each case the age-related effects on different types of memory and cognitive variables were

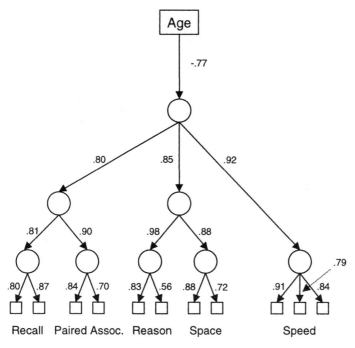

Figure 8
Hierarchical structural model for data from Salthouse, Fristoe, and Rhee (1996).

Table 1
Fit statistics and predicted age correlations for the hierarchical structure model for data set 1

$\chi^2(N = 259, df = 47) = 84.28$
NNFI = .97, CFI = .98, RMSEA = .06

	Age correlations	
	Predicted	Observed
Recall trial 2	−.40	−.47
Recall trial 6	−.43	−.45
PA 1	−.47	−.51
PA 2	−.39	−.35

NNFI: nonnormed fit index.
CFI: comparative fit index.
RMSEA: root mean square error of approximation.
PA: paired-associates recall.

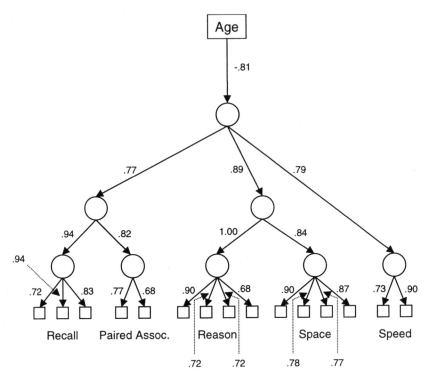

Figure 9
Hierarchical structural model for data from Salthouse (2001).

Table 2
Fit statistics and predicted age correlations for the hierarchical structure model for data set 2

$\chi^2(N = 206, \mathrm{df} = 97) = 161.91$
NNFI = .96, CFI = .97, RMSEA = .06

	Age correlations	
	Predicted	Observed
Recall 1	−.42	−.34
Recall 2	−.55	−.57
Recall 3	−.49	−.51
PA 1	−.39	−.37
PA 2	−.35	−.35

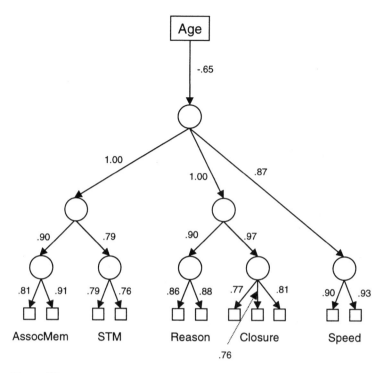

Figure 10
Hierarchical structural model for data from the normative sample of the Woodcock-Johnson Psycho-educational Test Battery.

Table 3
Fit statistics and predicted age correlations for the hierarchical structure model for data set 3

$\chi^2(N = 1580, \mathrm{df} = 47) = 551.21$
NNFI = .95, CFI = .96, RMSEA = .08

	Age correlations	
	Predicted	Observed
Memory for names	−.47	−.49
Visual-auditory learning	−.53	−.49
Memory for sentences	−.41	−.29
Memory for words	−.39	−.38

not independent, but instead most of the age-related variance on the different variables was shared. Moreover, in the hierarchical analyses the age differences in various episodic-memory variables were accurately predicted with a single age-related influence operating on all variables.

To summarize, the evidence discussed above strongly suggests that changes are needed in the nature of the explanations proposed to account for age-related effects on memory. In particular, because direct or unique effects associated with increased age on memory-specific processes contribute relatively little to the overall age-related effects on measures of episodic memory, memory-specific interpretations appear to be limited in their ability to account for age-related influences. However, because it now seems that age-related effects on memory variables do not occur in isolation, but rather in the context of age-related effects on a wide variety of cognitive variables, interpretations based on broad and general types of influences are likely to become more prominent, as will explanations of how these influences are manifested in the processes affecting particular memory tasks.

Let me now conclude by returning to the major question of what is responsible for adult age differences in episodic memory. I have suggested that there are two quite different approaches to this question. The dominant perspective at the current time can be termed the micro approach, as researchers within this perspective attempt to identify which specific aspect of task performance is most affected by increased age. This approach has relied on task analysis and various experimental decomposition procedures to attempt to specify the processes involved in successful task performance that are most affected by increased age.

The second approach can be termed the macro approach, because the goal of researchers within this perspective is to determine whether the age-related effects on the age-sensitive processes in the task are unique and specific to those processes, or are shared with processes involved in other types of tasks. If shared effects are identified, then the macro researcher would seek explanations for what might be responsible for those effects. The primary analytical tools used within the macro perspective are a variety of correlation-based statistical-control procedures.

In this chapter I have focused on the second approach, and the results I have described suggest that a substantial proportion of the age-related effects on episodic memory are shared with age-related effects on other types of cognitive variables. Evidence consistent with this inference was obtained in mediational analyses, in shared-influence analyses, and in analyses based on hierarchical structures of variables.

Among the speculations that might be proposed to account for the large proportions of age-related influences that appear to be shared across different types of variables are the following:

• General reductions in cognitive efficiency, as implied by hypotheses about processing resources

• Impairments in specific cognitive processes, such as formation of an internal representation or maintenance of a goal

• Declines in a critical cognitive construct, such as working memory or inhibition

• Decreases in neural efficiency, perhaps due to loss of myelin or reduced quantity of neurotransmitters

• Alterations in the functioning of particular neuroanatomical structures, such as the dorsolateral prefrontal cortex

• Disruption of a neural circuit, such as the dopaminergic pathway

• Reduced effectiveness of coordinating and monitoring cognitive processes or neural information.

All of these speculations are obviously very crude and tentative, however, and they are neither exhaustive nor mutually exclusive. An important goal for the future should therefore be the formulation and investigation of explicit hypotheses to account for shared age-related influences across memory and other types of cognitive variables.

References

Carroll, J. B. (1993). *Human cognitive abilities: A survey of factor analytic studies*. New York: Cambridge University Press.

Cattell, R. B. (1987). *Abilities: Their structure, growth, and action*. Amsterdam: North-Holland.

Cohen, J., & Cohen, P. (1983). *Applied multiple regression/correlation analysis for the behavioral sciences*. Hillsdale, N.J.: Lawrence Erlbaum.

Gustafson, J. E. (1984). A unifying model for the structure of mental abilities. *Intelligence, 8*, 179–203.

Horn, J. L., & Hofer, S. M. (1992). Major abilities and development in the adult period. In R. J. Sternberg & C. A. Berg (Eds.), *Intellectual development* (pp. 44–99). New York: Cambridge University Press.

Rabbitt, P. (1993). Does it all go together when it goes? The nineteenth Bartlett Memorial Lecture. *Quarterly Journal of Experimental Psychology, 46A*, 385–434.

Salthouse, T. A. (1993). Speed mediation of adult age differences in cognition. *Developmental Psychology, 29*, 722–738.

Salthouse, T. A. (1996). General and specific speed mediation of adult age differences in memory. *Journal of Gerontology: Psychological Sciences, 51B*, P30–P42.

Salthouse, T. A. (1998). Independence of age-related influences on cognitive abilities across the life span. *Developmental Psychology, 34*, 851–864.

Salthouse, T. A. (2001). Structural models of the relations between age and measures of cognitive functioning. *Intelligence, 29*, 93–115.

Salthouse, T. A., Fristoe, N., & Rhee, S. H. (1996). How localized are age-related effects on neuropsychological measures? *Neuropsychology, 10*, 272–285.

Salthouse, T. A., Hambrick, D. Z., & McGuthry, K. E. (1998). Shared age-related influences on cognitive and noncognitive variables. *Psychology and Aging, 13*, 486–500.

Salthouse, T. A., Toth, J., Daniels, K., Parks, C., Pak, R., Wolbrette, M., & Hocking, K. (2000). Effects of aging on the efficiency of task switching in a variant of the Trail Making Test. *Neuropsychology, 14*, 102–111.

Salthouse, T. A., Toth, J. P., Hancock, H. E., & Woodard, J. L. (1997). Controlled and automatic forms of memory and attention: Process purity and the uniqueness of age-related influences. *Journal of Gerontology: Psychological Sciences, 52B*, P216–P228.

Wechsler, D. (1997a). *WMS-III (Wechsler Memory Scale*, 3rd Ed.). San Antonio: Psychological Corporation.

Wechsler, D. (1997b). *WAIS-III (Wechsler Adult Intelligence Scale*, 3rd Ed.). San Antonio: Psychological Corporation.

9

Autobiographical Memory across the Lifespan

David C. Rubin

A Brief History

Galton describes the first procedure he used to cue memories as follows. "I walked leisurely along Pall Mall, a distance of 450 yards, during which time I scrutinised with attention every successive object that caught my eyes, and I allowed my attention to rest on it until one or two thoughts had arisen through direct association.... Samples of my whole life passed before me" (1879, p. 151). He then moved from the "real world" into the "laboratory." Galton produced sheets of paper, each with one word on it, waited a few days, placed a sheet with a word on it partially under a book so that it was blocked from view until he would lean forward to see it. He recorded his associations and his reaction times to 75 words on four occasions. "It was a most repugnant and laborious work" (1879, p. 153). Of the 124 different associations he obtained, 48 were from "boyhood and youth," 57 were from "subsequent manhood," and 19 were from "quite recent events."

Crovitz and Schiffman (1974) revived Galton's technique. About the same time Robinson (1976) independently came upon the same procedure. People were asked to think of an autobiographical memory in response to each word presented to them. They were then asked to return to their memories and date each one as accurately as possible.

The distribution of memories over the lifespan of the undergraduate can be described as a power function of the time since the event occurred (Crovitz & Schiffman, 1974). Figure 1 is of a typical plot. The power function (i.e., $y = at^{-b}$) is a simple two parameter curve that has often been used in psychology (Newell & Rosenbloom, 1981; Stevens, 1975).

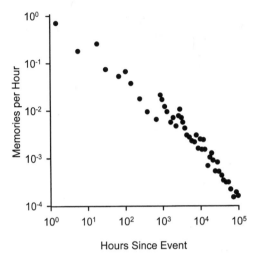

Figure 1
The relative number of autobiographical memories per hour reported by under-graduates as a function of the age of those memories. Both axes are logarithmic, so a straight line is a power function. (Adapted from Rubin, 1982, figure 2.)

When both axes are plotted as logarithmic scales, as they are in figure 1, the power function becomes a straight line (i.e., $\log(y) = -b \log(t) + \log(a)$). The fits to the curve are surprisingly good, with correlations usually over .95. If we assume that undergraduates encode an equal number of events each day of their lives, then the plot shown in figure 1 is a retention function. Because the power function is a common choice for a retention function (Anderson & Schooler, 1991; see Rubin & Wenzel, 1996, for a review), as a first approximation it appears that laboratory and autobiographical memory have similar patterns of for-getting (but see Rubin, Hinton & Wenzel, 1999).

A recurring theme can now be introduced (Rubin, 1989). Figure 1 presents some of the most regular data in memory research. Correlations over .95 are not all that common in cognitive psychology, especially when a two-parameter function is fit to over a dozen points and the function is a reasonable choice in terms of the existing literature. But figure 1 is of data that was collected with one of the least controlled experimental procedures in cognitive psychology. There are no restrictions or controls over the learning of the material or over which autobiographical memories people are to report. The function is not dependent on how the dating of memories is done; it does not change whether participants report the age of the memory with an estimate of the actual date in term of its month, day, and year or whether they use phrases of the form *n* hours, days, weeks, months, or years ago. The shape of the function does not depend on the cue words used, as it occurs when people respond to a single cue word, when they respond to different numbers of cue words, when odors are used instead of cue words, and when no cues are used at all—they respond to just a request for 50 autobiographical memories (Rubin, 1982; Rubin, Groth & Goldsmith, 1984). One reason for the regularity may be that the retention interval is large (from either 1 hour or 1 day ago to about 20 years ago) and the range of the dependent measure is large (often four orders of magnitude). Such large ranges on scales can be more easily obtained outside the laboratory.

Scott Wetzler, then a graduate student in clinical psychology, wondered what would happen if older adults were tested. After all, the undergraduates had only about 20 years of life on which to report. Would the retention function remain the same or perhaps just change its slope or intercept parameter? Would the whole shape of the function change? Robert Nebes, who was then at Duke, had data, and Scott wrote to other people for their data. They were all generous in their cooperation (their original articles were published as Fitzgerald & Lawrence, 1984; Franklin & Holding, 1977; Zola-Morgan, Cohen & Squire, 1983).

The results for older adults with a mean age of 70 are shown in figure 2. They were a surprise. No one had plotted the data this way before, and so we could find no earlier empirical demonstration of the non-monotonic plot. The shape of the curve also appeared replicable, because it appeared in the plots of the data from 70-year-old participants from each of the three laboratories that were summed to provide figure 2 and also in the plots from three laboratories for adults who were 50 years old (Rubin, Wetzler & Nebes, 1986). For figure 2, about one half of the memories were dated as occurring within the last year and were not plotted because they would make all decades but the last have very low values; they are, however, considered in detail when retention functions for the most recent decade are plotted. The large number of memories from the recent past also shows that older adults are not "living in the

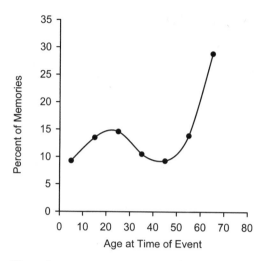

Figure 2
The distribution of autobiographical memories over the lifespan for older adults. Events dated as occurring in the most recent year are excluded. (Data from Rubin et al., 1986.)

past." From the shape of the plot and the retention-function fit for undergraduates, we assumed that the curve had three components: retention, childhood amnesia, and a *bump* or increase in the number of memories recalled from adolescence and early adulthood. Because the topic of this chapter, the increase in memories from ages 10 to 30, is defined empirically by what is left after the retention and childhood amnesia components are removed, these two components are considered briefly before concentrating on the nonmonotonic component.

The first component is a retention function that covers the whole lifespan, but that has most of its memories distributed over the most recent two decades of life; for periods more than two decades ago, it is too small to produce a measurable number of memories. If one assumes that the retention function of figure 1 holds for people of all ages without systematic age changes in the slope (an assumption supported by considerable data, e.g., Rubin et al., 1986; Rubin & Schulkind, 1997a, 1997b), then for a typical slope of $-.8$, the number of memories per hour decreases by a factor of .57 every time the retention interval doubles. If from a month that occurred three months ago an older adult recalled 10 memories, from months that occurred $\frac{1}{2}$, 1, 2, 4, 8, 16, 32, and 64 years ago that adult would recall 6, 3, 2, 1, .6, .4, .3, .2, and .1 memories. Thus, without some modification of the function, older adults would recall little from their youth.

The second component is childhood amnesia. When undergraduates were tested, there was an inflection in the power-function curve (Wetzler & Sweeney, 1986), but it is hard to argue that some other curve would not naturally fit this inflection. However, when adults of different ages were tested, it became clear that a function was needed that went to zero at or near the birth of the person no matter whether their birth was 20, 50, or 70 years before the date of testing. Thus a childhood-amnesia component based on age at the time of the event rather than time since the event had to be added to ensure that the curves of people of different ages all went to zero at birth. In mathematical terms, there had to be a function in terms of age at the time or the event (or equivalently, retention interval − current age) in addition to a function in terms of retention interval (i.e., $f(t - \text{age})$ as well as $f(t)$, where t is the time since the event). This component is very stable over numerous studies, having the same basic shape no matter what method is used to produce the data, as long as the participants come from the United States (Rubin, 2000). Thus, as with the retention component, the data are remarkably regular, though the experimental procedure has minimal control. The childhood-amnesia component is, however, affected by culture, and within some cultures by gender (Mullen, 1994; MacDonald, Uesiliana & Hayne, 2000). Figure 3 provides a sample plot.

The third component is the increase in memories from when older adults were between 10 and 30 years old compared to what would be expected from the other two components or from any monotonically decreasing function. We termed it "the bump" to emphasize our lack of theoretical understanding, a lack due to the paucity of an organized existing literature. Our later searches of the literature, however, found a multitude of possible theoretical explanations that could have predicted the bump, but that somehow did not lead to empirical tests.

The initial description of the bump was based on data from several laboratories. Since that time there have been consistent findings using the word-cue technique with older adults (Hyland & Ackerman, 1988;

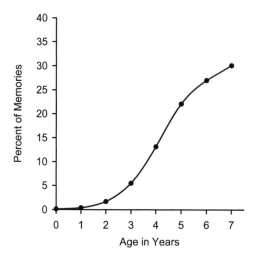

Figure 3
The distributions of 10,118 memories dated as occurring before age 8 from published studies. (Data from Rubin, 2000.)

Jansari & Parkin, 1996; Rubin & Schulkind, 1997a, 1997c; see Rubin, 1999, and Rybash, 1999, and the articles that follow in his special issue of the *Journal of Adult Development* for reviews). Minor differences exist in the shape of the distribution with changes in procedure and subject population, but the bump appears repeatedly, even for individuals (Rubin & Schulkind, 1997c). This literature indicates that the bump occurs when as few as 10 to 20 and as many as 900 word cues are given to each person; so the bump is not caused by just a few highly available memories.

The word-cue technique is useful to help people produce memories. It helps ensure that each memory is not cued mainly by the memories recalled previously, and thus provides a wider sampling of memories. But this is only one way to access autobiographical memories and not the one most commonly used in everyday life. A series of studies from Denmark first demonstrated that the bump occurs even when a life narrative is obtained from older adults and the distribution of experimenter-defined events from that life study is plotted (Fromholt & Larsen, 1991; Fromholt, Larsen & Larsen 1995; see Schrauf & Rubin, 2000, for a replication).

Differences in the Properties of Autobiographical Memories

The summary of this section is that there are few differences in the memories retrieved over the lifespan and none that distinguish the bump period. Basically, there are just more memories from the bump period. It is as if there were increased availability or accessibility for these memories (Tulving & Pearlstone, 1966). The properties that lead to this ease of retrieval do not change with the age of the memories.

Rubin and Schulkind (1997a) tested adults of different ages: 60 seventy-year-old adults, 20 thirty-five-year-old adults, and 40 twenty-year-old adults. Each adult provided a memory to each of 124 cue words. No consistent differences in reaction time as a function of the age of the memories were found, though the younger adults were much faster. Thus, participants were not spending more time trying to get memories from the bump period, or any other period. This observation argues against strategies that involve more elaborate searchs by subjects for various life periods and supports the interpretation of the bump as an increase in the ease of accessing memories from between the ages of 10 and 30 rather than as the result of a search strategy. There were also no gender differences in this data (Rubin, Schulkind & Rahhal, 1999).

One autobiographical memory from each of the 14 five-year periods of each older adult's life was selected. Each participant was asked to rate these 14 memories on several properties. There were five seven-point scales: vividness, pleasantness, significance, novelty of the event, and frequency of rehearsal. A three-point emotionality scale was calculated as the absolute value of the difference of the pleasantness rating from neutral. Separate analyses were performed for each scale, but none of the scales provided statistically significant differences in the bump period, even though there was considerable statistical power when all 60 older participants were combined. Conway and Haque (1999) obtained similar findings for ratings on three scales similar in wording to the ones Rubin and Schulkind (1997a) used: significance, novelty of the event, and frequency of rehearsal, as well as a scale that directly measured emotional intensity. This observation supports the interpretation of the bump as an increase in the ease of accessing memories from between the ages of 10 and 30 rather than as the result of a specific properties of memories from that period increasing their recall.

Rubin and Schulkind (1997b) investigated whether differences in the properties of the cue words produced differences in the autobiographical memories obtained. Imagery, concreteness, and meaningfulness ratings of the cue words correlated .34, .38, and .47, with the average age of the memory (i.e., the time between the date of the event and the date of the recall) for the 40 twenty-year-old participants and .25, .28, and .29 for the 60 seventy-year-old participants. For the 20 thirty-five-year-old participants, the correlations were smaller, perhaps because the smaller number of participants produced less reliable data. For reaction time, the correlations with imagery, concreteness, and meaning were −.37, −.36, and −.43 for the twenty-year-old participants and −.67, −.65, and −.64 for the older participants. In contrast to these fairly large correlations, the correlations of the percentage of memories that fell in the 10-to-29 bump period with imagery, concreteness, and meaning were .22, .18, and .14. None of the ratings of goodness or emotionality correlated greater than .20 with age of memory, reaction time, or percentage of memories in the bump period. Thus, the properties of the cue words did not differentiate memories that came from the bump from other memories. This observation also supports the interpretation that the bump results from an increase in the ease of accessing memories from between the ages of 10 and 30 rather than from specific properties of the cues used to prompt the memories.

Rybash and Monaghan (1999) asked 40 alumni of Hamilton College to recall an autobiographical memory associated with each of 18 cue words. For each memory, they were also asked to indicate whether they had a recollective experience in which they seemed to reexperience some of the same emotions, perceptions, and thoughts that they had at the time of the original event (i.e., whether they had a "remember" memory) or whether they just knew the event without any sense of reliving, even though they might know a good deal about the details of the event. There was a clear reminiscence bump, but no difference in the shape of the bump between the recollective or "remember" memories and the "know" memories. Their data, which are shown in figure 4, argue that

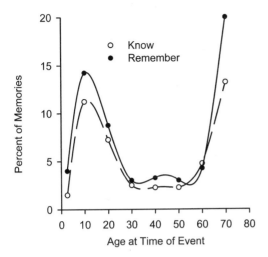

Figure 4
The distribution of older adults' lifespan autobiographical memories judged as remembered versus judged as just known. (Data from Rybash & Monaghan, 1999.)

this especially important phenomenological property of autobiographical memories does not differ over the lifespan.

The Role of Emotions

The effect of emotional states on the recall of autobiographical memories and the recall of the emotions present in autobiographical memories have been studied from many perspectives (for reviews, see Christianson & Safer, 1996; Robinson, 1996; and Williams, 1996). Less attention has been paid to the effect of emotions on the distribution of autobiographical memories over the lifespan. The studies cited in the previous section found no differences across the lifespan in the ratings of pleasantness, emotional intensity, or a sense of reliving, which was defined to include emotional reliving.

There are studies that examine the effect of clinical disorders involving emotional state on the distribution of autobiographical memory. The only data in which bump memories appear to be different than recent memories is in a study of older adults who suffered their first major depression. These patients provided brief life narratives, both during the period of their depression and six months later (Fromholt et al., 1995). Alzheimer's patients from an earlier study (Fromholt et al., 1991) were included in addition to healthy controls in an attempt to provide data that could aid in the differential diagnosis between dementia and depression in older adults. All three groups of participants showed a clear bump, but the depressed patients had more recent memories than the other two groups. Depressed patients also had less temporal coherence in their life narratives than the other two groups. As might be expected, depressed patients had more emotionally negative memories, though the increase in negative memories came only from the most recent five years. Depressed patients reported memories similar in emotional tone to the other two groups for memories older than five years, which was well before the onset of their depression. After six months, when most of the depressed patients had recovered, the recent memories of the depressed patients had the same emotional tone as their older memories and as the recent memories of the other groups. Thus, for older adults suffering from their first depression, memories retrieved from the bump did not change in emotional tone during the depression, though more recent memories did.

In addition to depression, posttraumatic-stress disorder differentially affects autobiographical memory across the lifespan. Vietnam War veterans with posttraumatic-stress disorder had more memories from the time of the Vietnam War than did veterans without posttraumatic-stress disorder (McNally, Lasko, Macklin & Pitman, 1995). In addition, veterans with posttraumatic-stress disorder, like patients with depression (Williams, 1996), had difficulty recalling specific autobiographical memories and had more difficulty producing specific memories when the cue words were positive traits as opposed to negative traits. The differences in the distribution of autobiographical memories and in the specificity of those memories were greatest for those veterans with posttraumatic-stress disorder who wore Vietnam War regalia to the testing sessions. These veterans did not differ from the other veterans with posttraumatic-stress disorder in terms of depression, anxiety, and combat experience, excluding these factors as an explanation. Thus, although there are no differences in the ratings of emotional intensity of autobiographical memories across the lifespan in most populations, in some populations differences can be observed.

The Role of Language

One way to study the role of language in autobiographical memory is to test sequential bilinguals who learn their two languages at different periods of their lives. By asking sequential bilinguals to recall autobiographical memories from across their lifespan in both of their languages, the extent to which autobiographical memory is stored in a language as opposed to other forms of representation can be studied. Clinicians have observed that childhood and traumatic memories are more easily accessed in bilinguals' first language (Aragno & Schalet, 1996; Javier, 1995; Schrauf, 2000), and thus childhood amnesia may be greater for bilinguals tested in their second language. For memories in general (Bugelski, 1977) and for autobiographical memories in particular (Marion & Neisser, 1997), sequential bilinguals tend to recall older memories in the first language.

Schrauf and Rubin (1998, 2000) tested older sequential bilinguals who were highly proficient and literate in both Spanish and English. These bilinguals failed to produce older memories when they were cued and asked to respond in their first language. However, when they were asked about the "internal language" of the memory, that is, the language in which the memory came to them as opposed to the external language of the testing session, their first language produced older memories. Similar findings occurred with Polish-Danish sequential bilinguals who learned Danish in their early 20s. Those who learned Danish in their early 30s and who had become less proficient in Danish had earlier memories when cued in Polish in addition to showing the "internal language" effect. Figure 5 shows a typical result. Taken together, these studies show that autobiographical memories are to some extent coded in a language or at least have language as a sensory or phenomenological quality (Larsen, Schrauf, Fromholt & Rubin, 2002).

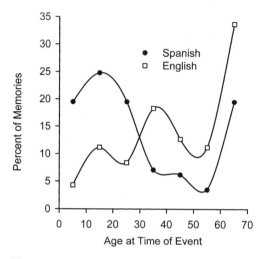

Figure 5
The distribution of memories that came to the participant in each language independent of the language being spoken in the session.

Is the Bump Just for Autobiographical Memory?

The studies reviewed so far are all about autobiographical memory. But
once one starts to look, one finds plots similar to the bump in autobiographical memory in other domains as well. A full explanation of the
bump needs to take such plots into account and decide whether they are
relevant to processes occurring in autobiographical memory. The oldest
such plot I know about appears in Ribot (1882). He claims that for most
people, imagination rises and drops in a fashion similar to the plots
shown for autobiographical memory. For a select few, such as Ribot, I
assume, it continues at a high level though old age. Like the bump, it has
components. Early in the lifespan, imagination is used for play, then for
sexual fantasy, and finally for more mature use.

Other classic theories also have peaks that correspond to those in the
bump. Identity formation in personality theories is the most obvious
(Erickson, 1950). Ideas similar to the bump are common, especially
when the effects of narrative on autobiographical memory are considered
(Holmes & Conway, 1999; Fitzgerald, 1988; Gergen & Gergen, 1983;
Robinson, 1996). However, even evolutionary theory would predict a

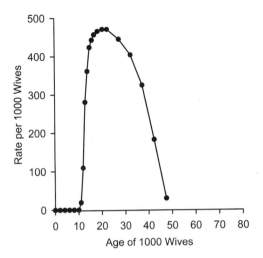

Figure 6
Births per 1,000 wives in traditional societies as a function of the age of the wife. (Data from Menken, Trussell & Larsen, 1986.) The data up to age 20 are hypothetical values based on the percentage of women reaching menarche. (Data from Komura, Miyake, Chen, Tanizawa & Yoshikawa, 1992.)

bump if the increase in memories is due to increases in cognitive abilities that happen to occur when we are most likely to be making decisions about childbearing and child raising. Figure 6 is a plot of when in the lifespan births occur in traditional societies without modern birth control. Such evolutionary ideas are not without behavioral support. We are faster during the period in which the bump occurs, as shown in figure 7. We also do better on standardized memory tests, such as the Wechsler Memory Scale, and so need more items correct during this period to obtain any percentile score, as shown in figure 8. A more recent theoretical plot was presented by Fredrickson and Carstensen (1990) to account for social contact and for the observation that it is most varied in early adulthood. In the course of a normative life in our culture, two motives for social contact peak near the peak of the bump: self-concept development and information seeking.

In summary, many empirically observed abilities, and the many theoretical constructs needed to explain them, peak at about the same time as the bump (for others see, Rubin, Rahhal & Poon, 1998). But so do many

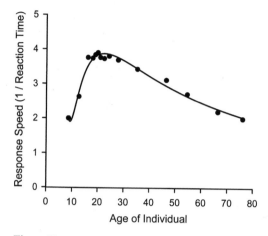

Figure 7

The reciprocal of the reaction times of people of different ages in a simple task. (Data from Noble, Baker & Jones 1964.)

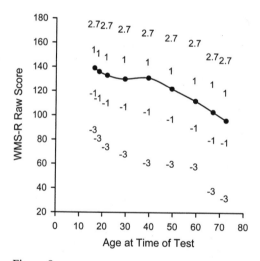

Figure 8

The raw scores needed on the Wechsler Memory Scale to score as average for a given age. Included without a line are the raw scores needed to be 2.7 and 1 standard deviation above the mean and 1 and 3 standard deviations below the mean.

other forms of memory or preference. People are more accurate in recalling public events (Rubin et al., 1998) and music (Schulkind, Hennis & Rubin, 1999) that occurred when they were between 10 and 30 years old. They prefer or are personally most affected by music (Holbrook & Schindler, 1989; Schulkind et al., 1999), films (Sehulster, 1996), and books (Larsen, 1996) from this period. They judge public events that occurred when they were in this period of life to be more important (Schuman, Belli & Bischoping, 1997). They concentrate on this period when choosing important events in their lives in psychology experiments (Fitzgerald, 1996; Fromholt & Larsen, 1991, 1992; Rubin & Schulkind, 1997a) and in written autobiographies (Mackavey, Malley & Stewart, 1991). Some of these findings are more directly related to the bump in autobiographical memory than others, but they all point to an increase in memory and preference for events from the bump period.

How to Explain These Findings

As usual in developmental processes, there are two broad classes of explanation: nature and nurture. As usual, it is impossible and unwise to separate them; their interaction is the important factor. On the side of nature or biological maturation, as reviewed in the previous section, people are faster and better at simple memory tasks in the bump period. On the side of nurture or environment, also as reviewed in the previous section, the bump period is a time of many culturally defined important events, a time of identity formation, and a time of the formation of a sense of generation. Using standard principles of experimental psychology, we postulated the cognitive theory of the bump (Rubin et al., 1998) to explain how such events would lead to increased recall of memories.

Events from the bump period are remembered best because they occur when rapid change is giving way to relative stability that lasts at least until retrieval. In times of rapid change many novel events are encountered. Such events benefit from three major processes that increase their encoding: (1) increased effort to understand the event, i.e., effort after meaning (Bartlett, 1932), (2) minimal proactive interference (see Rubin, 1995, for a brief review of this large literature), and (3) distinctiveness (Hunt & Smith, 1996). Periods of stability produce less encoding but have two major beneficial effects for retrieval: (1) a memory organization that is the same at encoding as it is at retrieval, i.e., encoding specificity (Tulving & Thomson, 1973), and (2) more retrieval, especially more spaced retrieval (Braun & Rubin, 1988; Dempster, 1988). The cognitive theory as just formulated falls into the nurture camp. However, if during this period people are also best at encoding new information because of maturation, the effects would be even stronger. To cloud the nature-nurture distinction even further, the cognitive theory could be extended to include the adolescent period of rapid change followed by relative stability in biology, as well as in a person's interactions with his environment.

The cognitive theory can explain other bump-period findings. The events on which people first base their understandings of the world should be judged as more important than other events and should come to mind more easily when the recall of an important event is requested. In addition, preference can be based on familiarity and understanding (see Bornstein, 1989, and Zajonc, 1980, for reviews).

Showing That the Environment Has an Effect

Superior memory ability can be demonstrated for the bump period from standardized tests. How can we show that environmental change also affects the bump and thus that the bump is not a purely maturational effect. From the perspective of the cognitive theory of the bump, the ideal experiment to do would be to introduce a major disruption followed by a period of stability at a time after the bump should have occurred. This would both remove the stability needed for spaced practice and provide a second period in which many new things would be learned and practiced.

According to the cognitive theory, such a major disruption should make the standard bump smaller because spaced practice is removed, but it should create a second, later bump. Such experiments cannot be planned, but they can be observed in the world. Immigration often changes a person's physical environment, his culture, and the language used to code and report new events. If we collapse over the language of testing in the data from immigrants discussed in the section on language (because it is not the question of interest here and because in most cases it did not affect the distribution of memories over the lifespan), we can

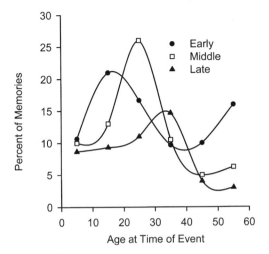

Figure 9
The distribution of events reported in a life narrative for people who immigrated around ages 21 (early), 26 (middle), and 34 (late).

ask how the distribution of autobiographical memories of people who immigrated at different times in their lives differ. Such data provide strong support for the cognitive theory. Figure 9 provides a sample plot. Conway and Haque (1999) provide similar results from a study after the Bangladeshi fight for independence, which involved major changes in a political system but did not involve changes in language or location.

Future Directions: Multiple Systems across the Lifespan

Up to this point autobiographical memories have been considered as single entities. An alternative view is that they consist of information stored in component processes, each process occurring in a separate behaviorally and neurally defined system (Rubin, 1995, 1998; Rubin & Greenberg, 1998, in press, 2000; Rubin, Greenberg & Schrauf, 2000). According to available evidence, these component processes are an integrative memory system (which is classically attributed to the hippocampus and more recently expanded to include the frontal lobes), imagery in each individual modality and a multimodal spatial-imagery system, language, narrative reasoning, and emotions. On this view, having a full-blown autobiographical memory requires the use of the integrative memory system, at least one modality-specific imagery system (usually visual imagery), spatial imagery, to varying degrees imagery in the other senses, language, narrative reasoning, and emotions. For different memories within an individual and for different clinical populations, the degree to which each system contributes varies. Thus, for instance, flashbulb memories are more likely to have considerable visual and spatial imagery, and people who are depressed or who have posttraumatic-stress disorder are likely to have voluntary memories that lack sensory details and narrative coherence. In contrast, the intrusive memories of people with posttraumatic-stress disorder are likely to have considerable sensory detail and, compared to other memories, sensory details in the olfactory and gustatory system. There is considerable support for this view from behavior (Rubin, Greenberg & Schrauf, 2000) and neuropsychology (Rubin & Greenberg, 1998, 2000), but what does it mean for understanding the bump?

How do the individual processes needed to produce a full-blown autobiographical memory develop over the lifespan? It is hard to know for sure because the processes are usually not studied developmentally in a way that would provide a direct answer. Figure 10 is my best guess. It is based on a what has been measured and some poorly supported assumptions, which I will make explicit. Figure 10 serves to clarify our level of ignorance and to frame questions for future investigation. I assume that the integrative memory system develops and declines something like fluid intelligence, that the language system develops something like vocabulary, that the narrative reasoning system and especially the narrative skills needed to tell a life story develop more slowly than language (Habermas & Bluck, 2000), and that visual imagery declines with age. I have no idea of how to plot the development of the system that processes emotion. From figure 10, the bump would result from the interaction of the component systems and how they interact with the environment present at the time. For example, under such a view, flashbulb memories, which require a strong visual component, would be more likely to form earlier in the lifespan (see Cohen, Conway & Maylor, 1994, for some support), and childhood memories should have less narrative coherence. Similarly, the same traumatic event would be more

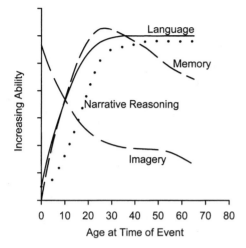

Figure 10
Hypothetical developmental trajectories of abilities needed to form autobiographical memories.

likely to produce a vivid intrusive memory not well integrated into the person's life story if it occurred early in the lifespan, when imagery was fully functioning and narrative coherence was not, as opposed to if it occurred later in the lifespan, when the imagery system was weaker and narrative reasoning was stronger.

Earlier the section "Differences in the Properties of Autobiographical Memories" provided evidence that the ratings of memories do not differ over the lifespan; there are just more memories from the bump period. There is an apparent discrepancy between this finding and the theory just put forth. If, for instance, visual-imagery ability decreases and narrative-reasoning ability increases over the lifespan, then one might expect older adults to rate memories from youth higher in imagery and lower in narrative coherence. Two possible resolutions exist. First, the ratings we have are measures of the ability of older adults now to produce a visual image and a coherent narrative from what was encoded a long time ago. Thus, the effects of differences in encoding might be minimal in comparison with the effects of current retrieval abilities. As reviewed earlier, we know that cuing with high-imagery words does produce older memories, and so it still might be the case that cues that differentially tap systems may be able to access memories from periods when a particular system was functioning best.

The second possible resolution is that if all memories could be accessed, there might be differences in the properties of the memories across the lifespan, whereas for the memories that come most easily to mind, this is not observed, because what makes the memories easy to recall is that they are high on several of the properties rated. An experiment to approximate an exhaustive search would have older adults spend an hour or two recalling and rating memories from a single year from when they were 10, 25, and 50. One might expect the memories from age 10 to be rated higher on imagery and lower on narrative coherence relative to the memories from age 50, whereas the bump memories might rated highly on both scales. I know of no data on these issues.

Phenomenon-Centered Research

I gave this chapter a semihistorical presentation partly because it reports on a program of research that I and my collaborators stumbled into, one observation at a time, without a strong theory to guide us. I wanted to portray a research program that is less common than the hypothetical-deductive one favored for the final reporting of research in most journals and required for the planning of research in grant proposals. Though less favored, I believe that it is one approach that needs to be used if science is to advance in an efficient manner. In his intellectual autobiography, my thesis adviser, Roger Brown, wrote, "While no one seems to recommend a phenomenoncentered approach to research, it can be argued that its record is at least as good in psychology as that of theory-centered work.... My research style ... has always started with some phenomenon and only later become theoretical.... I have tended to pick some mystery and poke it and prod it and turn it all around in an effort to figure it out" (1989, p. 50). I have expressed similar ideas less eloquently (Rubin, 1989, 1992, 1995). Here I hope I have shown by example that the phenomenoncentered approach is an efficient way to add to our knowledge of human behavior and even to theory.

The strength of the approach used here is that it documents and notes the limits of a robust phenomenon. The weakness is that a theoretical account of the data is not as easy to obtain as it is when all experiments are derived from a single theory. At its current level of understanding, cognitive psychology needs both robust findings and good theories (see Newell, 1973). We cannot obtain a useful or complete description of cognition if we limit ourselves to a collection of phenomena or to a collection of theories, each of which accounts for a limited set of experimental procedures. Both the phenomenon-centered approach and the theory-driven approach must be expanded and integrated. One advantage of the bump is that it is a robust phenomenon that stretches the limits of current theories and thus invites a wide range of theoretical speculation.

Acknowledgments

I wish to thank Herb Crovitz, Dan Greenberg, and Bob Schrauf for their comments and the National Institute on Aging for grant number RO1 AG16340.

References

Anderson, J. R., & Schooler, L. J. (1991). Reflections of the environment in memory. *Psychological Science*, 2, 396–408.

Aragno, A., & Schlachet, P. J. (1996). Accessibility of early experience through the language of origin: A theoretical integration. *Psychoanalytic Psychology*, 13, 23–34.

Baltes, P. B. (1997). On the incomplete architecture of human ontogeny: Selection, optimization, and compensation as foundation of developmental theory. *American Psychologist*, 52, 366–380.

Bartlett, F. C. (1932). *Remembering: A study in experimental and social psychology*. Cambridge: Cambridge University Press.

Bornstein, R. F. (1989). Exposure and affect: Overview and meta-analysis of research, 1968–1987. *Psychological Bulletin*, 106, 265–289.

Braun, K., & Rubin, D. C. (1988). The spacing effect depends on an encoding deficit, retrieval, and time in working memory: Evidence from once presented words. *Memory*, 6, 37–65.

Brown, R. (1989). Roger Brown. In G. Lindzey (Ed.), *A history of psychology in autobiography* (vol. 8, pp. 36–60). Stanford: Stanford University Press.

Bugelski, B. R. (1977). Imagery and verbal behavior. *Journal of Mental Imagery*, 1, 39–52.

Christianson, S.-A., & Safer, M. A. (1996). Emotional events and emotions in autobiographical memory. In D. C. Rubin (Ed.), *Remembering our past: Studies in autobiographical remembering* (pp. 218–243). Cambridge: Cambridge University Press.

Cohen, G., Conway, M. A., & Maylor, E. A. (1994). Flashbulb memories in older adults. *Psychology and Aging, 9*, 454–463.

Conway, M. A., & Haque, S. (1999). Overshadowing the reminiscence bump: Memories of a struggle for independence. *Journal of Adult Development, 6*, 35–44.

Crovitz, H. F., & Schiffman, H. (1974). Frequency of episodic memories as a function of their age. *Bulletin of The Psychonomic Society, 4*, 517–551.

Dempster, F. N. (1988). The spacing effect: A case study in the failure to apply the results of the psychological research. *American Psychologist, 43*, 627–634.

Erickson, E. (1950). *Childhood and society*. New York: Norton.

Fitzgerald, J. M. (1988). Vivid memories and the reminiscence phenomenon: The role of a self-narrative. *Human Development, 31*, 261–273.

Fitzgerald, J. M. (1996). Intersecting meanings of reminiscence in adult development and aging. In D. C. Rubin (Ed.), *Remembering our past: Studies in autobiographical memory* (pp. 360–383). Cambridge: Cambridge University Press.

Fitzgerald, J. M., & Lawrence, R. (1984). Autobiographical memory across the lifespan. *Journal of Gerontology, 36*, 692–698.

Franklin, H. C., & Holding, D. H. (1977). Personal memories at different ages. *Quarterly Journal of Experimental Psychology, 29*, 527–532.

Fredrickson, B. F., & Carstensen, L. L. (1990). Choosing social partners: How old age and anticipated endings make people more selective. *Psychology and Aging, 5*, 335–347.

Fromholt, P., & Larsen, S. F. (1991). Autobiographical memory in normal aging and primary degenerative dementia (dementia of the Alzheimer's type). *Journal of Gerontology: Psychological Sciences, 46*, 85–91.

Fromholt, P., & Larsen, S. F. (1992). Autobiographical memory and life history narratives in aging and dementia (Alzheimer type). In M. A. Conway, D. C. Rubin, H. Spinnler & W. A. Wagenaar (Eds.), *Theoretical perspectives on autobiographical memory* (pp. 413–426). Dordrecht: Kluwer Publishing.

Fromholt, P., Larsen, P., & Larsen, S. F. (1995). Effects of late-onset depression and recovery on autobiographical memory. *Journal of Gerontology: Psychological Sciences, 50*, 74–81.

Galton, F. (1879). Psychometric experiments. *Brain, 2*, 149–162.

Gergen, K. J., & Gergen, M. M. (1983). Narratives of the self. In T. R. Sarbin & K. E. Scheibe (Eds.), *Studies in social identity* (pp. 254–273). New York: Praeger.

Habermas, T., & Bluck, S. (2000). Getting a life: The emergence of the life story in adolescence. *Psychological Bulletin, 126*, 748–769.

Holbrook, M. B., & Schindler, R. M. (1989). Some exploratory findings on the development of musical tastes. *Journal of Consumer Research, 16,* 119–124.

Holmes, A., & Conway, M. A. (1999). Generation identity and the reminiscence bump: Memories for public and private events. *Journal of Adult Development, 6,* 21–34.

Hunt, R. R., & Smith, R. E. (1996). Accessing the particular from the general: The power of distinctiveness in the context of organization. *Memory and Cognition, 24,* 217–225.

Hyland, D. T., & Ackerman, A. M. (1988). Reminiscence and autobiographical memory in the study of the personal past. *Journal of Gerontology: Psychological Sciences, 43,* 35–39.

Jansari, A., & Parkin, A. J. (1996). Things that go bump in your life: Explaining the reminiscence bump in autobiographical memory. *Psychology and Aging, 11,* 85–91.

Javier, R. A. (1995). Vicissitudes of autobiographical memories in a bilingual analysis. *Psychoanalytic Psychology, 12* (3), 429–438.

Komura, H., Miyake, A., Chen, C., Tanizawa, O., and Yoshikawa, H. (1992). Relationship of age at menarche and subsequent fertility. *European Journal of Obstetrics and Gynecology and Reproductive Biology, 44,* 201–203.

Larsen, S. F. (1996). Memorable books: Recall of reading and its personal context. In M. S. MacNealy & R. Kreuz (Eds.), *Empirical approaches to literature and aesthetics* (pp. 583–599). Norwood, N.J.: Ablex.

Larsen, S. F., Schrauf, R. W., Fromholt, P., & Rubin, D. C. (2002). Inner speech and bilingual autobiographical memory: A Polish-Danish cross-cultural study. *Memory, 10,* 45–54.

Mackavey, W. R., Malley, J. E., & Stewart, A. J. (1991). Remembering autobiographically consequential experiences: Content analysis of psychologists' accounts of their lives. *Psychology and Aging, 6,* 50–59.

Marian, V., & Neisser, U. (1997). Autobiographical memory in bilinguals. Poster session presented at the 38th Annual Meeting of the Psychonomic Society, Philadelphia.

MacDonald, S., Uesiliana, K., & Hayne, H. (2000). Cross-cultural and gender differences in childhood amnesia. *Memory, 8,* 365–376.

Menken, J., Trussell, J., & Larsen, U. (1986). Age and infertility. *Science, 233,* 1389–1394.

Mullen, M. K. (1994). Earliest recollections of childhood: A demographic analysis. *Cognition, 52,* 55–79.

Newell, A. (1973). You can't play 20 questions with nature and win: Projective comments on the papers of this symposium. In W. G. Chase (Ed.), *Visual information processing* (pp. 283–308). New York: Academic Press.

Newell, A., & Rosenbloom, P. S. (1981). Mechanisms of skill acquisition and the law of practice. In J. R. Anderson (Ed.), *Cognitive skills and their acquisition* (pp. 1–55). Hillsdale, N.J.: Erlbaum.

Noble, C. E., Baker, B. L., & Jones, T. A. (1964). Age and sex parameters in psychomotor learning. *Perceptual and Motor Skills, 19*, 935–945.

Ribot, T. (1882). *Diseases of memory: An essay in the positive psychology.* New York: D. Appleton.

Robinson, J. A. (1976). Sampling autobiographical memory. *Cognitive Psychology, 8*, 578–595.

Robinson, J. A. (1996). Perspective, meaning, and remembering. In D. C. Rubin (Ed.), *Remembering our past: Studies in autobiographical remembering* (pp. 199–217). Cambridge: Cambridge University Press.

Rubin, D. C. (1982). On the retention function for autobiographical memory. *Journal of Verbal Learning and Verbal Behavior, 21*, 21–38.

Rubin, D. C. (1989). Issues of regularity and control: Confessions of a regularity freak. In L. W. Poon, D. C. Rubin & B. A. Wilson (Eds.), *Everyday cognition in adult and later life* (pp. 84–103) Cambridge: Cambridge University Press.

Rubin, D. C. (1992). Constraints on memory. In E. Winograd & U. Neisser (Eds.), *Affect and accuracy in recall: Studies of "flashbulb" memories* (pp. 265–273). New York: Cambridge University Press.

Rubin, D. C. (1995). *Memory in oral traditions: The cognitive psychology of epic, ballads, and counting out rhymes.* New York: Oxford University Press.

Rubin, D. C. (1998). Beginnings of a theory of autobiographical remembering. In C. P. Thompson, D. J. Herrmann, D. Bruce, J. D. Reed, D. G. Payne, and M. P. Toglia (Eds.), *Autobiographical memory: Theoretical and applied perspectives* (pp. 47–67). Mahwah, N.J.: Erlbaum.

Rubin, D. C. (1999). Autobiographical memory and aging. In D. Park & N. Schwartz (Eds.) *Aging and cognition: A student primer* (pp. 131–149). Philadelphia: Psychology Press.

Rubin, D. C. (2000). The distribution of early childhood memories. *Memory, 8*, 265–269.

Rubin, D. C., & Greenberg, D. (1998). Visual memory-deficit amnesia: A distinct amnesic presentation and etiology. *Proceedings of the National Academy of Sciences, 95*, 5413–5416.

Rubin, D. C., & Greenberg, D. L. (in press). The role of narrative in recollection: A view from cognitive and neuropsychology. In G. Fireman, T. McVay & O. Flanagan (Eds.), *Narrative and Consciousness: Literature, Psychology, and the Brain.* New York: Oxford University Press.

Rubin, D. C., Groth, L., & Goldsmith, D. (1984). Olfactory cuing of autobiographical memory. *American Journal of Psychology, 97*, 493–507.

Rubin, D. C., Rahhal, T. A., & Poon, L. W. (1998). Things learned in early adulthood are remembered best. *Memory and Cognition, 26*, 3–19.

Rubin, D. C., & Schulkind, M. D. (1997a). Distribution of important and word-cued autobiographical memories in 20, 35, and 70 year-old adults. *Psychology and Aging, 12,* 524–535.

Rubin, D. C., & Schulkind, M. D. (1997b). Properties of word cues for autobiographical memory. *Psychological Reports, 81,* 47–50.

Rubin, D. C., & Schulkind, M. D. (1997c). The distribution of autobiographical memories across the lifespan. *Memory and Cognition, 25,* 859–866.

Rubin, D. C., Schulkind, M. D., & Rahhal, T. A. (1999). A study of gender differences in autobiographical memory: Broken down by age and sex. *Journal of Adult Development, 6,* 61–72.

Rubin, D. C., & Wenzel, A. E. (1996). One hundred years of forgetting: A quantitative description of retention. *Psychological Review, 103,* 734–760.

Rubin, D. C., Wetzler, S. E., & Nebes, R. D. (1986). Autobiographical memory across the adult lifespan. In D. C. Rubin (Ed.), *Autobiographical Memory* (pp. 202–221). Cambridge: Cambridge University Press.

Rybash, J. M., & Monaghan, B. E. (1999). Episodic and semantic contributions to older adults' autobiographical recall. *Journal of General Psychology, 126,* 85–96.

Rybash, J. M. (1999). Aging and autobiographical memory: The long and bumpy road. *Journal of Adult Development, 6,* 1–10.

Schrauf, R. W. (2000). Bilingual autobiographical memory: Experimental studies and clinical cases. *Culture and Psychology, 6,* 387–417.

Schrauf, R. W., & Rubin, D. C. (1998). Bilingual autobiographical memory in older adult immigrants: A test of cognitive explanations of the reminiscence bump and the linguistic encoding of memories. *Journal of Memory and Language, 39,* 437–457.

Schrauf, R. W., & Rubin, D. C. (2000). Internal languages of retrieval: The bilingual encoding of memories for the personal past. *Memory & Cognition, 28,* 616–623.

Schulkind, M. D., Hennis, L. K., & Rubin, D. C. (1999). Music, emotion and autobiographical memory: They're playing your song. *Memory & Cognition, 27,* 948–955.

Schuman, H., Belli, R. F., & Bischoping, K. (1997). The generational basis of historical knowledge. In J. W. Pennebaker, D. Páez & B. Rimé (Eds.), *Collective memory of political events: Social psychological perspectives* (pp. 47–77). Hillsdale, N.J.: Erlbaum.

Sehulster, J. R. (1996). In my era: Evidence for the perception of a special period of the past. *Memory, 4,* 145–158.

Stevens S. S. (1975). *Psychophysics: Introduction to its perceptual, neural, and social prospects.* New York: John Wiley & Sons.

Tulving, E., & Pearlstone, Z. (1966). Availability versus accessibility of information in memory for words. *Journal of Verbal Learning and Verbal Behavior, 5,* 381–391.

Tulving, E., & Thompson, D. M. (1973). Encoding specificity and retrieval processes in episodic memory. *Psychological Review*, *80*, 352–373.

Wetzler, S. E., & Sweeney, J. A. (1986). Childhood amnesia: An empirical demonstration. In D. C. Rubin (Ed.), *Autobiographical memory* (pp. 191–200). Cambridge: Cambridge University Press.

Williams, M. J. G. (1996). Depression and the specificity of autobiographical memory. In D. C. Rubin (Ed.), *Remembering our past: Studies in autobiographical remembering* (pp. 244–267). Cambridge: Cambridge University Press.

Zajonc, R. B. (1980). Feeling and thinking: Preferences need no inferences. *American Psychologist*, *35*, 151–175.

Zola-Morgan, S., Cohen, N. J., & Squire, L. R. (1983). Recall of remote episodic memory in amnesia. *Neuropsychologia*, 21, 487–500.

10

Memory Development in Adulthood and Old Age: The Betula Prospective-Cohort Study

Lars-Göran Nilsson, Rolf Adolfsson, Lars Bäckman, Marc Cruts, Håkan Edvardsson, Lars Nyberg, and Christine Van Broeckhoven

The Betula project is a prospective-cohort study examining the development of memory and health in adulthood and old age. The project started in 1988 and is currently planned to continue until 2003. The chief objectives of the study are (1) to examine the development of health and memory in adulthood and old age, (2) to determine early preclinical signs of dementia, (3) to determine risk factors for dementia, and (4) to assess premorbid memory function in subjects who are in accidents or acquire diseases during the course of the study.

To accomplish these goals, the Betula study was designed on the basis of the assumption of continuous interactions between the individual and the environment in which the individual lives. The individual factors include medical and psychological parameters, age, gender, and genetic markers. The environmental factors include the events that the individual is exposed to and the experiences that the individual accumulates from these exposures throughout life. These environmental factors are manifested in family history, education, occupation, residential area, previous morbidity, risk factors, socioeconomical status, social networks, life styles and habits, and use and availability of social and medical facilities.

The design of the study includes three waves of data collection. The first of these waves was conducted in 1988–1990, the second in 1993–1995, and the third in 1998–2000. One sample of 1,000 subjects in these age cohorts underwent testing in 1988–1990 (100 subjects per cohort). This sample and two additional samples were tested in 1993–1995 and again in 1998–2000. A fourth sample was tested for the first time in 1998–2000.

This design presents clear advantages when compared to traditional cross-sectional or purely longitudinal designs. With this design it is possible to make cross-sectional, cross-sequential, cohort-sequential, time-sequential, and longitudinal analyses with proper control for practice effects. These analyses can be made after the third wave of data collection has been completed in 1998–2000.

In addition to an extensive examination of memory functions, the participants in the Betula study were given a health examination including blood-sample testing, an interview about health status and activities of daily living, and questionnaires about social and economic issues and about critical life events.

Health assessments were conducted by nurses on one occasion lasting 1.5 to 2 hours for each participant. Blood samples were taken for blood chemistry and were deep frozen for future use. The health examination was extensive so as to provide a good picture of the health of each subject. Our selection of lab tests aimed at disclosing unknown somatic disorders that might be associated with cognitive impairment and screening for abnormal laboratory values known to be associated with cognitive impairment (e.g., vitamin B12, blood folate, T4/TSH, blood glucose, serum calcium levels).

Assessment of memory function was based on a large-scale test battery. This battery was composed so that tests were theoretically motivated, and so that we could analytically explore a wide variety of processes and hypothetical memory systems. The memory tests and traditional psychometric tests selected were thoroughly described in Nilsson et al. (1997). A brief outline is presented here.

Some Results Relating to Memory Systems

Altogether, there were eight sets of episodic memory tasks included in the battery: prospective memory, face recognition, name recognition, action memory, sentence memory, word recall with or without a distractor task, source recall, and memory for activities. In the prospective memory task, participants were instructed to remind the experimenter at the end of the test session, when all tests had been completed, to sign a piece of paper. At the end of the memory testing the experimenter told the subject that the session was over as a cue for the subject to remind the experimenter to sign a paper. This is an event-based prospective memory task, which, in line with previous research (e.g., Einstein & McDaniel, 1990) revealed decreasing levels of performance as a function of age (Mäntylä & Nilsson, 1997).

In the recognition task for faces and names, participants were first presented with 16 color pictures of faces and made-up, regular, and frequent Swedish names. They were told to remember the faces and the surnames for a later recognition test. At this later test they were also asked to remember the first name of each face, which was thus incidentally learned in the study. Age differences in face-recognition performance have been demonstrated in several previous studies (e.g., Bartlett & Leslie, 1986; Larrabee & Crook, 1993; Smith & Winograd, 1978). Data from the present study confirm this pattern (Larsson, Nyberg, Bäckman & Nilsson, in press). Data also revealed age deficits in memory for names (Larsson et al., in press; Nilsson et al., 1997), in line with personal experiences by many and with several previous studies (e.g., Cohen & Faulkner, 1986; Larrabee & Crook, 1993).

For the action and sentence memory tasks, participants were first presented with two successive lists of short sentences in imperative form (e.g., roll the ball, break the match), with a free-recall test given immediately after each list. Each sentence, consisting of a verb and a noun, was presented visually on an index card. For one of these lists, subjects were instructed to enact each imperative presented, whereas for the other list of sentences, no such enactment was required. In addition to the test for free recall, cued-recall and recognition tests were also given. Age deficits were found in all these tasks (Nilsson et al., 1997; Rönnlund, Nyberg, Bäckman & Nilsson, 2000). In this context subjects were also tested on source recall. Following a paradigm of Johnson and Raye (1981), the participants were asked, at the time of the cued-recall test, whether each test item had been presented as an enacted or nonenacted sentence. Large age effects were obtained in the Betula study (Nilsson et al., 1997; Rönnlund et al., 2000).

The word-recall task, with or without a distractor task, was modeled after Baddeley, Lewis, Eldridge, and Thomson (1984). The basic idea behind this task was to explore the extent to which subjects can encode and retrieve information while being engaged in carrying out a concurrent task. Four different conditions constitute this task. In each of these four conditions subjects were auditorily presented a list of 12 common unrelated nouns with the instruction to learn these words for an immediate free-recall test. The concurrent task was to sort a deck of playing cards into two piles: one red and one black. In one condition this card sorting was done during both study and test. In another condition the card sorting was done at study only, not at test. In still another condition the card sorting was done at test but not at study. In the fourth condition there was no card sorting, neither at study nor at test. Nyberg, Nilsson, Olofsson and Bäckman (1997) demonstrated for the Betula data that age differences in memory performance were substantial under single-task conditions, but after correcting memory performance under dual-task conditions for differences in single-task performance, age did not predict performance. These results do not support the hypothesis that reduced attentional capacity in old age underlies age differences in episodic memory.

In still another episodic-memory task, subjects studied made-up facts about famous people (e.g., Astrid Lindgren collects stamps as a hobby). Statements of this sort were presented in one of four different ways: auditorily by means of a male voice or auditorily by means of a female voice or visually on a yellow card or visually on a red card. At test the information in the statements was presented again, but now in the form of questions (e.g., What is Astrid Lindgren's hobby?). This task is referred to as item recall of recently acquired facts. Participants were also questioned about how each item was presented; we refer to this task as source recall of recently acquired facts. The results obtained for this task at T1 (1988–1990) showed a substantial decrease in both item and source recall as a function of age (Nilsson et al., 1997; Erngrund et al., 1996). This result is in line with the results from a similar study by McIntyre and Craik (1987).

One final episodic-memory task used in the Betula study was called memory for activities. Participants were incidentally asked to report as many memory-task activities as possible of all those they had been engaged in during the whole test session. Previous research has demonstrated that this form of activity memory is highly age sensitive (Kausler,

1991; Kausler & Lichty, 1989). As shown by Nilsson et al. (1997) and Rönnlund et al. (2000), data from the Betula study revealed no exception to this rule.

In addition to these episodic-memory tasks, there were also three sets of semantic-memory tasks included in the Betula battery: word fluency, word comprehension, and general knowledge. There were four word-fluency tests. The task was to generate as many words as possible during a period of one minute for each of these four criteria: (a) words with the initial letter A, (b) five-letter words with the initial letter M, (c) words that are names of professions with the initial letter B, and (d) five-letter words that are names of animals with the initial letter S. Word-fluency tasks usually produce minor age deficits. Because there were time restrictions in responding, it was thought that age differences may occur (e.g., Hultsch et al., 1992; Salthouse, 1993). The data from the Betula study revealed significant age deficits. However, when number of years in formal education was used as a covariate in the analysis, the age differences were eliminated (Bäckman & Nilsson, 1996; Nilsson et al., 1997).

In the word-comprehension task, participants were presented with a list of 30 target words and 5 other words presented next to each target word. Among these 5 words there was one synonym to each target. The subjects were instructed to underline this synonym word. Seven minutes were allowed for this task. Previous research has demonstrated age deficits in this task (e.g., Arenberg, 1989; Berkowitz, 1953; Kausler & Puckett, 1980). Such a result was also obtained in the Betula study (Bäckman & Nilson, 1996; Nilsson et al., 1997). In the same way as for word fluency, the age deficit disappeared when education was used as a covariate. The third semantic-memory task included a set of general knowledge questions. Erngrund, Mäntylä and Nilsson (1996) demonstrated that the 75- and 80-year-olds showed a lower memory performance in this task than all other age cohorts.

A name-stem completion task was used for assessing priming. In this task, participants were presented with name stems and were asked to say the first word that came to mind for each stem they saw. The stems were two-letter stems of the surnames previously presented in the face-name recognition task. One set of stems served as targets for one half of the subjects in each cohort, and the other set served as distractors. For the other half of the subjects in each cohort, the target and distractor sets were reversed. The difference in completion rate between target names and distractor names is a measure of priming, which in turn is assumed to reflect one form of memory that does not require conscious recollection of a study episode. Data from the present study revealed no age deficits (Nilsson et al., 1997). Previous research has revealed a rather mixed picture regarding the effect of age on priming. Whereas some studies report age deficits in priming (e.g., Chiarello & Hoyer, 1988; Hultsch, Masson & Small, 1991), others do not (e.g., Light & Singh, 1987; Light, Singh & Capps, 1986).

General Cognition

An additional two tests of general cognitive function were also included in the test battery at T1. One of these tests was block design, which is a visuospatial task in which participants are required to place red and white blocks so that they form the same pattern as a target pattern shown to the subjects. This task constitutes one subtest of the Wechsler Adult Intelligence Scale or WAIS (Wechsler, 1981); it is used to assess construction ability and it is assumed to reflect "fluid intelligence." The block-design task is known to produce large age-related performance deficits (e.g., Kramer & Jarvik, 1979). A significant age deficit was also obtained in the Betula study (Herlitz, Nilsson & Bäckman, 1997).

Finally, the Mini-Mental State Examination test (MMSE; Folstein, Folstein & McHugh, 1975) was also included in the Betula battery. MMSE is a screening test for cognitive dysfunction. This test assesses orientation in time and space, short-term memory, episodic long-term memory, subtraction, ability to construct, and language ability. The maximum score in this test is 30; a score below 24 points is generally regarded as an indication of cognitive dysfunction. Data from the Betula study demonstrated a significant performance decrement as a function of age (Nilsson et al., 1997).

Memory Processing

Thus, the tests presented cover a wide range of memory processes and a large number of aspects of primary memory, episodic memory, the perceptual-representation system, and semantic memory. With respect to analyses of memory processes, several distinctions can be made. One such distinction is that between *encoding* and *retrieval*. The nature of the interaction between these two processes is of fundamental importance for analyzing the outcome in most episodic-memory tests.

Several tests were included in the battery to manipulate variables that are assumed to affect encoding. For example, in the name-recognition task, encoding of surnames was intentional in nature, whereas encoding of first names was incidental. Larsson et al. (in press) demonstrated that subjects benefitted from the intentional learning instruction and that there was no interaction with age. Another example is the encoding of short sentences with or without enactment. Enactment of such sentences is regarded as a means of providing cognitive support at the time of study. Rönnlund et al. (2000) demonstrated a higher recall performance after enacted encoding in the Betula study. This is indeed the most typical data pattern (see Nilsson, 2000, for a review). However, contrary to several studies (Bäckman & Nilsson, 1984, 1985) the ability to utilize enactment as a cognitive support at study did not interact with age in the Betula study (Rönnlund et al., 2000).

Still another task in the Betula study, with the experimental manipulation at study, is the word-list-recall task, with or without a distracting card-sorting task. Nyberg, Nilsson, Olofsson and Bäckman (1997) demonstrated that episodic-memory performance is substantially affected when the card-sorting task is given at the time of encoding. However, these data did not reveal any differential effects of division of attention across age, which is in line with some previous data (e.g., Craik, Govoni, Naveh-Benjamin & Anderson, 1996), but not in line with other data (e.g., Park, Smith, Dudley & Lafronza, 1989), where there was a stronger age effect when attention was divided at encoding. Differences of this sort might depend on what type of distractor task is used and on the nature of its interaction with the memory task used. However, the existence of this anomaly calls for further exploration.

Retrieval factors in episodic memory were explored in tasks providing different amounts of cue information at test. Subjects are tested in such tasks as free recall, cued recall, and recognition. In free recall there is very little cue information available at test, in cued recall more such cue information is available to support retrieval, and in recognition the cue information is further enriched by providing copy cues of the target items. In comparing free and cued recall after enacted and nonenacted encoding, Rönnlund et al. (2000) found that retrieval cues significantly increased performance in a similar way across age groups for both enacted and nonenacted encoding. Another experimental manipulation made at the time of test in the Betula study was that of assessing memory performance when subjects sorted cards as a distraction while retrieving words. Nyberg et al. (1996) found a small negative effect of this distractor task, and no differential effect across age.

Developmental effects in the episodic-memory tasks mentioned can easily be compared with developmental effects in the semantic-memory tasks. The semantic-memory tasks used in this study are first of all the four-word fluency tests and the word-comprehension test. As mentioned, age deficits were demonstrated in these semantic-memory tasks in the Betula study with subjects randomly selected from the population. As can be imagined, there are bound to be large differences in several demographic variables in such a sample in comparison with studies in which subjects in different age cohorts are matched with respect to all sorts of background variables.

Education is one such background factor. Whereas the youngest participants in the Betula study have been in school for about 14 years on the average, the oldest subjects at 90 years of age have been to school only for about half this time. When number of years in formal education is used as a covariate, the age differences in semantic-memory tasks disappear (Bäckman & Nilsson, 1996; Nilsson et al., 1997).

Bäckman and Nilsson (1996) reported that verbal fluency and vocabulary tests showed no variation between 35 and 50 years of age, followed by a gradual decline with increasing age. In a test of general knowledge, only the two oldest cohorts showed deficits. When educational level was controlled statistically, a different pattern of results was seen: the middle-aged adults performed at the highest level, and with the exception of one fluency test, no age-related deficits were observed before 75 years of age. These data suggest that, although there may be age-related deficits in semantic memory in the general population, education appears to be a more important factor than adult age per se for semantic-memory functioning.

Other Variables

These and many other variables for which data were collected in the Betula study are yet to be analyzed in relation to aging and memory. One study on other variables is a study by Herlitz, Nilsson and Bäckman (1997), who examined potential gender differences in episodic memory, semantic memory, primary memory and priming. There were no differences between men and women with regard to age, education, or global intellectual functioning. Men outperformed women on a visuospatial task, and women outperformed men on tests of verbal fluency. Most important, the results demonstrated that women consistently performed at a higher level than men on episodic-memory tasks, although there were no differences between men and women on the tasks assessing semantic memory, primary memory, or priming. Women's higher performance on the episodic-memory tasks could not be fully explained by their higher verbal ability.

Nyberg, Bäckman, Erngrund, Olofsson, and Nilsson (1996) explored whether an age effect existed in episodic memory, semantic memory, and priming after differences on various demographic, intellectual, and biological factors had been controlled for. Simple correlations of age with episodic-memory and semantic-memory performance were found to be significant, whereas no relationship was found between age and levels of priming. After controlling for differences on the background factors, age predicted episodic-memory performance but not semantic-memory performance.

Although we have stressed various forms of memory and how they are measured, it should be observed that the corpse of the data collected will make it possible to penetrate how these forms of memory might be differently affected by various forms of social and biological differentiation. With respect to social differentiation, we are interested in making an in-depth exploration of variability in factors like social class, education, professional life, and gender in relation to individual differences in memory performance. With respect to biological differentiation, we seek to study not only the issue of normal and pathological aging but also the question of how variation in memory performance can be associated to variation in different genetic markers in normally aged persons. Finally, we also recorded time of testing to determine possible effects of diurnal and circadian rhythm on memory performance.

Genetic Markers and Memory

In a first genetic study within the Betula project, Nilsson et al. (1996) studied associations between six serum protein polymorphisms (complement C3, haptoglobin, properdin factor B, orosomucoid, group-specific components, and transferrin C) and high versus low scoring on episodic-memory tasks in an attempt to identify quantitative trait loci (QTL) contributing to the heritability of. Of those six serum protein polymorphisms available at the time to relate to memory function, it was generally conceived that complement C3 and the acute-phase reactant haptoglobin should be of primary interest as immune response factors.

Because of the sex differences demonstrated by Herlitz et al. (1997), analyses for these polymorphisms were done separately for males and females. In females, significant differences between the high- and low-performers on episodic-memory tasks were found in four out of six marker systems (complement C3, haptoglobin, transferrin C, and group-specific component). In males, a significant difference was found only in the haptoglobin system. Significant differences from population frequencies were also demonstrated more frequently in females than in males. The strongest marker associations were found with complement C3 and the acute-phase reactant haptoglobin, which suggests that immune-response factors may be of importance in preserving episodic-memory function. In the haptoglobin system there was evidence of a primary phenotypic association involving heterozygotes (Nilsson et al., 1996). This means that haptoglobin may somehow be functionally involved in the preservation of episodic memory. An association involving heterozygotes indicates that linkage disequilibrium with alleles at other loci influencing memory function is unlikely. The association with complement C3 alleles may be due to either linkage disequilibrium or functional involvement on the protein level.

Our interest in the role of genetic markers for cognitive function has more recently turned to the role of ApolipoproteinE. ApoE4 is known as a strong risk factor for the development of Alzheimer's disease with late onset (Peterson et al., 1995) and a risk factor for cardiovascular disease in middle-age persons. The pathophysiological mechanism behind ApoE4 and Alzheimer's disease is still not yet fully determined; at least there is still no consensus among several alternative hypotheses. One general claim is that ApoE4 does not protect key neuronal structures from excessive phosphorylation, which thus leads to neuronal degeneration. Persons with ApoE2 and ApoE3, on the other hand, receive necessary neuronal protection and are much less likely to develop Alzheimer's disease.

The ApoE gene is located on chromosome 19. A protein on the surface of lipoproteins, it influences the metabolism of lipids, primarily cholesterol. There are three genetic forms of ApoE (alleles ε2, ε3, and ε4) coding for three forms of the protein (isoforms) ApoE2, ApoE3, and ApoE4. These isoforms differ in one or two amino acids at two codons. ApoE3 is the most common isoform, occurring in about three fourths of the population. ApoE2 and ApoE4 occur in about 10% and 15% of the population, respectively.

There is some evidence to show that the ApoE isoforms are involved in transporting lipids to cells in a continuous synthesis or repair of cellular membranes. ApoE is necessary for cellular membranes in response to neuronal damage. Stone et al. (1997, 1998) have shown that the ApoE2 and ApoE3 isoforms serve a more important role in this repair work than the ApoE4 isoform.

We are presently exploring the role of the three different alleles of ApoE in nondemented subjects. The three alleles of ApoE—ε2, ε3, and ε4—form six genotypes—22, 23, 24, 33, 34, and 44. In the results reported here, we have made a distinction between those participants who have at least one ε4 allele (i.e., those individuals with genotypes 24, 34, and 44) and those who have none (i.e., those individuals with genotypes 22, 23, and 33). Previous research (e.g., O'Hara et al., 1998) has demonstrated that subjects with the ε4 allele are more likely to develop Alzheimer's disease, and thus have a lower memory performance, since memory disorders are seen as a cardinal indicator of a developing disease. If one assumes a quantitative difference between normal aging and dementia (e.g., Bäckman & Small, 1998) rather than a qualitative difference (e.g., Bartlett et al., 1995; Weingartner, 1986), one might expect lower memory performances for individuals with the ε4 allele than individuals with the ε2 and ε3 alleles, even before a dementia diagnosis is determined. According to the view that there is a qualitative step between normal aging and dementia, preclinical loss of memory function should not necessarily be a critical factor.

The analyses to be reported here were based on cross-sectional data from the first wave of data collection in the Betula study, T1 for non-demented subjects. That is, demented persons who were randomly sampled to be included in the Betula study were excluded from the core sample of the 1000 subjects in the S1 sample before the testing started. The data for these nondemented subjects are presented in figures 1 and 2 and in table 1.

As can be seen first in figure 1, there is not much evidence for differences between the two groups of subjects with different allele compositions. If anything, it can be seen that the performance for participants with the ε4 allele is slightly superior to that of those who do not this allele. As judged from the two graphs in figure 1, subjects with the ε4 allele seem to perform slightly better than those without this allele in middle age for episodic-memory tasks and in both middle age and old age in semantic-memory tasks. For this latter category of tasks there is a slightly lower level of performance for participants with the ε4 allele among the 35-to-45-year-olds. A 2 (age group) × 2 (ApoE group) analysis of variance for episodic memory, with number of years in formal education, revealed a significant effect of age ($F(1, 941) = 98.53$, MSE = 1.03, $p < .001$). There was no significant main effect of ApoE ($p = .40$), and no interaction between age and ApoE ($p = .27$). The analysis of variance for semantic memory also revealed a significant effect of age ($F(1, 941) = 18.34$, MSE = .98, $p < .001$), but no main effect of ApoE ($p = .88$), and no interaction ($p = .63$).

Another way of analyzing data on the effects of genetic markers on cognitive performance is to divide subjects into two extreme groups with respect to cognitive performance and to examine the relative frequency of the ε4 allele and the non-ε4 alleles among high-performing and low-performing subjects. These data are presented separately for episodic-memory tasks and semantic-memory tasks in table 1. As can be seen from this table, the relative frequencies for high- and low-performing sub-

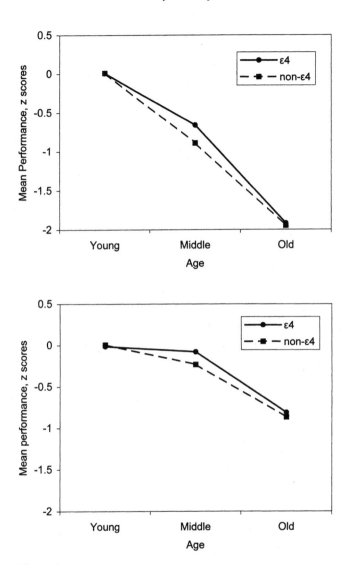

Figure 1
Mean recall performance, z scores, in episodic memory (top) and semantic memory (bottom) as a function of age for participants with and without the ε4 allele.

Table 1
Relative frequencies of Betula participants with ApoE alleles ε2, ε3, and ε4 by age group and by high and low performance in episodic-memory and semantic-memory tasks at T1

	35–45		50–60		65–80	
	High	Low	High	Low	High	Low
Episodic memory						
ε2	.10	.03	.05	.10	.10	.05
ε3	.78	.87	.73	.73	.83	.82
ε4	.12	.10	.23	.17	.07	.13
Semantic memory						
ε2	.10	.00	.13	.10	.13	.09
ε3	.73	.84	.70	.68	.74	.82
ε4	.17	.16	.17	.22	.13	.09

jects in each age group are relatively similar for both episodic-memory tasks and semantic-memory tasks. Thus, even with this type of analysis, the ApoE alleles do not seem to predict memory performance.

In this context the third step in analyzing the cross-sectional data from the first wave of data collection in the Betula study is to examine memory performance for participants who by the time of the second wave of data collection, five years later, had been diagnosed as demented, and to compare the performance of these persons at T1 with that of those persons who had not been diagnosed as demented.

At the time of T2 (1993–1995) there were 28 subjects of those 1,000 participating at T1 who had become demented. One of these participants was a 70-year-old who had been diagnosed as alcohol demented. Among the remaining 27 subjects in the demented group were 12 diagnosed as having Alzheimer's disease and 15 diagnosed as having vascular dementia.

The data depicted in figure 2 are based on these 27 subjects from the oldest age group and a total of 372 subjects in the same age group who had not been diagnosed as demented. As can be seen from this figure, it is quite clear that those who, during the five-year period following T1, developed dementia, performed at a much lower level already at T1 in comparison with those who did not develop dementia during the same

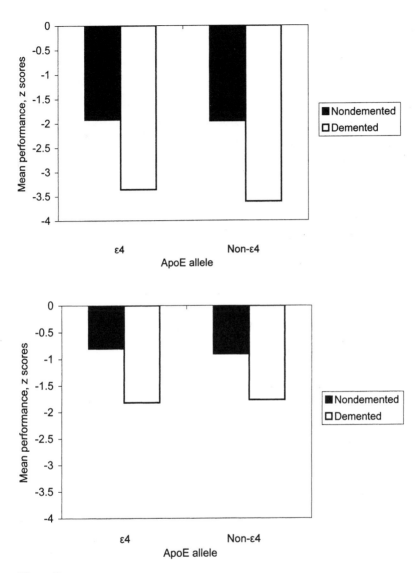

Figure 2
Mean recall performance, z scores, for demented and nondemented 65-to-80-year-old carriers of the ε4 allele and non-ε4 alleles in episodic-memory tasks (top) and semantic memory tasks (bottom).

period of time. From pure inspection of these data, there does not seem to be much of a difference between those participants with and those participants without the ε4 allele. Moreover, this data pattern is essentially the same for episodic-memory and semantic-memory tasks. The two analyses of variance carried out on these data revealed main effects of the dementia variable on episodic memory ($F(1, 380) = 37.57$, MSE $= 1.19$, $p < .001$) and on semantic memory ($F(1, 380) = 10.28$, MSE $= 1.14$, $p < .005$). The main effect of ApoE was nonsignificant on both episodic and semantic memory ($p = .76$ and $p = .71$, respectively). The interactions between dementia and ApoE were nonsignificant for both episodic memory and semantic memory ($p = .65$ and $p = .69$, respectively).

Obviously, these results will have to be confirmed in subsequent research before firm conclusions can be made. One opportunity to do this is after the third wave of data collection has been completed in the Betula study in year 2000. A word of caution should also be mentioned with respect to these first steps taken in the Betula study in trying to relate one single genetic marker to memory performance. Plomin (1997) emphasized when relating genetic markers to intelligence that the heritability of intelligence is more likely to be due to many genes with varying effects than to a few genes with a major effects. It is therefore likely that a multifactorial ability like memory should also be related to multiple genes rather than to a single gene. Environmental factors might also play a critical role in determining which genetic markers are associated with memory performance. It is indeed a challenging task to try to determine which genes determine a genetic component of memory functioning and which environmental factors may play a role in revealing these associations.

In sum, the data obtained demonstrate an age-related decline in memory performance for episodic memory. For semantic memory, the age-related decline disappears when background factors like education level are taken into account. There is some evidence in the Betula data showing that genetic markers may play an important role in determining memory performance. However, quite unexpectedly, the ApoE gene seems to play a rather minor role in determining memory performance in the cross-sectional data from the first wave of data collection in the Betula study.

Acknowledgments

This research was supported by grants from the Bank of Sweden Tercentenary Foundation, the Swedish Council for Research in the Humanities and the Social Sciences, the Swedish Council for Planning and Coordination of Research, and the Swedish Council for Social Research.

References

Arenberg, D. (1989). Longitudinal changes in memory performance. Poster session presented at the fifth meeting of the International Study Group on the Pharmacology of Memory Disorders Associated with Aging.

Bäckman, L., & Nilsson, L.-G. (1984). Aging effects in free recall: An exception to the rule. *Human Learning*, 3, 53–69.

Bäckman, L., & Nilsson, L.-G. (1985). Prerequisites for lack of age differences in memory performance. *Experimental Aging Research*, 11, 67–73.

Bäckman, L., & Nilsson, L.-G. (1996). Semantic memory functioning across the adult life span. *European Psychologist*, 1, 27–33.

Bäckman, L., & Small, B. J. (1998). A continuity view of episodic memory impairment: Illustrations from Alzheimer's disease and major depression. In C. Von Euler, I. Lundberg & R. Llinás (Eds.), *Basic mechanisms in cognition and language* (pp. 243–260). New York: Pergamon.

Baddeley, A. D., Lewis, V., Eldridge, M., & Thomson, N. (1984). Attention and retrieval from long-term memory. *Journal of Experimental Psychology: General*, 113, 518–540.

Bartlett, J. C., Halpern, A. R., Dowling, W. J. (1995). Recognition of familiar and unfamiliar melodies in normal aging and Alzheimer's disease. *Memory and Cognition*, 23, 531–546.

Bartlett, J. C., & Leslie, J. E. (1986). Aging and memory for faces versus single views of faces. *Memory & Cognition*, 14, 371–381.

Berkowitz, B. (1953). The Wechsler-Bellevue performance of white males past 50. *Journal of Gerontology*, 8, 76–80.

Brooks, B., & Gardiner, J. (1994). Age differences in memory for prospective compared with retrospective tasks. *Memory & Cognition*, 22, 27–33.

Chiarello, C., & Hoyer, W. J. (1988). Adult age differences in implicit and explicit memory: Time course and encoding effects. *Psychology and Aging*, 3, 358–366.

Cohen, G., & Faulkner, D. (1986). Memory for proper names: Age differences in retrieval. *British Journal of Developmental Psychology*, 4, 187–197.

Cohen, R. L., Sandler, S. P., & Schroeder, K. (1987). Aging and memory for words and action events: Effects of item repetition and list length. *Psychology and Aging*, 2, 280–285.

Craik, F. I. M., Govoni, R., Naveh-Benjamin, M., Anderson, N. D. (1996). The effects of divided attention on encoding and retrieval processes in human memory. *Journal of Experimental Psychology: General, 2*, 159–180.

Dick, M. B., Kean, M.-L., & Sands, D. (1989). Memory for action events in Alzheimer type dementia: Further evidence for an encoding failure. *Brain and Cognition, 9*, 71–87.

Einstein, G. O., & McDaniel, M. A. (1990). Normal aging and prospective memory. *Journal of Experimental Psychology: Learning, Memory, and Cognition, 16*, 717–726.

Erngrund, K., Mäntylä, T., & Nilsson, L.-G. (1996). Adult age differences in source recall: A population-based study. *Journal of Gerontology: Psychological Sciences, 51B*, P335–P345.

Folstein, M. G., Folstein, S. E., & McHugh, P. R. (1975). "Mini-Mental State": A practical method for grading the cognitive state of patients for the clinician. *Journal of Psychiatric Research, 12*, 189–198.

Guttentag, R. E., & Hunt, R. R. (1988). Adult age differences in memory for imagined and performed actions. *Journal of Gerontology: Psychological Sciences, 43*, 107–108.

Herlitz, A., Nilsson, L.-G., Bäckman, L. (1997). Gender differences in episodic memory. *Memory and Cognition, 25*, 801–811.

Hultsch, D. F., Hertzog, C., Small, B. J., McDonald-Miszczak, L., & Dixon, R. A. (1992). Short-term longitudinal change in cognitive performance in later life. *Psychology and Aging, 7*, 571–584.

Hultsch, D. F., Masson, M. E., & Small, B. J. (1991). Adult age differences in direct and indirect tests of memory. *Journal of Gerontology: Psychological Sciences, 46*, 22–30.

Johnson, M. K., & Raye, C. L. (1981). Reality monitoring. *Psychological Review, 88*, 67–85.

Kausler, D. H. (1991). *Experimental Psychology, cognition, and human aging.* 2nd ed. New York: Springer-Verlag.

Kausler, D. H., & Lichty, W. (1988). Memory for activities: Rehearsal-independence and aging. In M. L. Howe & C. J. Brainerd (Eds.), *Cognitive development in adulthood: Progress in cognitive development research* (pp. 93–131). New York: Springer-Verlag.

Kausler, D. H., & Puckett, J. M. (1980). Frequency judgments and correlated cognitive abilities in young and elderly adults. *Journal of Gerontology, 35*, 376–382.

Kramer, N. A., & Jarvik, L. (1979). Assessment of intellectual changes in the elderly. In A. Raskin & L. Jarvik (Eds.), *Psychiatric symptoms and cognitive loss in the elderly.* Washington, D.C.: Hemisphere.

Larrabee, G. J., & Crook, T. H. (1993). Do men show more rapid age-associated decline in simulated everyday verbal memory than do women? *Psychology and Aging, 8*, 68–71.

Larsson, M., Nyberg, L., Bäckman, L., & Nilsson, L.-G. (in press). Effects on episodic memory of stimulus richness, intention to learn, and extra-study repetition: similar profiles across the adult life span. *Journal of Adult Development*.

Light, L. L., & Singh, A. (1987). Implicit and explicit memory in young and older adults. *Journal of Experimental Psychology: Learning, Memory, and Cognition*, *13*, 531–541.

Light, L. L., Singh, A., & Capps, J. C. (1986). Dissociation of memory and awareness in young and old adults. *Journal of Clinical and Experimental Neuropsychology*, *8*, 62–74.

McIntyre, J. S., & Craik, F. I. M. (1987). Age differences in memory for item and source information. *Canadian Journal of Psychology*, *41*, 175–192.

Mäntylä, T., & Nilsson, L.-G. (1997). Remembering to remember in adulthood: A population-based study on aging and prospective memory. *Aging, Neuropsychology & Cognition*, *4*, 81–92.

Nilsson, L.-G. (2000). Memory of actions and words. In F. I. M. Craik & E. Tulving (Eds.), *Oxford handbook of memory*. Oxford: Oxford University Press.

Nilsson, L.-G., Bäckman, L., Erngrund, K., Nyberg, L., Adolfsson, R., Bucht, G., Karlsson, S., Widing, G., & Wilblad, B. (1997). The Betula prospective cohort study: Memory, health, and aging. *Aging, Neuropsychology, and Cognition*, *1*, 1–32.

Nilsson, L.-G., & Craik, F. I. M. (1990). Additive and interactive effects in memory for subject-performed tasks. *European Journal of Cognitive Psychology*, *2*, 305–324.

Nilsson, L.-G., Sikström, C., Adolfsson, R., Erngrund, K., Nylander, P.-O., & Beckman, L. (1996). Genetic markers associated with high versus low performance on episodic memory tasks. *Behavior Genetics*, *26*, 555–562.

Nyberg, L., Bäckman, L., Erngrund, K., Olofsson, U., & Nilsson, L.-G. (1996). Age differences in episodic memory, semantic memory, and priming: Relationships to demographic, intellectual, and biological factors. *Journal of Gerontology: Psychological Sciences*, *51B*, P234–P240.

Nyberg, L., Nilsson, L.-G., Olofsson, U., & Bäckman, L. (1997). Effects of division of attention during encoding and retrieval on age differences in episodic memory. *Experimental Aging Research*, *23*, 137–143.

Nyberg, L., Maitland, S., Rönnlund, M., Bäckman, L., Dixon, R., Wahlin, Å., & Nilsson, L.-G. (2000). The structure of declarative memory: Competing theoretical models and measurement equivalence. Paper presented at 27th International Congress of Psychology, Stockholm, Sweden, July 23–28, 2000.

O'Hara, F., Yesavage, J. A., Kraemer, H. C., Meuricio, M., Friedman, L. F., Murphy, G. M., Jr. (1998). The ApoE epsilon 4 allele is associated with decline on delayed recall performance in community-dwelling older adults. *Journal of the American Geriatric Society*, *46*, 1493–1498.

Park, D. C., Smith, A. D., Dudley, W. N., & Lafronza, V. N. (1989). Effects of age and a divided attention task presented during encoding and retrieval on memory. *Journal of Experimental Psychology: Learning, Memory, and Cognition, 15*, 1185–1191.

Peterson, R. C., Smith, G. E., Ivnik, R. J., Tangalos, E. G., Schaid, D. J., Thibodeau, S. N., Kokmen, E., Waring, S. C., & Kurland, L. T. (1995). Apolipoprotein E status as a predictor of the development of Alzheimer's disease in memory-impaired individuals. *Journal of the American Medical Association, 273*, 1274–1278.

Plomin, R. (1997). Current directions in behavioral genetics: Moving into the mainstream. *Current Directions in Psychological Science, 6*, 85.

Rönnlund, M., Nyberg, L., Bäckman, L., Nilsson, L.-G. (2000). Recall of subject-performed tasks, verbal tasks, and cognitive activities across the adult life span: parallel age-related deficits. Submitted.

Salthouse, T. A. (1993). Speed mediation of adult age differences in cognition. *Developmental Psychology, 29*, 722–738.

Smith, A. D., & Winograd, E. (1978). Age differences in recognizing faces. *Developmental Psychology, 14*, 443–444.

Stone, D. J., Rozovsky, I., Morgan, T. E., Anderson, C. P., Hagop, H., & Finch, C. E. (1997). Astrocytes and microglia respond to estrogen with increased ApoE mRNA *in Vivo* and *in Vitro*. *Experimental Neurology, 143*, 313–318.

Stone, D. J., Rozovsky, I., Morgan, T. E., Anderson, C. P., Hagop, H., & Finch, C. E. (1998). Increased synaptic sprouting in response to estrogen via an Apolipoprotein E–dependent mechanism: Implications for Alzheimer's disease. *Journal of Neuroscience, 18*, 3180–3185.

Weingartner, H. (1986). Automatic and effort-demanding processing in depression. In L. E. Poon (Ed.), *Clinical memory assessment of older adults* (pp. 218–225). Washington, D.C.: American Psychological Association.

Wechsler, D. (1981). *Manual for the Wechsler Adult Intelligence Scale—Revised.* New York: Psychological Corporation.

11

The Nature and Course of the Memory Impairment in Alzheimer's Disease

Lars Bäckman, Brent J. Small, and Laura Fratiglioni

Introduction

Alzheimer's disease (AD) is a progressive, degenerative brain disorder that accounts for approximately 60% of all dementia cases (e.g., Ebly, Parhad, Hogan & Fung, 1994; Hendrie et al., 1995). The prevalence of AD exponentially increases with increasing age (a doubling every five years from age 65). Approximately 1% of the population between 65 and 69 years of age are diagnosed with dementia; the corresponding figure for the 90+ population is around 50% (e.g., Fichter, Meller, Schröppel & Steinkirchner, 1995; Ott, Breteler, van Harskamp, Grobbee & Hofman, 1995). In this chapter we discuss the cognitive repercussions of AD, with special emphasis on memory functioning. The focus is on the transition from normal aging to dementia—the preclinical phase of AD. However, to provide a basis for analyzing this transition, we first give a brief overview of the cognitive problems associated with early clinical AD.

Evidence indicates that AD is characterized by a global cognitive impairment. Even early on in the disease process, AD patients typically exhibit deficits across multiple cognitive domains, including attention, memory, verbal ability, visuospatial skill, problem solving, and reasoning (for reviews, see Morris, 1996; Nebes, 1992; Small, Herlitz & Bäckman, 1998). Yet it is clear that the largest and most consistent cognitive deficit in early clinical AD is seen within the domain of memory. No form of memory is completely spared from the negative effects of AD. Thus, AD-related deficits have been documented in tasks assessing procedural memory (e.g., Dick, 1992), different forms of priming (e.g.,

Fleischman & Gabrieli, 1998), primary memory (e.g., Morris, 1986), working memory (e.g., Baddeley, Logie, Bressi, Della Sala & Spinnler, 1986), semantic memory (e.g., Hodges, Salmon & Butters, 1992), and episodic memory (e.g., Herlitz & Viitanen, 1991).

Despite the seemingly global nature of the memory impairment in AD, there is variability across different varieties of memory with regard to the size of the AD-related deficit. Specifically, numerous studies employing discriminant-analysis procedures indicate that episodic memory tasks are most effective in distinguishing between the normal old person and the mild-AD patient (e.g., Almkvist & Bäckman, 1993; Herlitz, Hill, Fratiglioni & Bäckman, 1995; Storandt & Hill, 1989; Welsh, Butters, Hughes, Mohs & Heyman, 1992).

Episodic Memory in Early Clinical AD

Episodic memory involves conscious retrieval of information acquired in a particular place at a particular time (Tulving, 1983). In tasks assessing episodic memory, the participant is typically required to recall or recognize some information acquired in the experimental setting (e.g., lists of words, pictures of faces).

The influence of cognitive support

Episodic-memory tasks vary in terms of the level of cognitive support provided. Such variation may be seen with regard to the encoding conditions (e.g., standard instructions versus organizational instructions), the materials (e.g., words versus objects), and the retrieval conditions (e.g., free recall versus cued recall). Thus, whereas some episodic tasks offer little cognitive support (e.g., free recall of unrelated words), others may provide considerable support for remembering (e.g., recognition of objects).

It is well established that normal old persons are able to benefit from supportive performance conditions in episodic-memory tasks. This indicates a potential for memory improvement—a cognitive reserve capacity—in normal aging (for reviews, see Bäckman, Mäntylä & Herlitz, 1990; Craik & Jennings, 1992). Early research demonstrated that AD patients were unable to utilize supportive conditions for remembering, which suggests a marked AD-related reduction in cognitive reserve capacity (for a review, see Herlitz, Lipinska & Bäckman, 1992). However, more recent studies have demonstrated that plasticity of episodic memory in normal aging and AD is not an either-or issue (for a review, see Bäckman & Herlitz, 1996). Specifically, research indicates that AD patients, under some conditions, are able to benefit from cognitive support in episodic-memory tasks, although they typically require more support than their healthy aged counterparts to demonstrate memory facilitation. In particular, several studies have shown that it is vital to provide cognitive support at both encoding and subsequent retrieval to demonstrate memory improvement in AD. Such results have been obtained when retrieval support has been combined with encoding support in the form of a rich stimulus input (Herlitz, Adolfsson, Bäckman & Nilsson, 1991), guidance to engage in categorical processing (Bird & Luszcz, 1991, 1993; Lipinska & Bäckman, 1997), organizational structure in the materials (Herlitz & Viitanen, 1991), activation of appropriate preexperimental knowledge (Lipinska, Bäckman & Herlitz, 1992), and more study time (Almkvist, Fratiglioni, Agüero-Torres, Viitanen & Bäckman, 1999).

A clear illustration of this pattern of performance is provided by Almkvist et al. (1999). In their study, normal old adults and early AD patients were presented with words at a rapid or slow rate and memory performance was assessed with both free recall and recognition. As shown in figure 1, when memory was tested with free recall, the normal old, as opposed to the AD patients, performed better with the slowly presented words than with the rapidly presented words. That is, the patients apparently failed to take advantage of more study time in order to engage in rehearsal or other elaborative encoding activities. However, when memory for the same information was tested with recognition, a rather different data pattern emerged. In this case both groups showed beneficial effects of about the same magnitude from more study time (see figure 2). Thus, the AD patients had obviously acquired more information from the slowly presented word list in comparison with the rapidly presented word list, although the impoverished retrieval conditions prevailing in free recall may have masked the effect. However, with the provision of more retrieval support in the recognition test, the memory

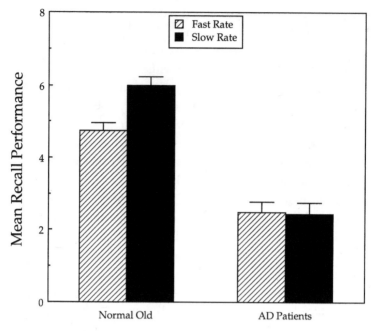

Figure 1
Mean free recall performance (d') for AD patients and normal old adults as a function of study time. Bars represent standard errors around the means. (Adapted from Almkvist, Fratiglioni, Agüero-Torres, Viitanen & Bäckman, 1999. Copyright 1999 by Swets and Zeitlinger.)

traces could be activated more easily, and facilitative effects from more study time were observed also in the AD patients.

Two further points should be noted concerning the relationship between cognitive support and episodic memory in normal aging and AD. First, as a result of the decreased cognitive reserve capacity in AD, dementia-related deficits in episodic memory may be larger for more supported tasks than for less supported tasks (e.g., Branconnier, Cole, Spera & DeVitt, 1982; Herlitz & Viitanen, 1991). This is an interesting observation that runs counter to the intuitively appealing assumption that difficult memory tasks should be most sensitive in differentiating between normal and memory-impaired individuals. Second, the fact that AD is associated with a reduced potential for memory improvement does not make this group of memory-impaired individuals unique. In fact, the

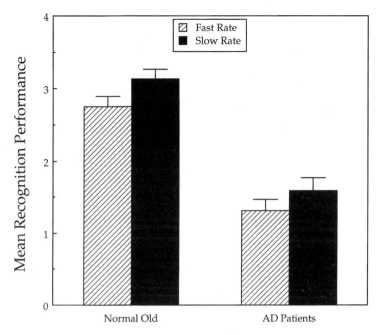

Figure 2
Mean recognition performance (d') for AD patients and normal old adults as a function of study time. (Adapted from Almkvist, Fratiglioni, Agüero-Torres, Viitanen & Bäckman, 1999. Copyright 1999 by Swets and Zeitlinger.)

correlation of overall episodic memory ability with the degree of performance gains from cognitive support has been observed for multiple clinical conditions of varying severity, including Korsakoff's syndrome, schizophrenia, and clinical depression, and also for individual-difference variables within the normal population, such as education, social-activity levels, and verbal ability (for an overview, see Bäckman, Small, Wahlin & Larsson, 1999).

Reduced effects of individual-difference variables
Before shifting the focus to the transition phase between normal aging and AD, we would like to highlight an intriguing observation regarding the influence of individual-difference variables on episodic-memory functioning in AD. It is well established that individual differences within the demographic domain (e.g., age, sex, education), social domain (e.g.,

activity levels), cognitive domain (e.g., processing speed, working-memory capacity), and biological domain (e.g., circulatory factors, vitamin status) play an important role in memory performance among normal old adults (for reviews, see Bäckman, Small, et al., 1999; Hultsch, Hertzog, Dixon & Small, 1998). Interestingly, research indicates that the influence of various subject characteristics on memory functioning is markedly reduced in AD. For example, investigators have examined whether onset age (which, of course, is highly related to chronological age) influences performance at a given point in time or rate of cognitive decline in AD. Although some research suggests that early-onset patients may be more impaired and exhibit a faster rate of decline than late-onset patients, perhaps because of more severe and widespread brain lesions (e.g., Hansen, De Teresa, Davies & Terry, 1988; Mann, 1994; Wilson, Gilley, Bennett, Beckett & Evans, 2000), the bulk of empirical evidence indicates that onset age has a negligible effect on cognitive functioning in AD (e.g., Bäckman, Hill, Herlitz, Fratiglioni & Winblad, 1994; Heston, Mastri, Anderson & White, 1981; Hill, Bäckman, Wahlin & Winblad, 1995; Katzman et al., 1983; Rubin et al., 1993; Small & Bäckman, 1998; Small, Viitanen, Winblad & Bäckman, 1997; Teri, McCurry, Edland, Kukull & Larson, 1995).

The fact that most research has failed to document a systematic relationship between onset age and different aspects of memory and other cognitive functioning in AD indicates that onset age acts much like many other potentially relevant individual-difference variables in this disease. Several studies demonstrate that variables known to influence cognitive performance in normal aging have little or no influence on performance in AD once severity of dementia is controlled. This includes education (Bäckman et al., 1994; Burns, Jacoby & Levy, 1991; Katzman et al., 1983), sex (e.g., Buckwalter, Sobel, Dunn, Diz & Henderson, 1993; Teri, Hughes & Larson, 1990), as well as a variety of biological variables, e.g., blood pressure, vitamin B_{12}, folic acid, thyroid stimulating hormone (Bäckman et al., 1994; Hill, Bäckman, et al., 1995; Small & Bäckman, 1998; Small, Viitanen, et al., 1997). A likely reason for the lack of association between these variables and cognitive functioning in AD is that the influence of demographic and other subject characteristics may be overshadowed by the pathogenetic process itself. In other words, and perhaps not surprisingly, the devastating effects of dementia appear to make people more cognitively similar.

Cognitive Deficits in Preclinical AD

In recent years, much cognitive dementia research has been directed at investigating whether persons who will develop dementia show deficits prior to the time at which a diagnosis may be rendered. The basic design in research addressing this issue involves following a group of non-demented older persons across a certain time period. In most instances, the retest interval ranges between 2 and 3 years, although some studies have employed considerably longer follow-up periods (La Rue & Jarvik, 1987; Elias et al., 2000). At the follow-up examination, some of the examined participants have likely developed AD, and the issue of interest concerns whether these incident AD cases differed in cognitive performance already at baseline assessment from those who remained non-demented over the interval covered by the retest.

The available evidence demonstrates a clear lowering of cognitive performance among incident AD cases several years before actual diagnosis. Such preclinical deficits in AD have been demonstrated in numerous studies employing global indicators of cognitive performance (e.g., Aronson et al., 1990; Yoshitake et al., 1995; Small, Viitanen & Bäckman, 1997). Within specific cognitive domains, preclinical deficits in AD have been documented for tasks assessing psychomotor speed (Masur et al., 1994), verbal ability and reasoning (Jacobs et al., 1995), and visuospatial skill (Small, Herlitz, Fratiglioni, Almkvist & Bäckman, 1997).

The primacy of episodic memory

However, as is true in early clinical AD, the largest and most consistent cognitive deficits observed before the diagnosis of AD occur within the domain of episodic memory (Grober et al., 2000; Hodges, 1998). Both before and after clinical diagnosis of this disease, several cognitive functions are affected, but the largest degree of impairment is seen for episodic memory. This pattern of results was illustrated by Small, Herlitz, et al. (1997). In their study, those who would develop AD across a three-year follow-up interval showed baseline cognitive deficits across a variety of tasks, including those assessing not only episodic memory but also visuoperceptive skill, visuoconstructive skill, letter fluency, and category fluency. However, when all measures were entered into a logistic-regression analysis, the tasks assessing episodic memory (e.g., word recall, face recognition) were found to dominate the prediction model.

Furthermore, the episodic-memory deficit in persons who will develop AD appears to be highly generalizable across different materials and testing conditions. Specifically, preclinical episodic-memory deficits have been observed for both verbal materials (Linn et al., 1995; Tierney et al., 1996) and nonverbal materials (Fuld et al., 1990; Small, Herlitz, et al., 1997), as well as across different retrieval conditions, including free recall (Howieson et al., 1997; Grober et al., 2000), cued recall (Linn et al., 1995; Bäckman & Small, 1998), and recognition (Fuld et al., 1990; Small, Herlitz, et al., 1997).

The global nature of the impairment

Notwithstanding the global nature of the episodic-memory deficit in preclinical AD, some tasks may still be more effective than others in signaling an impending dementia disease. As noted, episodic-memory tasks vary naturally with regard to the degree of cognitive support provided for remembering. If we analyze the effects of preclinical AD on episodic-memory performance in terms of the provision of cognitive support, three principal outcomes can be conceived.

First, the size of the memory deficit in preclinical AD may be greater in more supported tasks (e.g., cued recall) than in less supported tasks (e.g., free recall). Such an outcome would indicate that a reduction in cognitive reserve capacity is a salient feature of preclinical AD, much as it is in early clinical AD. Small, Herlitz, et al. (1997) found some support for this notion by demonstrating that measures of cued recall and recognition did a better job than measures of free recall in differentiating between incident AD cases and control subjects three years prior to diagnosis. In addition, intervention research in the area of fluid intelligence (Baltes, Kuhl, Gutzmann & Sowarka, 1995; Baltes, Kuhl & Sowarka, 1992) has demonstrated that persons classified as being at risk for developing AD showed smaller training-related gains than control subjects.

By contrast, the opposite result (that persons in a preclinical phase of AD show greater deficits in less supported tasks than in more supported tasks) would suggest that these individuals are particularly penalized under highly demanding task conditions. Although this pattern of results may be conceivable and has received some empirical support (Howieson et al., 1997), it would run counter to the finding that the degree of memory impairment typically increases with increasing cognitive support in early clinical AD (e.g., Branconnier, Cole, Spera & DeVitt, 1982; Herlitz & Viitanen, 1991). Finally, an outcome indicating that the magnitude of the episodic memory impairment for persons in the preclinical phase of AD is invariant across different levels of cognitive support could be interpreted to mean that a general impairment of episodic memory precedes reductions in memory plasticity in the early pathogenesis of AD.

The mixed evidence concerning this issue likely reflects the fact that task conditions have not been manipulated in a systematic manner, and the fact that some comparisons have involved tasks with different measurement properties (e.g., number of words recalled versus d' scores) and set sizes. To circumvent these problems, we (Bäckman & Small, 1998) compared groups of incident AD cases and control subjects on four episodic-memory tasks that varied systematically with regard to the degree of cognitive support provided: free recall of rapidly presented random words, free recall of slowly presented random words, free recall of organizable words, and cued recall of organizable words. These four tasks may be viewed as instances along a continuum of cognitive support, where more study time, organizability, and semantic retrieval cues are incrementally added to the memory task.

Subjects were tested both at baseline and at a three-year follow-up, at which time the incident AD cases were diagnosed. The main findings from this study are shown in figure 3. Several aspects of these data should be highlighted. First, although the normal old declined slightly over the three-year retest interval, they showed proficient utilization of all three forms of cognitive support at both times of measurement, with performance gradually increasing with the addition of more study time, organizability, and retrieval cues. Second, the incident AD cases showed a clear performance deficit at baseline, which was further exacerbated at

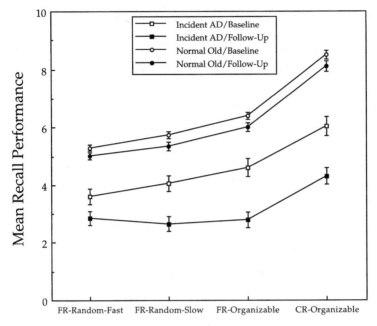

Figure 3
Episodic memory performance (*d'*) in normal old adults and incident AD patients across levels of cognitive support at baseline (three years before diagnosis) and follow-up (diagnosis). Bars represent standard errors around the means. (Adapted from Bäckman & Small, 1998. Copyright 1998 by the American Psychological Association.)

follow-up. The latter finding indicates that the time period just preceding the diagnosis of AD is characterized by a marked decline of episodic-memory functioning. Third and most interesting, although they were impaired at baseline assessment, the incident AD cases still showed the same qualitative pattern as the controls: performance gradually increased with increasing levels of cognitive support. Finally, at the time of diagnosis, the incident AD cases failed to benefit from more study time and organizability in free recall; here, performance gains were observed only in the most supportive condition, where an organizational structure was combined with retrieval cues. This result was expected, as several studies have demonstrated that it may be necessary to provide support at both encoding and retrieval for AD cases to show memory improvement in early clinical AD (for a review, see Bäckman & Herlitz, 1996).

The important point to be gathered from these results is that the size of the preclinical episodic memory impairment in AD does not seem to vary as a function of the level of cognitive support. As shown in figure 2, the deficit was highly generalizable across important dimensions of episodic memory, such as presentation time, organizability, and retrieval cues. The fact that the incident AD cases showed a normal pattern of utilization of cognitive support, although they performed worse than the controls at baseline, indicates that losses in cognitive reserve capacity may occur somewhat later in the pathogenesis of AD than a general episodic-memory impairment. Thus, in the presence of a general episodic-memory deficit, reductions in the ability to utilize cognitive support for remembering may not be expected three years prior to the time at which a diagnosis is possible.

In the Bäckman and Small (1998) study, we also analyzed free recall of random words in terms of the relative contribution of primary and secondary memory. These analyses revealed that the preclinical deficit among the incident AD cases was confined to secondary memory. To be sure, preclinical deficits in primary-memory functioning should not be expected, since this form of memory is relatively little affected even in early clinical AD (e.g., Simon, Leach, Winocur & Moscovitch, 1995; Spinnler, Della Sala, Bandera & Baddeley, 1988). The presence of clear secondary-memory deficits along with preserved primary-memory performance suggests that persons in a preclinical phase of AD have special difficulties in transferring information from a temporary representation to a more permanent representation, although the ability to hold information for a relatively brief period of time is spared.

The biological basis of the impairment

The above pattern of findings is relevant to determining neural correlates of memory deficits in preclinical AD. The histopathological hallmarks of AD, neurofibrillary tangles and amyloid plaques, are found in large numbers in the hippocampus; these changes are accompanied by gross atrophy of the hippocampal formation (e.g., West, Coleman, Flood & Troncoso, 1994). Of particular interest is the finding that changes in the brains of persons who will later develop AD may start in the entorhinal cortex and hippocampus before progressing to the neocortical association cortices (e.g., Braak & Braak, 1991, 1995; Van Hoesen et al., 1999). Given this pattern of neural changes in the preclinical phase of AD, it makes perfect sense that episodic memory should be affected prior to the time of the dementia diagnosis. This is so because both lesion studies (e.g., Squire, 1992; Vargha-Khadem et al., 1997) and brain-imaging studies (e.g., Grady et al., 1995; Nyberg et al., 1996) have linked the hippocampal formation to proficient encoding, consolidation, and retrieval of episodic information.

The observation that the hippocampal formation is severely affected early in AD is confirmed by magnetic-resonance-imaging (MRI) studies, which indicate volume losses of 25% or more already in mildly demented cases (e.g., Killiany et al., 1993; Lehericy et al., 1994). Further, the extent of hippocampal atrophy correlates with the degree of memory impairment in AD patients (Deweer et al., 1995; Laakso et al., 1997). In an interesting MRI study, Fox et al. (1996) examined seven at-risk members of a familial AD pedigree associated with the mutation of amyloid precursor protein 717 valine to glycine. Across a three-year follow-up interval, three subjects received a clinical diagnosis of AD. Volumetric measurement of the hippocampal formation in these subjects revealed atrophy before the appearance of clinical symptoms. Most interesting, the reduction in hippocampal volume occurred in parallel with decline in measures of episodic memory.

In a recent functional-imaging study, persons in a preclinical or very early clinical phase of AD and normal old adults were scanned under baseline (non-memory-retrieval) and cued-recall conditions (Bäckman, Andersson, et al., 1999). As expected, the behavioral data showed no group differences in the baseline condition, although the normal old outperformed the AD patients in cued recall.

The imaging data indicated increased activity during episodic retrieval in comparison with the baseline for control subjects and AD patients alike in a variety of brain structures, including the orbital and dorso-lateral prefrontal cortices as well as distinct parietal (precuneus) and cerebellar regions. Note that these regions are typically activated during episodic retrieval in young adults too (for an overview, see Cabeza & Nyberg, 2000). Thus, a widespread network subserving episodic-memory retrieval appears to function relatively normally in preclinical

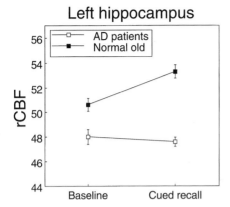

Figure 4
Brain activity in the left hippocampus during baseline and cued recall in normal old adults and AD patients. Bars represent standard errors around the means. rCBF = normalized regional cerebral blood flow (mL/[minutes × 100 mL]). (Adapted from Bäckman, Andersson, Nyberg, Winblad, Nordberg & Almkvist, 1999. Copyright 1999 by the American Academy of Neurology.)

and early clinical AD. Most interesting, however, the normal old, but not the AD patients, showed increased activity in the left hippocampus during cued recall, relative to the baseline (see figure 4).

Thus, there is evidence from histopathological, as well as structural and functional, brain-imaging studies that disease-related changes in the hippocampus play an important role in the episodic-memory difficulties experienced in preclinical and early clinical AD. However, the current focus on the medial-temporal lobe in understanding the biological origins of the AD-related memory impairment should not be taken to mean than other brain regions are unimportant. Indeed, considering (a) the wide variety of neuroanatomical and neurochemical changes associated with AD (for an overview, see Friedland & Wilcock, 1999), and (b) the interconnectedness of brain regions involved in episodic remembering (Cabeza & Nyberg, 2000), it is unrealistic to expect that changes in the medial-temporal lobe would be solely responsible for the memory deficits seen in AD. However, from the converging evidence reviewed above, it should be clear that early lesions in the hippocampus and related structures constitute a major source of the failure to acquire and recollect information in this beginning phase of AD.

The course of the impairment

Although the research reviewed above has yielded important insights with regard to the cognitive transition from normal aging to dementia, there are some shortcomings that need to be addressed. Foremost among these is the fact that the bulk of studies demonstrating preclinical cognitive deficits in AD have included only one preclinical measurement occasion. In some studies in which subjects have been assessed multiple times prior to diagnosis, the focus of the analyses has been on the single point in time at which preclinical deficits are first detectable. Thus, even though some research indicates that preclinical cognitive deficits in AD may be observed as long as 10–20 years before diagnosis (La Rue & Jarvik, 1987; Elias et al., 2000), these studies are not very informative concerning the progression of memory deficits before the diagnosis of AD. In some studies, persons have been assessed both before diagnosis and at the time of diagnosis. The results from this research indicate that patients in a preclinical phase of AD exhibit precipitous cognitive decline during the time period just preceding diagnosis (Bäckman & Small, 1998; Fox et al., 1998; Rubin et al., 1998; Small, Viitanen & Bäckman, 1997). However, these studies leave unanswered the question of whether those who will develop AD show disproportionate cognitive decline longer before diagnosis. Such knowledge should be important to further our understanding of the course of the early development of AD. Indeed, this issue is at the heart of AD, as the diagnostic criteria require an insidious onset, with individuals exhibiting changes from a previous level of functioning.

In a recent study (Bäckman, Small & Fratiglioni, 2001), we assessed persons from a population-based study on three occasions over six years. On the last occasion, some individuals were diagnosed with AD, although the entire study sample was nondemented at the first two times of measurement. The key issue in this study was whether preclinical AD is characterized by accelerated memory decline relatively long before diagnosis. If this is the case, difference scores on memory performance six years versus three years prior to diagnosis may be more effective in signaling an impending dementia in comparison with static performance scores. In addition, to obtain further evidence regarding the ability of different episodic-memory tasks to identify persons at risk for developing AD, we administered tests of verbal free recall and recognition at both

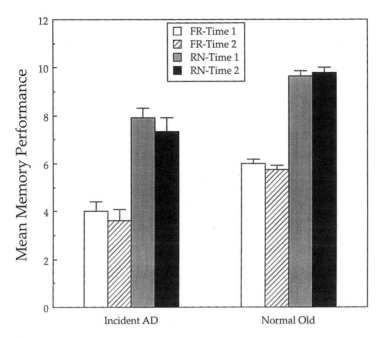

Figure 5
Mean free recall (FR) and recognition (RN) performance (d') for normal old and incident AD persons six years (time 1) and three years (time 2) before the diagnosis of dementia. Bars represent standard errors around the means. (Adapted from Bäckman, Small & Fratiglioni, 2001. Copyright 2001 by Oxford University Press.)

preclinical measurement points. Missing data at the time of diagnosis precluded group comparisons on memory scores at that time point.

The results from this study are shown in figure 5. We would like to highlight four aspects of the data in this figure. First, the normal old performed at about the same level on both measurement occasions. This is consistent with the results from several longitudinal studies, which indicates that decline in episodic memory may not be observed in normal aging over relatively short follow-up periods (e.g., Hultsch et al., 1992; Zelinski et al., 1997). Second, the incident AD cases showed clear deficits already six years before the time of diagnosis. Third and most interesting, although they exhibited clear deficits in the episodic-memory tests already at the first time of measurement, the incident AD cases did not decline selectively between time 1 and time 2. Thus, the data suggest that the episodic-memory deficit in preclinical AD is characterized by an early onset followed by relative stability, at least until a few years before a diagnosis can be rendered. Finally, the impairment in preclinical AD generalized across the two episodic-memory tests. In fact, the free recall and recognition tests were equally effective in discriminating between the two groups both six and three years before diagnosis. From a different perspective, the magnitude of performance gains from recall to recognition was similar in both groups. This finding is in agreement with the results of Bäckman and Small (1998) indicating that episodic-memory functioning in general may be affected before losses in cognitive reserve capacity are observed in the development of AD.

Relatedly, both recall and recognition made independent contributions to group classification in logistic-regression analyses. A common conception among memory theorists is that both recall and recognition involve decision processes, although recall taxes search processes to a greater extent than recognition (Gillund & Shiffrin, 1984; Hintzman, 1988). Yet the recognition test contributed significantly to the regression models, independently of recall. The interesting question, then, is what cognitive operations may be involved in recognition that are not similarly involved in recall. One possibility is that recognition constitutes a purer measure of the amount of information actually encoded in comparison with recall. Since the episodic-memory deficit in preclinical AD is largely related to the encoding phase (Bäckman & Small, 1998; Grober et al., 2000), recognition may be expected to contribute to predicting the development of AD over and above recall. However, if this were to be the main explanation of this intriguing finding, we would have expected larger group differences in recognition than in recall. This was not the case.

Another possibility is that an influence of unconscious processes underlies the additional contribution of the recognition test in predicting the development of AD. Although this account is highly speculative, there is ample evidence that recognition memory draws on a combination of conscious recollection and implicit processes, such as familiarity and perceptual fluency, whereas free recall largely depends on conscious recollection (Jacoby, 1991; Jacoby et al., 1993). There is also evidence that various implicit-memory processes, such as perceptual priming, are affected in early clinical AD (for reviews, see Fleischman & Gabrieli, 1998; Meiran & Jelicic, 1995). Brain imaging research with young and normal old adults indicates that perceptual priming is associated with decreased neural activity in the posterior neocortex (e.g., Bäckman et al., 1997; Buckner et al., 1995). This result has been interpreted to mean that less neural energy is required to process a particular stimulus after prior exposure (e.g., Ungerleider, 1995). In a recent study (Bäckman, Almkvist, Nyberg & Andersson, 2000), it was found that preclinical- and early-clinical-AD patients failed to exhibit decreased neural activity in the posterior neocortex during priming, which possibly reflects inadequate initial stimulus processing. Bringing together these observations with the finding that recognition contributed to the prediction of AD independently of recall, we can hypothesize that unconscious memory operations are influenced already in the preclinical phase of AD. Future research in which specific tests of implicit memory are included in prospective research on AD should clarify this issue.

As noted, memory performance was not assessed at the time of diagnosis in the Bäckman et al. (2001) study. In addition, the sample size in the incident AD group was relatively small, which limited the generalizability of the findings. To address these issues, we conducted a parallel study involving large samples of incident AD cases and control subjects, who were assessed six and three years before diagnosis, but also at the time of diagnosis (Small, Fratiglioni, Viitanen, Winblad & Bäckman, 2000). In this study, however, the assessment of cognitive performance was restricted to the Mini-Mental State Examination or MMSE (Folstein, Folstein & McHugh, 1975), which is a global screening instrument for cognitive dysfunction. This instrument assesses multiple cognitive abilities, including orientation to time and place, immediate and delayed word recall, naming, verbal repetition, reading, writing, and spatial ability,

At both preclinical measurement points, the incident AD cases showed deficits on one item only, delayed recall. This result provides additional support for the view that the earliest cognitive deficits in preclinical AD are seen within the domain of episodic memory. However, from the three-year point to the time of diagnosis, the incident AD group exhibited

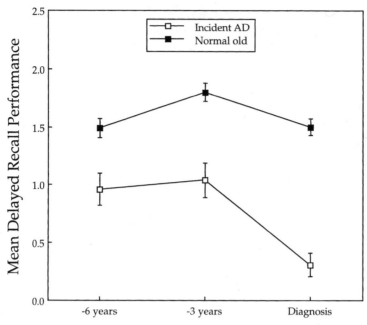

Figure 6
Mean performance on the delayed recall item from the Mini-Mental State Examination in incident AD patients and normal old adults six years before diagnosis, three years before diagnosis, and at the time of diagnosis. Bars represent standard errors around the means. (Adapted from Small, Fratiglioni, Viitanen, Winblad & Bäckman, 2000. Copyright 2000 by the American Medical Association.)

disproportionate declines across most cognitive domains assessed in the MMSE.

The results for the delayed-recall item in this study are shown in figure 6. In agreement with the recall and recognition data of Bäckman et al. (2001), the incident AD cases did not exhibit selective decline from six to three years before diagnosis in delayed recall, despite the fact that they performed at a considerably lower level than the nondemented persons at the initial measurement occasion. However, during the last retest interval, precipitous decline in the incident AD group was evident. These results corroborate the notion that AD is associated with a long preclinical period during which episodic-memory deficits are detectable, although accelerated decline in performance may not be expected until the time period preceding diagnosis.

The data portrayed in figure 6 begs the question of when the preclinical period actually begins; in other words, when the two curves in this figure approach each other. Do they ever meet? To address this issue, it is of interest to consider evidence from the Nun Study indicating that measures of linguistic skill assessed in early adulthood were highly predictive of who would develop AD more than 50 years later (Snowdon et al., 1995). In a similar vein, histopathological data demonstrate that initial signs of the formation of neurofibrillary tangles (i.e., cytoskeletal changes) may emerge in the medial-temporal lobe already in early adulthood (Braak et al., 1993). If we bring together these observations with the findings described above, it seems that the neural changes eventually leading to clinical AD progress at a very slow rate, and that accelerated memory decline may not be expected until various biological events (e.g., neurofibrillary tangles and amyloid plaques) have accumulated to reach a certain threshold. When this threshold is reached, precipitous decline in episodic memory and other cognitive functions will be observed. Also relevant to this lifespan view of the development of AD are recent findings that deleterious socioeconomic and environmental influences early in life may increase the risk of developing AD in late life (Hall et al., 2000; Moceri et al., 2000).

Concluding Points

In this final section, we would like to highlight the key points in this overview of the nature and course of the memory impairment in AD. First, although early clinical AD is characterized by a global cognitive impairment, the largest and most consistent deficit is seen for episodic memory. This deficit is accompanied by a reduced ability to benefit from supportive conditions in memory tasks. Specifically, to exhibit performance gains from cognitive support, mild AD patients appear to require guidance at both encoding and subsequent retrieval.

Episodic-memory deficits dominate also in preclinical AD, which thus indicates continuity in terms of the locus of cognitive impairment from the preclinical to the clinical stage of the disease. However, an important difference between these two stages is that the ability to utilize cognitive support for remembering appears to be little affected preclinically. This suggests that a generalized episodic-memory impairment may precede losses in the potential for memory improvement in the early development of AD.

There is converging evidence from histopathological research as well as from both structural- and functional-brain-imaging studies that the hippocampal formation is affected in the preclinical phase of AD, and that these changes are exacerbated as the disease process progresses into the clinical stage. The vital importance of this brain region for successful encoding, storage, and retrieval of episodic information is well documented in both lesion and imaging research. Thus, lesions in the hippocampal complex may largely underlie the episodic-memory deficits observed in both preclinical and early clinical AD.

An intriguing observation is that memory deficits among persons who will develop AD may be observed several decades prior to the time at which a diagnosis is made. However, despite this long preclinical period, the size of the memory impairment appears to be quite stable up until the time period just preceding diagnosis. These somewhat paradoxical phenomena may reflect the fact that those neural changes that eventually lead to clinically diagnosed AD progress at a very slow rate. As a result, precipitous decline during the preclinical phase is observed only when these neural changes have accumulated to reach a certain threshold.

Acknowledgments

The writing of this chapter was supported by grants from the Swedish Council for Research in the Humanities and the Social Sciences, the Swedish Medical Research Council, and the Swedish Council for Social Research to Lars Bäckman and Laura Fratiglioni.

References

Almkvist, O., & Bäckman, L. (1993). Progression in Alzheimer's disease: Sequencing of neuropsychological decline. *International Journal of Geriatric Psychiatry, 8*, 755–763.

Almkvist, O., Fratiglioni, L., Agüero-Torres, H., Viitanen, M., & Bäckman, L. (1999). Cognitive support at episodic encoding and retrieval: Similar patterns of utilization in community-based samples of Alzheimer's disease and vascular dementia patients. *Journal of Clinical and Experimental Neuropsychology, 21,* 816–830.

Aronson, M. K., Ooi, W. L., Morgenstern, H., Hafner, A., Masur, D., Crystal, H., Frishman, W. H., Fisher, D., & Katzman, R. (1990). Women, myocardial infarction, and dementia in the very old. *Neurology, 40,* 1102–1106.

Bäckman, L., Almkvist, O., Nyberg, L., & Andersson, J. L. R. (2000). Functional changes in brain activity during priming in Alzheimer's disease. *Journal of Cognitive Neuroscience, 12,* 134–141.

Bäckman, L., Almkvist, O., Andersson, J. L. R., Nordberg, A., Winblad, B., Reineck, R., & Långström, B. (1997). Brain activation in young and older adults during implicit and explicit retrieval. *Journal of Cognitive Neuroscience, 9,* 378–391.

Bäckman, L., Andersson, J. L. R., Nyberg, L., Winblad, B., Nordberg, A., & Almkvist, O. (1999). Brain regions associated with episodic retrieval in normal aging and Alzheimer's disease. *Neurology, 52,* 1861–1870.

Bäckman, L., & Forsell, Y. (1994). Episodic memory functioning in a community-based sample of old adults with major depression: Utilization of cognitive support. *Journal of Abnormal Psychology, 103,* 361–370.

Bäckman, L., & Herlitz, A. (1996). Knowledge and memory in Alzheimer's Disease: A relationship that exists. In R. G. Morris (Ed.), *The cognitive neuropsychology of Alzheimer-type dementia* (pp. 89–104). Oxford: Oxford University Press.

Bäckman, L., Hill, R. D., Herlitz, A., Fratiglioni, L., & Winblad, B. (1994). Predicting episodic memory performance in dementia: Is severity all there is? *Psychology and Aging, 9,* 520–527.

Bäckman, L., Mäntylä, T., & Herlitz, A. (1990). The optimization of episodic remembering in old age. In P. B. Baltes & M. M. Baltes (Eds.), *Successful aging: Perspectives from the behavioral sciences* (pp. 118–163). Cambridge: Cambridge University Press.

Bäckman, L., & Small, B. J. (1998). Influences of cognitive support on episodic remembering: Tracing the process of loss from normal aging to Alzheimer's disease. *Psychology and Aging, 13,* 267–276.

Bäckman, L., Small, B. J., & Fratiglioni, L. (2001). Stability of the preclinical episodic memory deficit in Alzheimer's disease. *Brain, 124,* 96–102.

Bäckman, L., Small, B. J., Wahlin, Å., & Larsson, M. (1999). Cognitive functioning in very old age. In F. I. N. Craik & T. A. Salthouse (Eds.) *Handbook of aging and cognition* (vol. 2, pp. 499–588). Mahwah, N.J.: Erlbaum.

Baddeley, A. D., Logie, R., Bressi, S., Della Sala, S., & Spinnler, H. (1986). Dementia and working memory. *Quarterly Journal of Experimental Psychology, 38,* 603–618.

Baltes, M. M., Kuhl, K. P., Gutzmann, H., & Sowarka, D. (1995). Potential of cognitive plasticity as a diagnostic instrument: A cross-validation and extension. *Psychology and Aging, 10*, 167–172.

Baltes, M. M., Kuhl, K. P., & Sowarka, D. (1992). Testing for limits of cognitive reserve capacity: A promising strategy for early diagnosis of dementia? *Journal of Gerontology: Psychological Sciences, 47*, 165–167.

Bird, M., & Luszcz, M. (1991). Encoding specificity, depth of processing, and cued recall in Alzheimer's disease. *Journal of Clinical and Experimental Neuropsychology, 13*, 508–520.

Bird, M., & Luszcz, M. (1993). Enhancing memory performance in Alzheimer's disease: Acquisition assistance and cue effectiveness. *Journal of Clinical and Experimental Neuropsychology, 15*, 921–932.

Braak, H., & Braak, E. (1991), Neuropathological staging of Alzheimer-related changes. *Acta Neuropathologica, 82*, 239–259.

Braak, H., & Braak, E. (1995). Staging of Alzheimer's disease–related neurofibrillary tangles. *Neurobiology of Aging, 16*, 271–284.

Braak, E., Braak, H., & Mandelkow, E. M. (1993). Cytoskeletal alterations demonstrated by the antibody AT8: Early signs for the formation of neurofibrillary tangles in man. *Society of Neuroscience Abstracts, 19*, 228.

Branconnier, R. J., Cole, J. O., Spera, K. F., & DeVitt, D. R. (1982). Recall and recognition as diagnostic indices of malignant memory loss in senile dementia: A Bayesian analysis. *Experimental Aging Research, 8*, 189–193.

Buckner, R. L., Petersen, S. E., Ojemann, J. G., Miezin, F. M., Squire, L. R., & Raichle, M. E. (1995). Functional anatomical studies of explicit and implicit memory retrieval tasks. *Journal of Neuroscience, 15*, 12–29.

Buckwalter, J. G., Sobel, E., Dunn, M. E., Diaz, M. M., & Henderson, V. W. (1993). Gender differences on a brief measure of cognitive functioning in Alzheimer's disease. *Archives of Neurology, 50*, 757–760.

Burns, A., Jacoby, R., & Levy, R. (1991). Progression of cognitive impairment in Alzheimer's disease. *Journal of the American Geriatrics Society, 39*, 39–45.

Cabeza, R., & Nyberg, L. (2000). Imaging cognition. II: An empirical review of 275 PET and fMRI studies. *Journal of Cognitive Neuroscience, 12*, 1–37.

Craik, F. I. M., & Jennings, J. M. (1992). Human memory. In F. I. M. Craik & T. A. Salthouse (Eds.), *The handbook of cognitive aging* (pp. 51–110). Hillsdale, N.J.: Erlbaum.

Deweer, B., Lehericy, S., Pillon, B., Baulac, M., Chiras, J., Marsault, C., et al. (1995). Memory disorders in probable Alzheimer's disease: The role of hippocampal atrophy as shown with MRI. *Journal of Neurology, Neurosurgery, and Psychiatry, 58*, 590–597.

Ebly, E. M., Wolf, P. A., D'Agostino, R. B., Cobb, J., & White, L. R. (1994). Prevalence and types of dementia in the very old: Results from the Canadian Study of Health and Aging. *Neurology, 44*, 1593–1600.

Elias, M. F., Beiser, A., Wolf, P. A., Au, R., White, R. F., & D'Agostino, R. B. (2000). The preclinical phase of Alzheimer's disease: A 22-year prospective study of the Framingham cohort. *Archives of Neurology*, *57*, 808–813.

Fichter, M. M., Meller, I., Schröppel, H., & Steinkirchner, R. (1995). Dementia and cognitive impairment in the oldest old in the community: Prevalence and comorbidity. *British Journal of Psychiatry*, *166*, 621–629.

Fleischman, D. A., & Gabrieli, J. D. E. (1998). Repetition priming in normal aging and Alzheimer's disease: A review of findings and theories. *Psychology and Aging*, *13*, 88–119.

Folstein, M. F., Folstein, S. E., & McHugh, P. R. (1975). "Mini-Mental State": A practical method for grading the cognitive state of patients for the clinician. *Journal of Psychiatric Research*, *12*, 189–198.

Fox, N. C., Warrington, E. K., Freeborough, P. A., Hartikainen, P., Kennedy, A. M., Stevens, J. M., & Rossor, M. N. (1996). Presymptomatic hippocampal atrophy in Alzheimer's disease. *Brain*, *119*, 2001–2007.

Fox, N. C., Warrington, E. K., Sieffer, A. L., Agnew, S. K., & Rossor, M. N. (1998). Presymptomatic cognitive deficits in individuals at risk of familial Alzheimer's disease: A longitudinal prospective study. *Brain*, *121*, 1631–1639.

Friedland, R. P., & Wilcock, G. K. (1999). Dementia. In J. G. Evans, T. F. Williams, B. L. Beattie, J.-P. Michel & G. K. Wilcock (Eds.), *Oxford textbook of geriatric medicine* (2nd ed., pp. 922–932). Oxford: Oxford University Press.

Fuld, P. A., Masur, D. M., Blau, A. D., Crystal, H. A., & Aronson, M. K. (1990). Object-memory evaluation for prospective detection of dementia in normal functioning elderly. *Journal of Clinical and Experimental Neuropsychology*, *12*, 520–528.

Gillund, G., & Shiffrin, R. M. (1984). A retrieval model for both recognition and recall. *Psychological Review*, *91*, 1–67.

Grady, C. L., McIntosh, A. R., Horwitz, B., Maisog, J. M., Ungerleider, L. G., Mentis, M. J., Pietrini, P., Schapiro, M. B., & Haxby, J. V. (1995). Age-related reductions in human recognition memory due to impaired encoding. *Science*, *269*, 218–221.

Grober, E., Lipton, R. B., Hall, C., & Crystal, H. (2000). Memory impairment on free and cued selective reminding predicts dementia. *Neurology*, *54*, 827–832.

Hall, K. S., Gao, S., Unverzagt, F. W., & Hendrie, H. C. (2000). Low education and childhood rural residence: Risk for Alzheimer's disease in African Americans. *Neurology*, *54*, 95–99.

Hansen, L. A., De Teresa, R., Davies, P., & Terry, R. D. (1988). Neocortical morphometry, lesion counts, and choline acetyltransferase levels in the age spectrum of Alzheimer's disease. *Neurology*, *38*, 48–54.

Herlitz, A., Adolfsson, R., Bäckman, L., & Nilsson, L.-G. (1991). Cue utilization following different forms of encoding in mildly, moderately, and severely demented patients with Alzheimer's disease. *Brain and Cognition*, *15*, 119–130.

Herlitz, A., Hill, R. D., Fratiglioni, L., & Bäckman, L. (1995). Episodic memory and visuospatial skill in detecting and staging dementia in a community-based sample of very old adults. *Journal of Gerontology: Medical Sciences, 50,* 107–113.

Herlitz, A., Lipinska, B., & Bäckman, L. (1992). Utilization of cognitive support for episodic remembering in Alzheimer's disease. In L. Bäckman (Ed.), *Memory functioning in dementia* (pp. 73–96). Amsterdam: North-Holland.

Herlitz, A., & Viitanen, M. (1991). Semantic organization and verbal episodic memory in patients with mild and moderate Alzheimer's disease. *Journal of Clinical and Experimental Neuropsychology, 13,* 559–574.

Heston, L. L., Mastri, A. R., Anderson, V. E., & White, J. (1981). Dementia of the Alzheimer type: Clinical genetics, natural history, and associated conditions. *Archives of General Psychiatry, 38,* 1085–1090.

Hill, R. D., Bäckman, L., Wahlin, Å., & Winblad, B. (1995). Visuospatial performance in very old demented persons: An individual difference analysis. *Dementia, 6,* 49–54.

Hintzman, D. L. (1988). Judgments of frequency and recognition memory in a multiple-trace memory model. *Psychological Review, 95,* 528–551.

Hodges, J. R. (1998). The amnestic prodrome of Alzheimer's disease. *Brain, 121,* 1601–1602.

Hodges, J. R., Salmon, D. P., & Butters, N. (1992). Semantic memory impairment in Alzheimer's disease: Failure of access or degraded knowledge. *Neuropsychologia, 30,* 301–314.

Howieson, D. B., Dame, A., Camicioli, R., Sexton, G., Payami, H., & Kaye, J. A. (1997). Cognitive markers preceding Alzheimer's dementia in the healthy oldest old. *Journal of the American Geriatrics Society, 45,* 584–589.

Hultsch, D. F., Hertzog, C., Dixon, R. A., & Small, B. J. (1998). *Memory change in the aged.* Cambridge: Cambridge University Press.

Hultsch, D. F., Hertzog, C., Small, B. J., McDonald-Miszczak, L., & Dixon, R. A. (1992). Short-term longitudinal change in cognitive performance in later life. *Psychology and Aging, 7,* 571–584.

Jacobs, D. M., Sano, M., Dooneif, G., Marder, K., Bell, K. L., & Stern, Y. (1995). Neuropsychological detection and characterization of preclinical Alzheimer's disease. *Neurology, 25,* 317–324.

Jacoby, L. L. (1991). A process dissociation framework: Separating automatic from intentional uses of memory. *Journal of Memory and Language, 30,* 513–541.

Jacoby, L. L., Toth, J. P., & Yonelinas, A. P. (1993). Separating conscious and unconscious influences on memory: Measuring recollection. *Journal of Experimental Psychology: General, 122,* 139–154.

Katzman, R., Brown, T., Thal, L. J., Fuld, P., Aronson, M., Butters, N., Klauber, M. R., Wiederholt, W., Pay, M., Renbing, X., Ooi, W. L., Hofstetter, R., &

Terry, R. D. (1983). Comparison of annual change of mental status scores in four independent studies of patients with Alzheimer's disease. *Annals of Neurology, 24*, 384–389.

Killiany, R. J., Moss, M. B., Albert, M. S., Sandor, T., Tieman, J., & Jolesz, F. (1993). Temporal lobe regions on magnetic resonance imaging identify patients with early Alzheimer's disease. *Archives of Neurology, 50*, 949–954.

Laakso, M. P., Soininen, H., Partanen, K., Lehtovirta, M., Hallikainen, M., Haenninen, T., Helkala, E.-L., Vainio, P., & Riekkinen, P. J., Sr. (1997). MRI of the hippocampus in Alzheimer's disease: Sensitivity, specificity, and analysis of the incorrectly classified subjects. *Neurobiology of Aging, 19*, 23–31.

La Rue, A., & Jarvik, L. F. (1987). Cognitive function and prediction of dementia in old age. *International Journal of Aging and Human Development, 25*, 75–89.

Lehericy, S., Baulac, M., Chiras, J., Pierot, L., Martin, N., Pillon, B., Deweer, B., Dubois, B., & Marsault, C. (1994). Amygdalohippocampal MR volume measurements in the early stages of Alzheimer's disease. *American Journal of Neuroradiology, 15*, 927–937.

Linn, R. T., Wolf, P. A., Bachman, D. L., Knoefel, J. E., Cobb, J. L., Belanger, A. J., Kaplan, E. F., & D'Agostino, R. B. (1995). The "preclinical phase" of probable Alzheimer's disease. *Archives of Neurology, 52*, 485–490.

Lipinska, B., & Bäckman, L. (1997). Encoding-retrieval interactions in mild Alzheimer's disease: The role of access to categorical information. *Brain and Cognition, 34*, 274–286.

Lipinska, B., Bäckman, L., & Herlitz, A. (1992). When Greta Garbo is easier to remember than Stefan Edberg: Influences of prior knowledge on recognition memory in Alzheimer's disease. *Psychology and Aging, 7*, 214–220.

Mann, D. M. A. (1994). Pathological correlates of dementia in Alzheimer's disease. *Neurobiology of Aging, 15*, 357–360.

Masur, D. M., Sliwinski, M., Lipton, R. B., Blau, A. D., & Crystal, H. A. (1994). Neuropsychological prediction of dementia and the absence of dementia in healthy elderly persons. *Neurology, 44*, 1427–1432.

Meiran, N., & Jelicic, M. (1995). Implicit memory in Alzheimer's disease: A meta-analysis. *Neuropsychology, 9*, 291–303.

Moceri, V. M., Kukull, W. A., Emanuel, I., van Belle, G., & Larson, E. B. (2000). Early-life risk factors and the development of Alzheimer's disease. *Neurology, 54*, 415–420.

Morris, R. G. (1986). Short-term forgetting in senile dementia of the Alzheimer's type. *Cognitive Neuropsychology, 3*, 77–97.

Morris, R. G. (Ed.). (1996). *The cognitive neuropsychology of Alzheimer's disease*. Oxford: Oxford University Press.

Nebes, R. D. (1992). Cognitive dysfunctions in Alzheimer's disease. In F. I. M. Craik & T. A. Salthouse (Eds.), *Handbook of aging and cognition* (pp. 373–446). Hillsdale, N.J.: Erlbaum.

Nyberg, L., McIntosh, A. R., Houle, S., Nilsson, L.-G., & Tulving, E. (1996). Activation of medial temporal structures during episodic memory retrieval. *Nature, 380,* 715–717.

Rubin, E. H., Storandt, M., Miller, J. P., Grant, E. A., Kinscherf, D. A., Morris, J. C., & Berg, L. (1993). Influence of age on clinical and psychometric assessment of subjects with very mild or mild dementia of the Alzheimer type. *Archives of Neurology, 50,* 380–383.

Rubin, E. H., Storandt, M., Miller, J. P., Kinscherf, D. A., Grant, E. A., Morris, J. C., & Berg, L. (1998). A prospective study of cognitive function and onset of dementia in cognitively healthy elders. *Archives of Neurology, 55,* 395–401.

Simon, E., Leach, L., Winocur, G., & Moscovitch, M. (1995). Intact primary memory in mild to moderate Alzheimer's disease: Indices from the California Verbal Learning Test. *Journal of Clinical and Experimental Neuropsychology, 16,* 414–422.

Small, B. J., & Bäckman, L. (1998). Predictors of longitudinal changes in memory, visuospatial, and verbal performance in very old demented adults. *Dementia, 9,* 258–266.

Small, B. J., Fratiglioni, L., Viitanen, M., Winblad, B., & Bäckman, L. (2000). The course of cognitive impairment in preclinical Alzheimer's disease: 3- and 6-year follow-up of a population-based sample. *Archives of Neurology, 57,* 839–844.

Small, B. J., Herlitz, A., & Bäckman, L. (1998). Cognitive development in Alzheimer's disease: Charting the decline process. In B. Edelstein (Ed.), *Comprehensive clinical psychology: Clinical geropsychology* (vol. 7, pp. 231–245). Oxford: Elsevier.

Small, B. J., Herlitz, A., Fratiglioni, L., Almkvist, O., & Bäckman, L. (1997). Cognitive predictors of incident Alzheimer's disease: A prospective longitudinal study. *Neuropsychology, 11,* 413–420.

Small, B. J., Viitanen, M., & Bäckman, L. (1997). Mini-Mental State Examination item scores as predictors of Alzheimer's disease: Incidence data from the Kungsholmen project, Stockholm. *Journal of Gerontology: Medical Sciences, 52,* 299–304.

Small, B. J., Viitanen, M., Winblad, B., & Bäckman, L. (1997). Cognitive changes in very old demented persons: The influence of demographic, biological, and psychometric variables. *Journal of Clinical and Experimental Neuropsychology, 19,* 245–260.

Snowdon, D. A., Kemper, S. J., Mortimer, J. A., Greiner, L. H., Wekstein, D. R., & Markesbery, W. R. (1996). Linguistic ability in early life and cognitive function and Alzheimer's disease in late life. *Journal of the American Medical Association, 275,* 528–532.

Spinnler, H., Della Sala, S., Bandera, R., & Baddeley, A. D. (1988). Dementia, aging, and the structure of human memory. *Cognitive Neuropsychology, 5,* 193–211.

Squire, L. R. (1992). Memory and the hippocampus: A synthesis from findings with rats, monkeys, and humans. *Psychological Review, 99*, 195–231.

Storandt, M., & Hill, R. D. (1989). Very mild senile dementia of the Alzheimer type. II: Psychometric test performance. *Archives of Neurology, 46*, 383–386.

Teri, L., Hughes, J. P., & Larson, E. B. (1990). Cognitive deterioration in Alzheimer's disease: Behavioral and health factors. *Journal of Gerontology: Psychological Sciences, 45*, 58–63.

Teri, L., McCurry, S. M., Edland, S. D., Kukull, W. A., & Larson, E. B. (1995). Cognitive decline in Alzheimer's disease: A longitudinal investigation of risk factors for accelerated decline. *Journal of Gerontology: Medical Sciences, 50*, 49–55.

Tierney, M. C., Szalai, J. P., Snow, W. G., Fisher, R. H., Nores, A., Nadon, G., Dunn, E., & St. George-Hyslop, P. H. (1996). Prediction of probable Alzheimer's disease in memory-impaired patients: A prospective longitudinal study. *Neurology, 46*, 661–665.

Tulving, E. (1983). *Elements of episodic memory.* Oxford: Oxford University Press.

Van Hoesen, G. W., Augustinack, J. C., & Redman, S. J. (1999). Ventromedial temporal lobe pathology in dementia, brain trauma, and schizophrenia. *Annals of the New York Academy of Sciences, 877*, 575–594.

Vargha-Khadem, F., Gadian, D. G., Watkins, K. E., Connelly, A., Van Paesschen, W., & Mishkin, M. (1997). Differential effects of early hippocampal lesions on episodic and semantic memory. *Science, 277*, 376–380.

Welsh, K. A., Butters, N., Hughes, J. P., Mohs, R. C., & Heyman, A. (1992). Detection and staging of dementia in Alzheimer's disease: Use of the neuropsychological measures developed for the Consortium to Establish a Registry for Alzheimer's Disease. *Archives of Neurology, 49*, 448–452.

West, M. J., Coleman, P. D., Flood, D. G., & Troncoso, J. C. (1994). Differences in the pattern of hippocampal neuronal loss in normal aging and Alzheimer's disease. *Lancet, 344*, 769–772.

Wilson, R. S., Gilley, D. W., Bennett, D. A., Beckett, L. A., & Evans, D. A. (2000). Person-specific paths of cognitive decline in Alzheimer's disease and their relation to age. *Psychology and Aging, 15*, 18–28.

Yoshitake, T., Kiyohara, Y., Kato, I., Ohmura, T., Iwamoto, H., Nakayama, K., Ohmori, S., Nomiyama, K., Kawano, H., Ueda, K., et al. (1995). Incidence and risk factors of vascular dementia and Alzheimer's disease in a defined elderly Japanese population: The Hisayama study. *Neurology, 45*, 1161–1168.

Zelinski, E. M., & Burnight, K. P. (1997). Sixteen-year longitudinal and time-lag changes in memory and cognition in older adults. *Psychology and Aging, 12*, 503–513.

V

The Adulthood Development of Prospective Memory

12

Prospective Memory across the Lifespan

Elizabeth A. Maylor, Richard J. Darby, Robert H. Logie, Sergio Della Sala, and Geoff Smith

The past few years have seen an increasing interest in prospective memory, or ProM (see Brandimonte, Einstein & McDaniel, 1996), which can be defined as remembering at some point in the future that something has to be done, without any prompting in the form of explicit instructions to recall. This contrasts with retrospective memory (RetM), which refers to remembering information from the past. It should be noted at the outset that all ProM tasks have a RetM component, so a pure ProM task probably does not exist. For example, if the task is to remember to give a message to someone when you next see him, you may fail because you forget the content of the message, which would be a RetM failure. In general, studies of ProM have deliberately attempted to make the RetM component as undemanding as possible to ensure that performance is more determined by ProM than by RetM (e.g., Maylor, 1998).

A ProM task can be divided into at least four phases (see Ellis, 1996): (1) the formation or encoding of an intention, (2) the retention interval, (3) the execution of an intention, and (4) the evaluation of the outcome. In this chapter, we will present experiments that were designed particularly to examine the second, third, and fourth of these phases.

It is clear that living independently in the community requires the successful functioning of both ProM and RetM. There has been a vast literature concerned with RetM and with its development in childhood (e.g., Schneider & Pressley, 1997) and its decline in old age (e.g., Hultsch, Hertzog, Dixon & Small, 1998) and dementia (e.g., Morris, 1996). But only recently have researchers turned their attention to investigating ProM across the lifespan, and most of this work has been concerned with normal aging (see Maylor, 1993b, 1996b, for reviews).

A Theoretical Framework

In 1986 Craik proposed what has become an influential framework for understanding age differences in memory tasks. Performance is determined by an interaction between two factors: (1) external factors such as cues and context (or more generally, environmental support), and (2) the type of mental operation required. The claim is that self-initiated mental activities (such as retrieval) become more difficult with increasing age. However, age-related deficits are reduced in situations in which environmental support is high. In the resulting hierarchy of memory tasks, "remembering to remember" (now ProM) is at the top of the hierarchy as having low environmental support, requiring a high degree of self-initiated activity, and consequently being the most impaired by old age. Next in the hierarchy come more traditional tests of RetM (free recall, cued recall, then recognition) usually involving the presentation of information that the subject is later asked to recall or recognize in response to some prompt from the experimenter. Finally, at the bottom of the hierarchy, priming involves the greatest environmental support, requires the least self-initiated activity, and is therefore least impaired by age.

Craik's (1986) hierarchy was largely drawn up on an intuitive basis: at the time, there was very little evidence on aging and ProM. But the clear prediction was that age-related memory impairments should be greater in ProM tasks than in RetM tasks. This is because prospective remembering, by definition, places a heavy demand on self-initiated retrieval processes in the absence of any prompt or cue from the environment. In fact, two more recent claims have been made about ProM, the first claim being less consistent with Craik's predictions than the second. The first, made by Einstein and McDaniel (1990), is that ProM is unusually spared in normal aging, that is, ProM appears to be an exception to typically found age-related decrements in memory. The second claim, by Huppert and Beardsall (1993), is that ProM tasks are particularly sensitive to the early stages of dementia, in other words, that ProM is disproportionately impaired in abnormal aging. If these two claims are confirmed, then they would obviously have enormous implications, particularly with regard to the diagnosis of dementia, but also for the debate on whether there is continuity or discontinuity between normal aging and dementia.

ProM and Normal Aging

What is the evidence from studies of ProM and normal aging? First, if we consider so-called naturalistic studies in which volunteers are asked to make a series of telephone calls or mail postcards from home, the results seem to show preserved ProM (see Maylor, 1993b, 1996b, for summaries), contrary to Craik's (1986) predictions. Many older people can perform at least as well as younger people in such ProM tasks, but they may achieve their success by using efficient cues (see, e.g., Maylor, 1990). These may be suitable for tasks such as important occasional appointments. However, many everyday ProM tasks probably have to be tackled without the use of alarm clocks, calendars, and so on, for obvious practical reasons. Thus, the finding that older people do not perform so well if they do not use cues (Maylor, 1990) may be quite important.

At least one problem with naturalistic studies is that there is little control over the other activities that volunteers have to carry out. We therefore have to turn to laboratory-controlled experiments to determine whether or not ProM is affected by normal aging. Einstein and McDaniel (1990) introduced a novel paradigm for investigating ProM in the laboratory. Participants were presented with lists of words that they had to recall (a short-term RetM task). Some time before the task began, they were instructed to press a key whenever a specified word appeared in the list (ProM target event). No significant difference was found between the performance of young and older adults in terms of the number of responses to the ProM target events. This was obviously a very surprising result with important implications for both the aging and memory literatures, and it led Crowder to suggest, "Here was a form of memory that seemed to obey different laws" (1996, p. 145). In other words, the result provided important evidence for a dissociation between RetM and ProM because old age significantly affected one but not the other.

Einstein et al. (1995) have since replicated the result and also have extended it by examining age differences in both event- and time-based ProM tasks (e.g., taking medicine after every meal versus every four hours, respectively). The event-based ProM task was as before, namely, to press a key whenever a particular word was presented. In the time-based

ProM task, participants were required to press a key every ten minutes. The clock was not visible while performing the background task; participants were required either to turn around to see the clock or to press a function key to reveal a clock on the screen. The results again revealed no age-related impairment in the event-based ProM task, but there was an age deficit in the time-based ProM task (see also Park et al., 1997). Einstein and collaborators interpreted these findings within Craik's (1986) framework by suggesting that age-related impairment is not apparent in the event-based task because the target event itself provided a strong external cue to support performance; self-initiated retrieval was therefore unnecessary. In contrast, in the time-based task, participants had to take active steps to monitor the clock; environmental support was low and self-initiated retrieval was high.

However, this cannot be the whole story because other studies in the literature have found age-related decrements in event-based ProM performance (e.g., Cherry & LeCompte, 1999; Einstein, Smith, McDaniel & Shaw, 1997; Kidder, Park, Hertzog & Morrell, 1997; Mäntylä, 1994; Maylor, 1993a, 1996a, 1998; West & Craik, 1999). For example, Maylor (1998) asked participants to name 120 famous people (RetM background task) and also to circle the trial number if the person was wearing glasses (event-based ProM task; $n = 8$ targets). There were three groups of participants: young, middle-aged, and old, with mean ages of 20, 59, and 76 years, respectively. As expected from studies of aging and proper-name retrieval (e.g., Maylor, 1997), the young and middle-aged were significantly more successful at naming the famous people than the old (53%, 54%, and 32% correct, respectively). ProM performance declined significantly from the young (77%) to the middle-aged (62%) to the old (26%). Note that when participants were questioned carefully at the end of the experiment, almost all of them were able to repeat the task instructions correctly. In other words, they all knew (and remembered) what they were required to do, but they simply forgot to do it at the appropriate time.

How, then, can we account for these different patterns of results? There may be several possibilities or issues that need to be addressed, but there is space here to mention only two. The first issue is that of the difficulty of the background task. Einstein and McDaniel (1990) deliberately reduced the cognitive demands of the background task for their older participants by presenting them with shorter word lists to remember (see also Cherry & LeCompte, 1999). In contrast, Maylor (1993a, 1996a, 1998) used a background task of naming that is known to be particularly difficult in old age (see Maylor, 1997). This raises the question of the relationship between the ProM task and the background task in which it is embedded (see Maylor, 1998). Second, perhaps another difference between studies could be crucial in accounting for mixed results, namely, that procedures vary in terms of the relationship between stimulus processing required to perform the background task and stimulus processing required to perform the ProM task. This has been termed the task-appropriate processing hypothesis (Maylor, 1996a). Thus, in Einstein and McDaniel's study, the background and ProM tasks required the same type or level of stimulus processing in order both to remember the word for the short-term memory task and to recognize it as the ProM target. In contrast, in Maylor's studies (see also Mäntylä, 1994), a shift was required in the level of stimulus analysis from the background naming task (the "semantic" level) to the ProM task (the "structural" level) in order both to name the person and to recognize the photograph as the ProM target (identified by a physical feature). Thus, Einstein and McDaniel may have failed to observe age differences, not because their ProM task was event-based (note that all of the tasks just described were event-based), but because there was considerable overlap between the stimulus processing necessary (although not sufficient) to perform each task.

A Test of the Task-Appropriate Processing Hypothesis

We designed an experiment to test these possibilities (Darby & Maylor, 1998). On each trial, participants were presented with a target word followed by six alternative responses (e.g., UNCTUOUS: anxious, ingratiating, undertone, unaware, maroon, uncover). The background task was either semantic (write down the word closest in meaning to the target word) or structural (write down the word that follows the target word in alphabetical order). The ProM task was similarly either semantic (circle the trial number if the name of a color appears) or structural (circle the trial number if a word with a double letter appears). Each participant was assigned to one of four conditions according to the combination of background tasks and ProM tasks: (1) semantic-semantic, (2) semantic-structural, (3) structural-semantic, and (4) structural-structural. There were two main questions of interest. First, we expected older participants to find the semantic background task easier than would the younger participants because of their superior crystallized intelligence (e.g., Schaie, 1996). This would allow a comparison between ProM performance across age groups in the context of a background task on which older participants were not impaired. Second, on the basis of the task-appropriate processing hypothesis, we predicted that age differences in ProM would be greater in conditions 2 and 3 (where a shift in the level of stimulus analysis was required to perform both the background and ProM tasks) than in conditions 1 and 4 (where no shift was required). There were 65 trials (10 seconds per trial). ProM targets appeared on trials 28 (maroon), 45 (green), and 62 (yellow).

There were two groups of participants. Younger participants ($n = 79$) were aged between 18 and 24 years (mean age = 19) and were psychology undergraduates whose participation in the study was a course requirement. Older participants ($n = 76$) were aged between 63 and 84 years (mean age = 72) and were selected from a panel of community-dwelling volunteers aged over 50.

The results for the background task are shown in figure 1, top graph, for each of the four background-ProM task conditions. It can be seen that the older participants performed considerably better than the younger participants in identifying synonyms (semantic background task, conditions 1 and 2), whereas the younger participants performed slightly better than the older participants in selecting the next word in alphabetical order (structural background task, conditions 3 and 4). There appeared to be little influence of the nature of the ProM task on background-task performance in either age group. An analysis of variance (ANOVA) was conducted on these background task data with age group (younger versus older), background task (semantic versus structural), and ProM task (semantic versus structural) as between-participant variables. There were significant effects of age group ($F(1, 147) = 5.42$, $p < .05$) and background task ($F(1, 147) = 141.40$, $p < .0001$). The in-

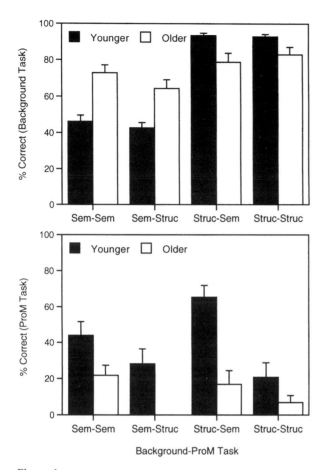

Figure 1
Data from a study by Darby and Maylor (1998). The four conditions represent the combination of background task (semantic or structural) and ProM task (semantic or structural). (a) Background task performance. In the *Sem*-Sem and *Sem*-Struc conditions, the background task was to select the word closest in meaning to the target word, whereas in the *Struc*-Sem and *Struc*-Struc conditions, the background task was to select the word that followed the target word in alphabetical order. (b) ProM task performance. In the Sem-*Sem* and Struc-*Sem* conditions, the ProM task was to respond to colors, whereas in the Sem-*Struc* and Struc-*Struc* conditions, the ProM task was to respond to words with double letters. ProM targets = maroon, green, and yellow in both tasks. Error bars represent 1 SE.

teraction between age group and background task was also significant ($F(1, 147) = 51.12$, $p < .0001$). There were no other significant effects (all remaining p values > .10). In summary, we succeeded in our aim of selecting background tasks that differed in their relative difficulty across age groups, thereby providing an interesting case for the comparison of age differences in ProM performance.

Figure 1, bottom graph, shows the results for the ProM task for each of the four background-ProM task conditions. It is clear that, regardless of the background task, the younger participants were more successful in responding to the ProM targets than the older participants. ProM performance was higher for the semantic task (color targets) than for the structural task (double-letter targets), despite the fact that the ProM targets were physically identical in the two tasks. More important and consistent with our predictions, the age difference in ProM appeared to be greater when a shift was required between the levels of stimulus analysis required by the background and ProM tasks (conditions 2 and 3) than when no shift was required (conditions 1 and 4). These effects were confirmed by an ANOVA with the same variables as before. There were significant effects of age group ($F(1, 147) = 37.55$, $p < .0001$) and ProM task ($F(1, 147) = 24.82$, $p < .0001$). The only other significant effect was the crucial three-way interaction between age group, background task, and ProM task ($F(1, 147) = 4.79$, $p < .05$). Thus, the age difference in ProM was 38% when a shift was required but only 18% when no shift was required.

To determine the extent to which the effects of age on ProM could be attributable to RetM failures in the older participants, the ProM data were reanalyzed after having excluded participants who were unable to select the correct ProM-task instructions in a recognition test at the end of the experiment. This led to the loss of 1 younger participant and 8 older participants. The ANOVA on ProM performance was very similar to before, except that the three-way interaction was now only marginally significant ($F(1, 138) = 3.75$, $p = .055$), with mean age differences in the shift and no-shift conditions of 36% and 17%, respectively.

To conclude, it is clear that ProM is not always spared in normal aging and that deficits can be observed even when (1) the background task is easier for older participants and (2) failures of RetM in retaining the task instructions are taken into account. In addition, there is evidence to support the task-appropriate processing hypothesis (Maylor, 1996a): age deficits are greater when a shift is required between the type of stimulus processing required by the background task and that required by the ProM task. An interesting subject for future research is whether this task-shifting deficit is particularly related to the loss of frontal functioning in old age (see West, 1996, on the frontal hypothesis of aging and McDaniel et al., 1999, on its relationship to ProM). In summary, the results from these and other studies converge on the conclusion that age deficits do vary across different ProM tasks. As with RetM, age deficits appear to be greatest when task demands are high (task-shifting being perhaps just one example of how tasks differ). In terms of Craik's (1986) framework, it is probably not the case that all ProM tasks are low in environmental support and high in self-initiated activity.

ProM and Dementia

To return to our two original claims, if ProM is sometimes affected by normal aging, then this weakens the case for poor ProM as an early indicator of dementia. But what about the claim that ProM may be disproportionately impaired by abnormal aging? There are certainly some anecdotal reports that when people consult their doctors because they are worried about possible symptoms of dementia in one of their relatives, it is often ProM problems in particular that they complain about (e.g., McKitrick, Camp & Black, 1992). However, to date, there have been very few experimental studies of ProM in dementia. One potential problem was briefly mentioned earlier, namely, that it is difficult to separate prospective failures from retrospective failures. So in a ProM task, you have to remember that something has to be done (ProM component), but also what has to be done, and when and where (RetM component). Usually, retention of the RetM component is nearly perfect in studies with normal participants, since the content is deliberately kept as simple as possible (such as marking the trial number if someone is wearing glasses). Unfortunately, remembering the task requirements may not be such a trivial task for patient populations. People with dementia may therefore perform poorly in a ProM task, not necessarily because of impaired ProM, but because of impaired RetM (see Maylor, 1995, for further discussion).

In a project based at the University of Aberdeen, we have taken two approaches to the study of ProM in dementia. The first was a questionnaire study to obtain reports on the frequency of ProM and RetM failures and associated frustration from patients with Alzheimer's disease (AD), from their carers, and from both younger and older controls (Smith, Della Sala, Logie & Maylor, 2000). Contrary to the anecdotal evidence, ProM failures were no more frequent than RetM failures in AD patients (from carers' ratings), although AD patients were rated near the ceiling for both, so this absence of a difference may be difficult to interpret. Significantly more ProM than RetM failures were reported in the remaining groups, and this effect was identical for younger and older controls. Patients' ProM and RetM failures were reported by carers as being equally frustrating to AD patients, whereas ProM failures of AD patients were reported as more frustrating for carers than their RetM failures. Thus, although ProM failures were rated as no more frequent than RetM failures in AD patients (i.e., both generally occurred very often), they may have greater impact on the lives of carers in terms of the resulting levels of frustration and therefore may be more likely to be reported as early indicants of the disease.

Our second approach to the study of ProM in dementia was to conduct laboratory-controlled experiments to compare ProM and RetM performance of AD patients with that of age-matched controls and young controls (Maylor, Smith, Della Sala & Logie, submitted). To illustrate with one example, the background task was to view a 17-minute film of scenes in and around Aberdeen. Participants were advised to watch the film carefully because there would be a recognition-memory test at the end of the film. Each participant was assigned to one of two ProM conditions. In the event-based condition, participants were asked to say "animal" whenever they saw an animal in the film. A cow, a horse, a dog, a pig, and a sheep appeared on the screen for 3 seconds at approximately 3, 6, 9, 12, and 15 minutes. In the time-based condition, participants were asked to stop a clock every three minutes throughout the film by pressing the space bar of a computer keyboard (which reset the clock to zero). A large clockface was displayed on a computer screen placed to the right of participants so that they were required to turn their heads to check the time.

There were three groups of participants: young, old, and AD patients. The AD patients were closely matched in age to the old participants. Several measures of RetM were obtained, including digit span, sentence span, and free recall. In addition, the recognition-memory test at the end of the film, in which 12 scenes from the film were presented together with 12 new scenes for old/new judgments, provided a further measure of RetM. The young and old groups did not differ significantly in terms of digit span, sentence span, and recognition. However, the young group achieved higher scores on the free-recall test than the old group. As expected, the AD patients performed significantly worse than the old group on all four measures of RetM.

Before summarizing the results for the ProM tasks, it is important to note that all participants were able to accurately recall the ProM instructions when questioned at the end of the experiment, although some AD patients required occasional prompting. In other words, ProM failures cannot be attributed to RetM failures in retaining the task instructions. ProM performance was scored as follows. For the event-based task, a response within 4 seconds of the animal's onset was counted as a ProM success. For the time-based task, stopping the clock between 2 seconds before and 2 seconds after the clock reached 3 minutes was counted as a ProM success. Young participants were significantly more successful than old participants, who themselves significantly outperformed the AD patients. Although the age decline between young and old was greater in the time-based task than in the event-based task (see Einstein et al., 1995; Park et al., 1997), this comparison was compromised by ceiling effects for the young group on this particular measure of performance. Comparing the old group with the AD patients, we found that the deficit was very similar across the two tasks. It might have been expected that the task more adversely affected by normal aging (i.e., time-based) would also be more adversely affected by abnormal aging. However, it should be acknowledged that larger age deficits in time-based tasks than event-based tasks are not always found (see, for example, d'Ydewalle, Luwel & Brunfaut, 1999), and that both event-based and time-based ProM tasks can probably vary (e.g., in terms of the degree of self-initiated activity required), with the result that some event-based tasks can be more demanding than some time-based tasks.

Perhaps of more interest here are the effects of normal and abnormal aging on ProM versus RetM. First, for normal aging (young versus old), this experiment revealed significant ProM deficits on both event-based and time-based tasks, along with significant declines in free recall, but no decline in measures of span or recognition. Thus, we again have evidence that ProM is not unusually spared in normal aging. Second, for abnormal aging (old versus AD patients), there were significant deficits for both event-based and time-based ProM tasks, but also for measures of RetM. To compare the effects of dementia on ProM and RetM directly, we calculated standardized scores for the AD patients and their age-matched controls. The differences between the two groups were very similar across the five memory measures, with no evidence of greater impairment for ProM than for RetM.

The conclusion from our experimental work on ProM and dementia is that there is no evidence that ProM is particularly impaired by AD in comparison with RetM. This would appear to conflict with Huppert and Beardsall's (1993) conclusion that ProM tasks are particularly sensitive to the early stages of dementia. However, it should be noted that the AD patients of Maylor et al. (submitted) were not necessarily in the early stages of dementia. It therefore remains possible that ProM failures may be earlier indicators of dementia than RetM failures, as argued by Huppert and Beardsall, because ProM tasks may require the use of more brain areas than RetM tasks (see also Glisky, 1996).

The Retention Interval

Clock-checking and self-rated thoughts

Our discussion so far has largely concerned the third phase of ProM tasks (i.e., intention execution), where we have seen clear deficits due to both normal aging and dementia. We turn now to consider the second phase, namely, the retention interval. The question of interest here is what is the status of the intention to carry out the ProM task during the period when the task cannot be carried out? And are there age and dementia differences here too? We have investigated behavior during the retention interval in a number of ways. First, following others, we examined clock-checking behavior in time-based ProM tasks. For example, in the time-based condition of Maylor et al. (submitted), we recorded the number of times participants checked the clock during each 30-second period leading up to successful ProM responses and to unsuccessful ProM responses. For successful ProM responses, considerably more checks were made in the final 30-second period than in the previous periods, as expected. In addition, clock-checking differed significantly across the three groups: young participants checked the clock less often than the old participants, who in turn checked the clock less often than the AD patients. These results for normal aging would appear to be inconsistent with those of both Einstein et al. (1995) and Park et al. (1997), who observed less clock-checking in their older age groups than in their younger age groups. However, these previous studies did not distinguish between clock-checking prior to ProM success and clock-checking prior to ProM failure. Note that older adults are more likely than younger adults to forget the ProM task and therefore fail to check the clock. Our results suggest that successful ProM performance is preceded by different overt behaviors in both normal aging and dementia.

A second method of investigating the retention interval was adopted by Maylor (1998). Participants were asked at the end of an event-based ProM experiment to rate how often they had thought about the ProM component during the task. Regression analyses relating such self-rated thoughts to ProM performance showed that even when participants reported the same level of thoughts about the ProM task, the older participants were still less successful in responding to ProM targets. Alternatively, for the same level of ProM performance, older participants reported thinking more often about the ProM task than younger participants.

The intention-superiority effect

For obvious reasons, it is probably not sufficient to rely entirely on self-ratings obtained retrospectively. A more direct method of investigating the status of ProM tasks during the retention interval is provided by Goschke and Kuhl (1993). Students were asked to memorize descriptions of different activities, such as setting the dinner table or clearing a messy desk. They were then informed which of these scripts they were later to execute (rather than simply observe). In a subsequent speeded recognition test for the words in the instructions, participants responded more quickly to words from the to-be-executed script than to words from the to-be-observed script. Goschke and Kuhl's (1993) results from four experiments suggested that representations of intentions are characterized by a "heightened level of subthreshold activation in long-term memory" (p. 1211). They demonstrated that this "intention-superiority effect" was neither the result of selective encoding nor differential rehearsal but instead reflected the "intrinsic property of representations of intentions to decay more slowly than representations of nonintended activities" (p. 1223).

We have recently attempted to extend the intention-superiority effect in a number of ways (see Maylor, Darby & Della Sala, 2000). First, we were interested in whether the effect applied to participants' own intentions as opposed to experimenter-imposed intentions. Second, we wondered whether the effect would occur for long-term intentions, that is, tasks to be carried out hours or days, rather than minutes, in the future. Third, we were obviously interested in possible differences between age groups in the intention-superiority effect. We employed a speeded fluency task to compare the production of tasks that have to be carried out in the future with the production of tasks that have already been carried out in the past. Participants were asked to recall as many instances as possible from a specified category in four minutes. There were two categories, with order counterbalanced across participants: (1) jobs, appointments, or things the participant did last week (RetM), and (2) jobs, appointments, or things the participant intends to do next week (ProM). Participants were instructed to summarize each memory in one or two words.

Young participants recalled slightly more ProMs than RetMs, thereby demonstrating a long-term intention-superiority effect for participants' own intentions. This is a particularly striking result for at least two reasons. First, the memory representations of events that have taken place are surely richer (e.g., they contain more sensory detail) than those of events that have yet to take place. Second, we do not plan everything we do a week in advance; thus, there are potentially many more memories available from the past than from the future. Despite these two considerations, the young participants displayed an intention-superiority effect. In contrast, middle-aged participants recalled similar numbers of RetMs and ProMs, whereas both older participants and AD patients actually recalled fewer ProMs than RetMs (an intention-inferiority effect). This pattern of results suggests that there are age differences in the relative status of intentions during the retention interval of ProM tasks.

Marsh, Hicks and Bryan (1999) have recently shown that two effects may contribute to the intention-superiority effect: the facilitation of ProMs and the inhibition of RetMs. The intention-inferiority effect observed in our older adults and AD patients could therefore be due to reduced facilitation of ProMs, reduced inhibition of RetMs, or indeed both. It is not possible to decide between these alternatives from the present data. However, there is some support from other paradigms for reduced inhibitory processing in normal aging (e.g., McDowd, Oseas-Kreger & Filion, 1995).

Although a direct link between the intention-superiority effect and ProM performance remains to be established, it seems reasonable to assume that successful prospective remembering depends at least partly on the level of resting activation of the intended action. We suggest that since the representations of intentions in older adults and AD patients are less characterized by some form of privileged status in long-term memory than in young adults, this may at least contribute to observed deficits in prospective remembering in normal aging and dementia.

ProM and Development

Clearly, ProM declines with normal aging and dementia. But how does ProM develop at the other end of the lifespan? So far there have been almost as few studies of ProM in children as there are studies of ProM in dementia. The existing handful of studies have used very different methodologies and have produced inconsistent results. Some have found little or no ProM improvement (e.g., Somerville, Wellman & Cultice, 1983) and therefore have argued that ProM develops at a much earlier age than RetM. However, others have found significant improvement (e.g., Passolunghi, Brandimonte & Cornoldi, 1985), in some cases attributable to greater use of effective external cues (Beal, 1985). Here, we briefly present two of our own attempts to look at the development of ProM.

First, we were interested in the extent to which any improvement in ProM with increasing age was related to changes in RetM. Children ($n = 200$) were asked to name teachers from their photographs (background task) and to indicate if the teacher was wearing glasses or if there was a plant in the picture (ProM task). The RetM task was immediate free recall of ten everyday objects.

There were significant improvements from 6 to 11 years for both ProM and RetM, and these improvements were very similar in terms of standardized scores (-0.55 to $+0.72$ for ProM, and -0.97 to 0.65 for RetM, from 6–11 years). The ProM data were further analyzed in terms of successful responses to each ProM target (glasses versus plant). Improvement with increasing age was more striking for the plant than for the glasses: the younger children were much less successful in responding to the plant than to the glasses. This was despite the fact that the plant was visually more prominent in the photographs than the glasses (e.g., in terms of size). A possible explanation is that young children may have particular difficulty when the ProM target event is not within the focus of attention for the background task (i.e., identifying and naming the person in the photograph). This would be consistent with the task-appropriate processing hypothesis discussed earlier with respect to aging. In other words, young children may be less likely to switch attention on every trial from stimulus processing required to perform the background task to stimulus processing required to respond to the ProM target.

A second experiment was based on a recent study by Einstein, McDaniel, Smith, and Shaw (1998) designed as a laboratory analogue of a habitual ProM task, that is, where the same ProM task has to be done on a regular basis, like remembering to feed the goldfish once a day. In habitual ProM tasks, we are particularly interested in the fourth phase of the task, that of evaluating the outcome. One possibility is that young children might fail to perform the task (an omission error) because they mistake thinking about feeding the goldfish with actually feeding the goldfish (an output or reality-monitoring error). Or children might think that they have performed the task because they are mistakenly recalling their memory of feeding the goldfish yesterday (a temporal-discrimination error). A related problem with habitual ProM tasks is repetition errors. Thus, children might feed the goldfish twice because they forgot that they had already fed them, or they might remember that they fed the goldfish but attribute the memory to yesterday rather than to today.

We asked 90 children aged 5–11 years to play a game in which points were scored by maneuvering a steel ball around an obstacle course. Each game lasted 90 seconds, and children were asked to play the game 10 times. The ProM task was to turn a counter over once on each trial; however, they were not allowed to turn the counter over during the first 20 seconds. A timer moved from start to stop over the course of each game. During the first 20 seconds, the timer pointed to a red zone; from 20 to 90 seconds, the timer pointed to a green zone. Participants were instructed to turn the counter over only when the timer reached the green zone. After each trial, participants were asked if they had remembered to turn the counter over on that trial.

Omission errors in the ProM task (i.e., failing to turn the counter over) were most frequent in the youngest children. There were few repetition errors (i.e., turning the counter over more than once), with no significant effect of age. We were particularly interested in the two types of outcome-evaluation errors: (i) the number of times children claimed to have turned the counter over but in fact had not, conditionalized on ProM failures and (ii) the number of times they claimed not to have turned the counter over when in fact they had, conditionalized on ProM successes. For the first type of error, there was a significant increase with age. This can be explained as follows: Children may fail to perform the ProM task but may think that they have because they are mistakenly recalling their ProM response from a previous trial (a temporal-discrimination error). This is more likely to occur in older children because a previous trial is more likely to be a ProM success than it is for younger children. The second type of error is particularly interesting because it could lead eventually to repetition errors. Most of these errors occurred in the last few trials, consistent with Einstein et al.'s (1998) conclusion that as a ProM task becomes habitual, it is more difficult to remember whether or not the ProM task has been performed. This second error type significantly decreased with age. There are two possible interpretations of this result: First, if younger children are more prone to temporal-discrimination errors, they would be more likely to attribute their memory of performing the task on the current trial to the previous trial. Second, younger children may be more prone to output-monitoring failures; in other words, they may simply forget that they performed the task, perhaps because it has become automatic. Further empirical work is required to distinguish between these two possibilities (see Einstein et al., 1998).

Conclusions

ProM research is still in its infancy, particularly with respect to changes in ProM across the lifespan. Nevertheless, although there have been some mixed results, it is clear that ProM does develop in childhood and decline in old age, with further decline in dementia. Both in development and in normal aging, it seems that ProM is more affected when the attentional demands of the task are high. For example, age effects are greater when attention switching is required between background-task and ProM-task demands (the task-appropriate processing hypothesis; Maylor, 1996a).

There is currently no evidence that ProM is more affected by dementia than RetM, at least in moderately demented patients. Careful longitudinal research is still required to provide an appropriate test of Huppert and Beardsall's (1993) suggestion that ProM failures may be earlier indicators of dementia than RetM failures. Whether or not ProM failures turn out to be more prevalent than RetM failures in the early stages of dementia, it is clear that patients' ProM failures are more frustrating to carers than their RetM failures. This finding may provide an explanation for the anecdotal evidence that relatives of patients note problems with ProM in particular when initially consulting their doctors.

During the retention interval between the formation and execution of an intention, ProM tasks are less represented in long-term memory by a heightened level of activation (relative to RetM tasks) in old age and dementia than in young adults, which accounts for at least some of the deficits observed. However, the reason for this (e.g., reduced facilitation of ProMs, reduced inhibition of RetMs, or both) is not yet clear. When ProM is successful in old age and dementia, it is achieved by greater effort during the retention interval, for example, in terms of more checks on the clock in a time-based task or more thoughts about the task in an event-based task.

A final issue is whether there is anything special about ProM or whether we can simply predict ProM changes across the lifespan on the basis of what we know about RetM changes. Initial studies suggested that ProM was exceptionally spared in old age, but subsequent studies have shown age deficits in ProM performance that are largely consistent with Craik's (1986) framework. Thus, deficits are greater when self-initiated activity is high and environmental support is low, both for ProM and RetM (although care must be taken to avoid circularity here). It certainly seems that findings in the RetM literature can help in understanding ProM data. For example, the development of temporal memory may be able to account for some of the outcome-evaluation errors observed in the study of habitual ProM.

Acknowledgments

Much of the work reported in this chapter was funded by the Medical Research Council at the University of Warwick (grants G9606610N and G9608199), and by The Wellcome Trust at the University of Aberdeen (grant 047065). We are grateful to Teresa McCormack for useful discussion of this work and to the following research assistants and undergraduate students for their help with data collection: Fiona Anderson, Jane Coomber, Christian Hempsall, Victoria Holman, Piers Jones, Lucy Richardson, and Joanne Rodger.

References

Beal, C. R. (1985). The development of knowledge about the use of cues to aid prospective retrieval. *Child Development, 56,* 631–642.

Brandimonte, M., Einstein, G. O., & McDaniel, M. A. (Eds.) (1996). *Prospective memory: Theory and applications.* Mahwah, N.J.: Erlbaum.

Cherry, K. E., & LeCompte, D. C. (1999). Age and individual differences influence prospective memory. *Psychology and Aging, 14,* 60–76.

Craik, F. I. M. (1986). A functional account of age differences in memory. In F. Klix & H. Hagendorf (Eds.), *Human memory and cognitive capabilities: Mechanisms and performances* (pp. 409–422). Amsterdam: Elsevier.

Crowder, R. G. (1996). Commentary: The trouble with prospective memory: A provocation. In M. Brandimonte, G. O. Einstein & M. A. McDaniel (Eds.), *Prospective memory: Theory and applications* (pp. 143–147). Mahwah, N.J.: Erlbaum.

Darby, R. J., & Maylor, E. A. (1998). Effects of the relationship between background and prospective memory task requirements on age differences in prospective memory. Poster presented at the Seventh Cognitive Aging Conference, April, Atlanta, Georgia.

D'Ydewalle, G., Luwel, K., & Brunfaut, E. (1999). The importance of on-going concurrent activities as a function of age in time- and event-based prospective memory. *European Journal of Cognitive Psychology, 11,* 219–237.

Einstein, G. O., & McDaniel, M. A. (1990). Normal aging and prospective memory. *Journal of Experimental Psychology: Learning, Memory, and Cognition, 16,* 717–726.

Einstein, G. O., McDaniel, M. A., Richardson, S. L., Guynn, M. J., & Cunfer, A. R. (1995). Aging and prospective memory: Examining the influences of self-initiated retrieval processes. *Journal of Experimental Psychology: Learning, Memory, and Cognition, 21,* 996–1007.

Einstein, G. O., McDaniel, M. A., Smith, R. E., & Shaw, P. (1998). Habitual prospective memory and aging: Remembering intentions and forgetting actions. *Psychological Science, 9,* 284–288.

Einstein, G. O., Smith, R. E., McDaniel, M. A., & Shaw, P. (1997). Aging and prospective memory: The influence of increased task demands at encoding and retrieval. *Psychology and Aging, 12,* 479–488.

Ellis, J. (1996). Prospective memory or the realization of delayed intentions: A conceptual framework for research. In M. Brandimonte, G. O. Einstein & M. A. McDaniel (Eds.), *Prospective memory: Theory and applications* (pp. 1–22). Mahwah, N.J.: Erlbaum.

Glisky, E. L. (1996). Prospective memory and the frontal lobes. In M. Brandimonte, G. O. Einstein & M. A. McDaniel (Eds.), *Prospective memory: Theory and applications* (pp. 249–266). Mahwah, N.J.: Erlbaum.

Goschke, T., & Kuhl, J. (1993). Representation of intentions: Persisting activation in memory. *Journal of Experimental Psychology: Learning, Memory, and Cognition, 19,* 1211–1226.

Hultsch, D. F., Hertzog, C., Dixon, R. A., & Small, B. J. (1998). *Memory change in the aged.* Cambridge: Cambridge University Press.

Huppert, F. A., & Beardsall, L. (1993). Prospective memory impairment as an early indicator of dementia. *Journal of Clinical and Experimental Neuropsychology, 15,* 805–821.

Kidder, D. P., Park, D. C., Hertzog, C., & Morrell, R. (1997). Prospective memory and aging: The effects of working memory and prospective memory task load. *Aging, Neuropsychology, and Cognition, 4,* 93–112.

Mäntylä, T. (1994). Remembering to remember: Adult age differences in prospective memory. *Journal of Gerontology: Psychological Sciences, 49,* P276–P282.

Marsh, R. L., Hicks, J. L., & Bryan, E. S. (1999). The activation of unrelated and canceled intentions. *Memory & Cognition, 27,* 320–327.

Maylor, E. A. (1990). Age and prospective memory. *Quarterly Journal of Experimental Psychology, 42A,* 471–493.

Maylor, E. A. (1993a). Aging and forgetting in prospective and retrospective memory tasks. *Psychology and Aging, 3,* 420–428.

Maylor, E. A. (1993b). Minimized prospective memory loss in old age. In J. Cerella, J. Rybash, W. Hoyer & M. L. Commons (Eds.), *Adult information processing: Limits on loss* (pp. 529–551). San Diego: Academic.

Maylor, E. A. (1995). Prospective memory in normal ageing and dementia. *Neurocase, 1,* 285–289.

Maylor, E. A. (1996a). Age-related impairment in an event-based prospective memory task. *Psychology and Aging, 11,* 74–78.

Maylor, E. A. (1996b). Does prospective memory decline with age? In M. Brandimonte, G. O. Einstein & M. A. McDaniel (Eds.), *Prospective memory: Theory and applications* (pp. 173–197). Mahwah, N.J.: Erlbaum.

Maylor, E. A. (1997). Proper name retrieval in old age: Converging evidence against disproportionate impairment. *Aging, Neuropsychology, and Cognition, 4,* 211–226.

Maylor, E. A. (1998). Changes in event-based prospective memory across adulthood. *Aging, Neuropsychology, and Cognition, 5,* 107–128.

Maylor, E. A., Darby, R. J., & Della Sala, S. (2000). Retrieval of performed vs. to-be-performed tasks: A naturalistic study of the intention-superiority effect in normal aging and dementia. *Applied Cognitive Psychology, 14,* S83–S98.

Maylor, E. A., Smith, G., Della Sala, S., & Logie, R. H. (submitted). Prospective memory in normal aging and dementia: An experimental study. Manuscript submitted for publication.

McDaniel, M. A., Glisky, E. L., Rubin, S. R., Guynn, M. J., & Routhieaux, B. C. (1999). Prospective memory: A neuropsychological study. *Neuropsychology, 13,* 103–110.

McDowd, J. M., Oseas-Kreger, D. M., & Filion, D. L. (1995). Inhibitory processes in cognition and aging. In F. N. Dempster & C. J. Brainerd (Eds.), *Interference and inhibition in cognition* (pp. 363–400). San Diego: Academic Press.

McKitrick, L. A., Camp, C. J., & Black, F. W. (1992). Prospective memory intervention in Alzheimer's disease. *Journal of Gerontology: Psychological Sciences, 47,* 337–343.

Morris, R. G. (1996). *The cognitive neuropsychology of Alzheimer-type dementia.* Oxford: Oxford University Press.

Park, D. C., Hertzog, C., Kidder, D. P., Morrell, R. W., & Mayhorn, C. B. (1997). Effect of age on event-based and time-based prospective memory. *Psychology and Aging, 12,* 314–327.

Passolunghi, M. C., Brandimonte, M. A., & Cornoldi, C. (1995). Encoding modality and prospective memory in children. *International Journal of Behavioral Development, 18,* 631–648.

Schaie, K. W. (1996). *Intellectual development in adulthood: The Seattle longitudinal study*. Cambridge: Cambridge University Press.

Schneider, W., & Pressley, M. (1997). *Memory development between two and twenty*. 2nd Edition. Mahwah, N.J.: Erlbaum.

Smith, G., Della Sala, S., Logie, R. H., & Maylor, E. A. (2000). Prospective and retrospective memory in normal aging and dementia: A questionnaire study. *Memory, 8*, 311–321.

Somerville, S. C., Wellman, H. M., & Cultice, J. C. (1983). Young children's deliberate reminding. *Journal of Genetic Psychology, 143*, 87–96.

West, R. L. (1996). An application of prefrontal cortex function theory to cognitive aging. *Psychological Bulletin, 120*, 272–292.

West, R., & Craik, F. I. M. (1999). Age-related decline in prospective memory: The roles of cue accessibility and cue sensitivity. *Psychology and Aging, 14*, 264–272.

13

Prospective and Retrospective Memory in Adulthood

Peter Graf, Bob Uttl, and Roger Dixon

Prospective memory (ProM) is a distinctive aspect of memory that forms the logical, natural complement of retrospective memory (RetM). ProM is required for carrying out planned activities, such as removing the pot before it boils over, getting groceries en route from work to home, and taking medication nightly at bedtime. However, despite the fact that it is intimately involved in many everyday activities and the fact that its breakdown seems as debilitating as impairments in RetM, ProM has received little attention by mainstream memory researchers, and the topic is frequently not even mentioned in introductory cognitive-psychology texts. We believe that this neglect of ProM has several causes, prominent among them are the absence in the literature of clear definitions of memory's prospective function and the lack of convincing empirical support for the claim that ProM is a distinct form of memory.

With the overall goal to increase the visibility of ProM, we begin this chapter by identifying and defining the uniquely prospective function of memory. This function appears to encompass a domain as wide as that of RetM. Therefore, we argue, ProM research should proceed with a divide-and-conquer strategy similar to that used for RetM research, that is, by identifying distinct subdomains (like episodic and semantic memory) and by pursuing research questions and theoretical accounts that focus on them. For the reasons that made it useful and even necessary to adopt clear subdomain labels and definitions for RetM, we believe that it will be equally useful and necessary in the future for ProM researchers to identify precisely which subdomain is targeted by each investigation.

In this chapter we focus on that subdomain of ProM that seems most directly analogous to James's (1890) memory proper, today more generally known as explicit episodic memory. We will identify this sub-domain of ProM, herein called ProM proper (see Graf & Uttl, 2001), specify exactly how it differs from explicit episodic RetM, and show how it can be operationalized and measured. In addition, we use this chapter to introduce a new methodology for measuring ProM proper. A major advantage of this new methodology is that it yields a continuous index of performance, in contrast to existing methods that produce primarily success/failure data. We report new research that employed this methodology to demonstrate that various experimental manipulations and subject variables have different effects on ProM proper and on explicit episodic RetM performance. The finding of such performance dissociations supports the claim that ProM proper is a distinct form of memory.

A final objective of this chapter is to report new research on the hypothesis that ProM task performance is more sensitive to age-related changes than RetM task performance. This hypothesis builds, first, on the widespread assumption that aging is associated with a decline in the attention resources required for performing a wide range of cognitive tasks (Hasher & Zacks, 1979; Salthouse, 1980, 1985) and, second, on the notion that performance of ProM tasks is more dependent on attention resources than performance on RetM tasks (Craik, 1986). According to Craik, performance on all memory tests is determined by a combination of processes that are either driven or guided by the environment or initiated and controlled by the subject. He proposed that subject-initiated processing is more resource-demanding than environmentally guided processing, and because ProM tests provide less environmental cues for supporting performance than other memory tests, age-related performance differences are larger on ProM than RetM tests.

Memory's Prospective Function

ProM has been described in many ways, including as intention memory (Goschke & Kuhl, 1996; Kvavilashvili & Ellis, 1996; Loftus, 1971), memory for future actions (Einstein & McDaniel, 1996; Mäntylä, 1996), and remembering that something has to be done (Dobbs & Rule, 1987; Maylor, 1996b). As in these examples, the prospective function of memory is defined by the to-be-remembered content. But a content-based definition is difficult to sustain because it raises obvious questions, such as these: How is memory for plans and intentions different from memory for anything else (i.e., memory for words, memory for music, memory for emotions)? Does a content-specific domain of episodic memory require a name of its own? In separate commentaries that appeared in the first book entirely devoted to ProM (Brandimonte, Einstein & McDaniel, 1996), Crowder (1996) and Roediger (1996) answered the latter question with an emphatic no, and we agree with this position.

To ferret out memory's uniquely prospective function, we examined the word "prospective," what it means to be a prospector, and the unique operational requirements of prospective memory tasks.

Prospectors are specialists, trained to see beyond the obvious (i.e., they see not just what is, but also what could be), their core task is to examine the environment for telltale signs of mineral deposits. Typically, the job of unearthing or recovering such deposits is left to the next set of specialists, miners. By analogy, we regard RetM, like the miner, as being concerned with specialized recovery operations, whereas unique to ProM is the capacity to see beyond the obvious, to recognize telltale signs (see Craik, 1986; Ellis, 1996; Einstein & McDaniel, 1990, 1996). Concretely, if the plan is to buy groceries en route home from work, ProM is required for recognizing the supermarket as relevant to this plan, even when attention is focused elsewhere (e.g., on driving or talking on the phone). If the plan is recollected in the presence of an appropriate cue, RetM is engaged to recollect the items on the grocery list (i.e., for recovery operations). On this understanding, the cues given for a memory test function like the telltale signs sought out by prospectors.[1] RetM begins with cues, with recognized telltale signs, and it uses these as guides for recovering prior episodes, events, and experiences (i.e., hidden knowledge deposits). By contrast, the prospective function of memory is required for situations where telltale signs have to be recognized before recovery operations can be initiated.

These characterizations of ProM and RetM tasks lend themselves to a task analysis. Any memory task may be defined as a request or a comparable situation (defined by the experimenter, the subject, ongoing activities, or the environment) that occurs in a particular context and that calls for, elicits, or recruits a particular type of responding. Consistent with this definition, any memory task is objectively describable in terms of cues, instructions, a context (e.g., spatial, emotional), and a response type (see Graf & Birt, 1996). Under some circumstances, a difference in a single property is sufficient for distinguishing between two types of memory tasks. In many previous investigations of implicit and explicit memory, for example, the memory tests differed only in terms of the instructions given to subjects. That is, both tests used the exact same cues, required the same response type, and were given in the same context (e.g., Graf & Mandler, 1984; Schacter & Graf, 1986). Similarly, we can conceive of ProM and RetM tasks that make use of the same cues and context. The context might be a laboratory room, and a cue for remembering might be the experimenter's giving the subject a printed form showing the initial letters of previously studied words. When cues and context are held constant in this manner, this serves to isolate the crucial differences between ProM and RetM tasks, in this case, the exact instructions given to subjects. For the RetM task, the instructions, delivered together with the test form, might direct subjects to write previously studied words on the test form. For the ProM task, the instructions, which would have been given earlier in the experiment, might be "After you receive the recall form later on, please request a red pen from me and use it to write your name on the test form."

Table 1 summarizes the core similarities and differences between ProM and two familiar RetM tasks—implicit and explicit. We make the assumption that the cues, the context, and the response type are held constant. If so, what differs between the tasks is, first, whether at the time of testing subjects are alerted to the cues and directed to work with them in a target/task-relevant manner, and second, whether subjects are specifically instructed to use the cues in a manner that is relevant to the prior study or planning phase. For all RetM tasks, subjects are aware of or are made aware of the cues at the time of testing, and they are given specific instructions on how to work with them. As the table shows, the critical difference between explicit and implicit tests is that for the former, subjects are specifically instructed to use the cues in a study/trial-relevant manner. That is, they are instructed to use the cues as aids for recollecting previously studied words. For implicit memory tests, subjects also are instructed on how to use the cues (e.g., subjects may be told to complete

Table 1
Properties of tests for explicit retrospective, implicit retrospective, and prospective memory

Type of memory test	Cues provided on test	At test, Ss are alerted to cues and instructed to work with them in a task-relevant manner	At test, Ss are alerted to the study/planning-phase relevance of cues
Retrospective			
Explicit	Yes	Yes	Yes
Implicit	Yes	Yes	No
Prospective	Yes	No	No

the cues with any words that come to mind), but the instructions do not draw attention to specific prior learning events and experiences (Graf & Schacter, 1985). By contrast, for ProM tasks, subjects may or may not be aware of the cues (the cues may be central or incidental to an ongoing task); what is critical is that at the time of testing, subjects are not instructed to work with the cues in a ProM-task-relevant manner. When driving by the supermarket, nothing alerts us to pay attention to this cue, and no one instructs us that this cue is relevant to a previously formed plan (e.g., to get the groceries en route from work to home). Instead, in ProM tasks the cues appear as a natural part of other tasks or situations; they are embedded in other ongoing activities. *What is unique about ProM tasks is that they require identifying or recognizing cues as telltale signs of previously formed plans and intentions when the cues occur as part of ongoing thoughts, actions, or situations* (Craik, 1986; Einstein & McDaniel, 1996; Graf & Uttl, 2001; Kidder, Park, Hertzog & Morrell, 1997; Kvavilashvili, 1987; Maylor, 1993; Mäntylä, 1996; Park & Kidder, 1996).

The uniquely prospective function of memory must not be confused with what is indexed by performance on commonly used ProM tasks, such as time-based versus event-based tasks (Einstein & McDaniel, 1990; Harris, 1983), or habitual versus episodic tasks (Einstein, McDaniel, Smith & Shaw, 1998). Performance on such tasks is not a "process pure" barometer of recognizing cues as telltale signs. This is highlighted by what can happen when the task is, for example, to get groceries en route from work to home. We can fail this task either because we did not recollect the intention (to get groceries) when driving by the supermarket or because we did not remember the items on the grocery list. It is widely acknowledged that only the first of these components—recollecting the intention—is clearly prospective (Dobbs & Rule, 1987; Einstein & McDaniel, 1996; Graf & Uttl, 2001); the latter seems part of retrospective memory and is not different from recollecting (or failing to recollect) a list of words upon request.

We have developed a new methodology that yields a separate index of each of these components. This methodology is described later in this chapter, together with new investigations of the relation between performance on ProM and explicit episodic RetM tasks.

Subdomains of ProM

An intuitive analysis reveals that different ProM activities are associated with different conscious experiences. For example, waiting for the pot to boil is a short-term task; it is likely to be kept active in working memory and to dominate conscious awareness. By contrast, if we plan in the morning to get groceries en route from work later in the day, this involves a different type of conscious experience. This plan is not likely to remain active and dominant in working memory; it is out of conscious awareness for most of the retention interval (i.e., the period between making the plan and executing it). Instead, the retention interval is filled with other activities, the ProM-task-relevant cue (e.g., the supermarket) appears incidentally as a natural part of these other activities (e.g., driving home from work), and what is of interest is whether the cue succeeds in bringing the previously formed plan back into conscious awareness (Einstein & McDaniel, 1996; Graf & Uttl, 2001; Kvavilashvili, 1998; Mäntylä, 1996; Meier & Graf, 2000).

The different conscious experiences associated with these different prospective activities seem analogous to the experiences that characterize performance on primary- and secondary-memory tasks, and thus it seems reasonable to proceed in the spirit of William James's work. James stipulated that "memory proper" requires "the knowledge of an event, or fact, of which meanwhile we have not been thinking, with the additional consciousness that we have thought or experienced it before" (1890, p. 684). By analogy, we propose to define *ProM proper as requiring that we are aware of a plan, of which meanwhile we have not been thinking, with the additional consciousness that we remember making the plan earlier.* By this definition, ProM proper does not encompass the prospective equivalent of primary memory, that is, when a plan or intention remains active in working memory throughout the retention interval. The latter situation is more typical of vigilance or monitoring tasks, and thus such labels seem more appropriate for the ProM equivalent of primary memory (cf. Baddeley & Wilkins, 1984; Craik & Kerr, 1996; Einstein & McDaniel, 1996; Meacham & Leiman, 1982).[2]

We regard vigilance and ProM proper as part of a continuum of possible prospective-memory activities. At one end of this continuum, the prospective task dominates working memory and conscious awareness during the retention interval. At the other end, the ProM-proper end, the plan is out of working memory during the retention interval and conscious awareness is focused on competing activities. We hypothesize that what varies along the continuum is the proportion of available processing resources allocated to the prospective task during the retention interval. For vigilance, all or most of the available resources are allocated to the prospective task, whereas for ProM proper, all or most of the available resources are allocated to competing activities. Other tasks, such as waiting for the arrival of a limousine or for the cupcakes to finish baking may fall between these extremes (see Ceci & Bronfenbrenner, 1985; Dobbs & Reeves, 1996; Harris & Wilkins, 1982). Such tasks may recruit a more equal allocation of resources to prospective and other activities.

The domain of ProM proper seems further circumscribed by the distinction between episodic and habitual tasks (Harris, 1983; Meacham, 1982), which appears analogous to the distinction between episodic and semantic memory tasks. Buying groceries en route from work is an episodic task, like an episodic-memory task, in the sense that the plan arose out of a single event and is to be executed only once. By contrast, taking medication and brushing one's teeth at bedtime are habitual tasks; they are similar to semantic-memory activities that have been shaped by many previous repetitions. Episodic and habitual tasks are radically different from each other: they arise out of different needs, they are associated with different conscious experiences, and they are marked by different histories (i.e., number of occasions for thinking about and practicing them). For these reasons, by analogy with Tulving's (1972) distinction between episodic and semantic memory, we use the label ProM proper only in reference to episodic or one-off tasks.

Our focus in this chapter is on ProM proper, specifically, on responding to cues as telltale signs of previously formed intentions. ProM proper seems to be the direct complement of explicit episodic RetM. For this reason, an investigation of ProM proper is most relevant to theoretical assumptions about age-related changes in prospective and retrospective memory (see Craik, 1986).

Assessing ProM Proper

ProM researchers have exercised considerable ingenuity in developing tasks for assessing various aspects of prospective memory (e.g., Einstein & McDaniel, 1990, 1996; Harris, 1983; Harris & Wilkins, 1982; Kvavilashvili & Ellis, 1996), but none of them have been designed specifically to focus on ProM proper. Our goal was to develop such a task. Furthermore, we wanted this task to be more sensitive to gradations in performance than the success/failure scores provided by existing tasks.

Our starting point for developing a new task was an investigation by Dobbs and Rule (1987). Their subjects were required to complete a questionnaire at home, and the ProM task was to write the time and date in the upper right corner of the form. Dobbs and Rule scored performance in two ways. By a strict criterion, both the time and the date had to be written in the correct location, and by a lenient criterion, performance was counted as successful if either the time or the date were in the correct location. According to Dobbs and Rule, the "lenient criterion provides some measure (albeit not perfect) of remembering to do something while placing minimum requirements on remembering the content of the task" (1987, p. 216). Dobbs and Rule found that the strict scores showed only a marginal influence due to age, but the lenient scores showed a significant, substantial age-related performance decline.

To our knowledge, Dobbs and Rule's (1987) study was the first investigation that attempted to estimate ProM proper in this manner, and by their own words, their lenient scores are far from being a perfect measure. Nevertheless, their approach underscores that ProM proper leaves a distinct signature on responding, and the methodological challenge is to magnify this signature and assess it independently of the RetM component. Toward this objective, we conducted an investigation that involved a series of attention, perception, and memory tasks (Uttl, Graf, Miller & Tuokko, 2001). The participants were 133 community-dwelling healthy adults between 65 and 95 years of age. To assess ProM proper, for one task, the Name task, subjects were told "In the course of the experiment, when I [the experimenter] say, 'This is the end of this task. I would like you to ask for a pen and a piece of paper, and then I would like you to write your name on the paper'." Following these instructions, subjects performed various activities, at the end of one of which the experimenter said, "This is the end of this task." In order to indicate that they recognized this cue as a telltale sign, subjects responded to it with comments like, "We need to stop here for another task," "Oh, there is something I have to do now," by explaining that they had to ask for something, or by asking for the pen and/or the paper. By this method, we elicited responses to the cue that are indicative of ProM proper. By contrast, explicit-episodic-RetM performance was indexed by whether or not subjects asked for the objects (e.g., the pen and piece of paper) and by whether or not they carried out the assigned task (i.e., write their name on the paper).

A subset of the results from our investigation appears in table 2. The top of the table shows the mean ProM proper scores for the name task, the ProM task described in the preceding paragraph. The means show a significant age-related decline in performance. The means for explicit episodic RetM on this task are not shown, because performance was at the ceiling, which indicates that most participants who remembered that they needed to perform a task were successful in remembering what objects they had to request (i.e., a pen and a piece of paper) and

Table 2
Mean levels of performance on one test of ProM proper and on two tests of explicit episodic RetM

Memory task	Subject age groups (in years)			
	65–69	70–74	75–79	80–95
Name[a]				
M	0.84	0.76	0.45	0.43
SD	0.37	0.43	0.50	0.51
Buschke 1–3[b]				
M	10.02	9.34	9.33	8.78
SD	1.00	1.21	1.46	1.37
RAVLT A1–5[c]				
M	9.82	9.19	8.99	8.46
SD	1.46	1.84	2.66	2.04

a. A test for assessing ProM proper: the ability to recognize cues as telltale signs of previously formed plans.
b. Buschke Selective Reminding Test (see Spreen & Strauss, 1991); average recall for trials 1 to 3.
c. Rey Auditory Verbal Learning Test (see Spreen & Strauss, 1991); average recall for trials 1 to 5 on List A.

what they had to do with these objects (i.e., write their name on the paper).

Table 2 includes the mean scores from two commonly used standardized tests of explicit episodic RetM that were included in our test battery: the Buschke Selective Reminding Test (BSRT) and the Rey Auditory Verbal Learning Test (RAVLT). Both of these tests were administered according to published instructions (Spreen & Strauss, 1991). The BSRT measures free recall of 12 unrelated concrete words across three trials, and one part of the RAVLT tracks learning of 15 unrelated words across five trials. Shown in table 2 are the performance levels achieved on the BSRT and on the RAVLT. Both sets of means show a noticeable age-related decline in performance.

Our investigation was intended to explore the relationship between age-related performance declines in ProM proper and explicit episodic RetM. In contrast to the expectation derived from Craik's (1986) view that aging has a more profound effect on ProM proper than on explicit episodic RetM, the means in table 2 point to declines of similar magnitudes (i.e., about 1 SD). Nevertheless, it appears that these declines are mediated by different mechanisms, as suggested by the outcomes of follow-up correlation analyses. The results showed a moderately strong correlation of $r = .70$ between performance on the two RetM tests, whereas the correlations between performance on these tests and performance on the name test (our index of ProM proper) were substantially smaller ($r = .18$ and $.24$ with the BSRT and the RAVLT, respectively).

The investigation by Uttl et al. (2001) convinced us that it is possible to assess ProM proper directly, reliably, and independently of explicit episodic RetM. The limits of this method became equally obvious, however, by our explorations of the correlations among tasks. Like all existing tasks, the method used by Uttl et al. provides only a success/failure index of ProM proper. This type of index is not sensitive to subtle influences on performance and is ill suited, for example, for systematic investigations of the factors (e.g., speed of processing) that mediate age-related declines in memory performance. For these reasons, we embarked on the development a new method that provides a continuous index of ProM proper.

The inspiration for the new method was the claim made earlier in this chapter, that the distinguishing feature of the prospective functions of memory is the requirement to identify cues as telltale signs when these occur as a natural part of other thoughts, actions, or situations. From this claim, it follows that to execute a previously formed plan, a first step is to stop or pause the ongoing activity, and so the action of stopping or pausing in response to a cue provides an index of ProM proper (Dobbs & Rule, 1987; Einstein & McDaniel, 1996; Graf & Uttl, 2001). This index would be a continuous variable if a cue were presented for an extended period of time, and if we tracked the time required to identify it as a telltale sign. A similar dependent variable would result if the same cue were presented repeatedly and if we counted the number of presentations required to identify it as a telltale sign. Stopping in response to a cue seems independent of the retrospective component of the task: it does not guarantee that we remember what needs to be done, just as stopping a colleague in the hallway does not guarantee that we remember a message we intended to convey.

For the research reported in the next section of this chapter, we required subjects to respond to a visual cue presented several times, with each successive version larger than the preceding display. The dependent variable was the number of displays, directly correlated with the size of the display, required until subjects recognized it as a sign for executing a previously formed intention, in this case, recalling a list of words memorized earlier in the experiment. The specific objectives of our work were, first, to examine whether or not performance on our new test of ProM proper would dissociate from performance on a standard test of explicit episodic RetM and, second, to investigate whether or not performance on these two test types is affected differently by age-related changes in cognition.

Dissociating ProM Proper from Explicit Episodic RetM

General method

We conducted two experiments with each using the same general method for assessing ProM proper and explicit, episodic RetM. Each experiment required subjects to complete a series of attention, perception, and memory tasks, including two ProM tasks that were designed to be analogous to remembering to get groceries en route home from work. We required subjects to learn a list of common concrete words, like a shopping list, and to recollect this list later in the experiment while they were engaged in an unrelated activity (i.e., an ongoing task like driving home from work). To ensure learning, the word list was presented for two study-test trials, with each trial structured according to the procedure used for the RAVLT. At the time of learning, subjects were instructed that their task was to recall the list later in the experiment whenever they saw the recall cue, which was a picture of a common object (e.g., a helicopter). The specific instructions were, "If at any time during this experiment you see a picture of a helicopter [or one of the other cues], stop whatever you are doing and recall the list you have just learned." These instructions were repeated until subjects were able to report what was required of them. Subjects were reminded that the instructions would not be repeated, that it was their responsibility to recall the list at the appropriate time.

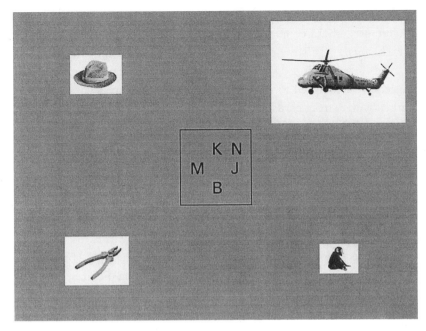

Figure 1
An example of the materials displayed for the card-sorting task and for assessing prospective memory.

ProM was tested later in the experiment, while subjects were engaged in a simple decision-making task. This task was modeled on Rabbitt's (1965) card-sorting task. We prepared two sets of 54 computer displays, each of which looked like a 7 × 7 cm playing card (see figure 1 for an example). Each card was divided into nine equal squares. For half of the cards in each set, one square had printed on it the target letter A, and the other cards had printed on them the target letter B. The target letters A and B were in capitals, printed in 28-point Helvetica font. Across the cards, they occupied each of the nine possible squares equally often. For one third of the cards from each set, the remaining squares were left blank. For another third of the cards, a random four additional squares were occupied by irrelevant or filler letters that were selected randomly and without replacement from the rest of the alphabet. And for the remaining cards, all eight additional squares were occupied with other letters from the alphabet. All letters from the alphabet (other than A and B) were used about equally often as fillers; they were assigned randomly to each square and were printed in the same manner as the targets. The 54 cards from each set were displayed randomly, one at a time, and subjects were required to sort them into two groups by separating cards marked with A from cards marked with B. The specific instructions were, "Press the left-arrow key if there is an A on the card, and press the right-arrow key if there is a B on the card." The critical dependent variable was the time required to sort each card, as well as the number of errors made in sorting the cards under each condition (i.e., cards with 0, 4, and 8 irrelevant letters).

The decision-making task had three blocks, each with 108 (i.e., 2 sets of 54) trials. For block 1, subjects were presented with cards, and they made AB decisions as described in the preceding paragraph. For block 2, each card was displayed together with four distracting pictures, arranged as shown in figure 1. The pictures were color photos of 128 common objects. Each display included 4 different objects, selected randomly from the pool of all available objects. As shown in figure 1, the photo displays differed in size; some were as small as 98×72 pixels, whereas others were as large as 336×252 pixels. Subjects were instructed to concentrate on making AB decisions and were informed that "this phase of the experiment assesses your ability to keep focused on the decision task despite the pictures." For block 3, the same method for constructing displays was used, except that this time one of the pictures was the ProM cue. This cue was shown for the first time on about the thirtieth trial of block 3, and thereafter on about every fourth trail (the actual number was a random choice between 3, 4, and 5 trials). On its first presentation, the ProM cue measured 98×72 pixels (i.e., the smallest picture in figure 1). It grew in width and height on every succeeding display in equal steps until it reached a maximum size of 336×252 pixels (i.e., the largest picture in figure 1) after 16 presentations.[3] For each presentation, the ProM cue appeared in a randomly chosen quadrant of the display. Consistent with the instructions given earlier in the test session, upon recognizing the ProM cue, subjects were expected to halt making decisions and to recall the word list learned earlier. The dependent variable for ProM proper was the cue size when it was detected.

Cue type and retention interval influences

The first experiment examined whether or not ProM proper and explicit episodic RetM are affected differently by a manipulation of the ProM cue type and by a manipulation of the length of the retention interval. The subjects were 72 undergraduate students who participated in return for course credit. They completed a battery of attention, perception, and memory tests, including two instances of the decision-making task described in the preceding paragraphs. The latter were separated from each other by at least 15 minutes spent on completing other battery items. The ProM task was to "recollect the list of words you are about to learn if you see a picture of a helicopter [i.e., one of the ProM cues] at any time during the experiment."

For each instance of the ProM task, the participants learned a different list of 18 common words, and ProM was cued either with a color picture or with a black and white picture. This manipulation of cue types was counterbalanced across subjects. For the retention manipulation, the ProM-instruction and list-learning phase occurred either immediately prior to administering block 1 of the card-sorting task or about 10 minutes earlier in the test session. In the latter condition, subjects completed two additional test-battery items after learning the to-be-remembered list and only then proceeded to block 1 of the card-sorting task. By this manipulation, the retention interval from list learning to the first display of the ProM cue averaged about 6 minutes in the immediate condition and about 20 minutes in the delayed condition. For subjects who interrupted the card-sorting task when they detected the ProM cue, they recollected the word list and then continued on with the card-sorting task. For subjects who did not notice the cue, they were asked to recall the word list immediately after completing the card-sorting task.

The critical findings for RetM and ProM test performance are shown respectively in figures 2 and 3. Figure 2 shows that the ProM cue-type manipulation had no effect on free-recall-test performance ($F(1, 66) = 0.10$, MSE $= 6.45$), and that free recall performance was not affected by the delay manipulation ($F(1, 66) = 0.71$, MSE $= 6.61$). Additional analyses examined recall performance after the first and second list-learning trials; they showed the expected increase from trial 1 (M $= 10.40$, SD $= 1.77$) to trial 2 (M $= 13.06$, SD $= 1.55$): $F(1, 66) = 216.92$, MSE $= 1.10$.

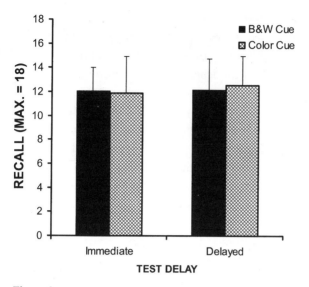

Figure 2
Average free recall of words as a function of ProM cue type and retention interval. (Error bars are standard deviations.)

Recall performance was higher immediately after the second learning trial than when it followed ProM cue detection ($F(1, 66) = 25.37$, $MSE = 1.06$). This general pattern of findings is consistent with previous evidence showing a rapid loss of information immediately after learning, followed by relatively stable performance across small differences (6 versus 20 minutes) in retention intervals.

Figure 3 shows ProM test performance. The top panel shows the proportion of participants who detected the ProM cue, and the bottom panel shows the level or size of the cue at the time it was detected. Although they draw attention to different aspects of performance, both panels show the same pattern of effects: a higher level of performance in the immediate condition than in the delayed condition, and when the ProM cue was in color rather than in black and white. The top panel reveals a performance-ceiling effect in the immediate testing condition, and for this reason, we focused statistical analyses on the data in the bottom panel of figure 3. For these analyses, subjects who failed to detect the ProM cue received a score of 18, that is, a value of one higher than

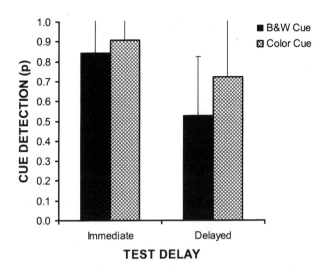

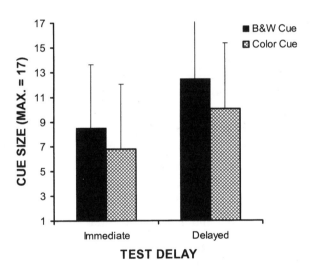

Figure 3
Average ProM test performance as a function of ProM cue type and retention interval. (Bars are standard deviations.) The top panel shows the proportion of participants who detected the ProM cue; the bottom panel shows the size of the ProM cue when it was detected.

the maximum cue size displayed in the experiment. The results showed that participants were able to detect the ProM cue on the basis of a smaller display when it was in color than black and white ($F(1,66) = 6.58$, MSE = 21.69), and when it occurred after a short retention interval rather than after a longer retention interval ($F(1,66) = 13.97$, MSE = 31.57). No other effects were significant.

The combined findings from this experiment are encouraging for theoretical and methodological reasons. The finding that two variables—cue type and retention interval—have different effects on ProM proper and on explicit episodic RetM implies mediation by different perceptual and/or cognitive processes. It is too early to speculate about the nature of these processes, however, until the generality of our findings is more firmly established. We anticipate that future research will show both similarities and differences between ProM proper and explicit episodic RetM. It seems likely, for example, that a longer-retention-interval manipulation would affect both forms of memory in similar ways. Other variables, that are known to influence explicit episodic RetM such as the nature of the to-be-remembered materials (e.g., related versus unrelated lists of words) or the type of learning phase activity (e.g., levels of processing manipulations), may have no effect on ProM proper. Future research will explore these possibilities.

The main goal of our experiment was methodological: concerned with providing evidence that our new method for assessing ProM proper works, that it is able to reveal performance dissociations between ProM proper and explicit episodic RetM. This goal has been achieved.

Age-related changes in ProM proper and in explicit episodic RetM

The main goal of this experiment was to test the hypothesis that ProM is more sensitive to aging than RetM, more specifically, to examine whether age-related changes in cognition have a larger effect on ProM proper than on explicit episodic RetM. We used the same basic method as for the experiment reported above. Each participant was tested in two sessions scheduled at least 24-hours apart. The retention-interval manipulation was not used. Instead, we manipulated the nature of the to-be-remembered materials by requiring subjects to learn a list of 15 unrelated common words for one session, and a list of 15 related common words (3 words each from 5 different categories, such as fruit or furniture) for the other session. The assignment of materials was counterbalanced.

The subjects were 111 community-living older adults who participated in the Victoria Longitudinal Study (VLS). (For a detailed description of this project and of the subjects, see Hultsch, Hertzog, Dixon & Small, 1998.) They were between 67 and 93 years of age, highly educated, and generally in good health. Brief descriptive data on the subjects are provided in table 3. As indicated by the table, the subjects were arranged into two groups, one consisting of young-old adults (67–74) and the other of old-old adults (75–93).

Table 3
Descriptive data on participants

| | Age group (years) | | Age effects[a] | |
	67–74	75–93	r^2	$F(1, 109)$
N	60	51		
Sex				
Men	21	21		
Women	39	30		
Education				
M	14.3	13.9	.007	0.77
SD	3.16	3.14		
ETS vocabulary				
M	43.0	44.5	<.001	0.06
SD	5.47	5.94		
WAIS-R Digit Symbol[b]				
M	43.2	39.5	.092	10.98*
SD	7.34	9.56		
Optimal overall health rating[c]				
M	1.75	1.59	.010	1.04
SD	0.70	0.67		

a. Age effects were computed by regression analysis.
b. WAIS-R Digit Symbol scores (Wechsler, 1981).
c. Participants used a 5-point scale to rate their health relative to "perfect health" (0 = very good to 4 = very poor).
* $p < .05$.

On the RetM test, the materials manipulation had the expected effect. Overall free recall was higher on the related list (M = 10.32, SD = 2.19) than on the unrelated list (M = 7.30, SD = 2.35): $F(1, 108) = 224.29$, MSE = 2.62. The recall-test means also show a higher level of performance for the young-old adults than for the old-old adults ($r^2 = .076$, $F(1, 109) = 8.93$, MSE = 51.24). Additional analyses that examined recall performance after the first and second list-learning trials showed the expected increase from trial 1 (M = 8.08, SD = 2.01) to trial 2 (M = 9.61, SD = 2.27): $F(1, 110) = 146.72$, MSE = 0.89. Recall that performance was higher immediately after the second learning trial than when it followed ProM cue detection (M = 8.64, SD = 2.48): $F(1, 110) = 69.88$, MSE = 0.74.

Figure 4 shows ProM test performance. The top panel shows the proportion of participants who detected the ProM cue, and the bottom panel shows the level or size of the cue at the time it was detected. Although they draw attention to different aspects of performance, both panels show the same pattern of effects: higher performance by the young-old group than the old-old group. There was no influence due to the materials manipulation. These observations were supported by the outcome of statistical analyses, which revealed a significant age effect on the cue detection data in the top panel ($r^2 = .068$, $F(1, 109) = 8.01$, MSE = 1, 12) and on the cue size data in the bottom panel ($r^2 = .078$, $F(1, 109) = 9.28$, MSE = 257.05). No other effects were significant.

We used hierarchical regression analyses to examine more directly the hypothesis that age-related changes in cognition have a larger effect on ProM proper than on explicit episodic RetM. In contrast to this expectation, the results showed comparable effects, revealing significant r^2 values of .078 and .066 for ProM and RetM, respectively.

In a final analysis, we explored the relationship between ProM proper and explicit episodic RetM, as well as the relationship between these and performance on the card-sorting task. Card sorting is a highly resource-demanding task. For this analysis, we used a separate index of sorting cards without distractors (CS-ND) versus sorting cards in the presence of distractors (CS-D). The results are summarized in table 4. The table corroborates the outcome of the regression analysis by showing similar

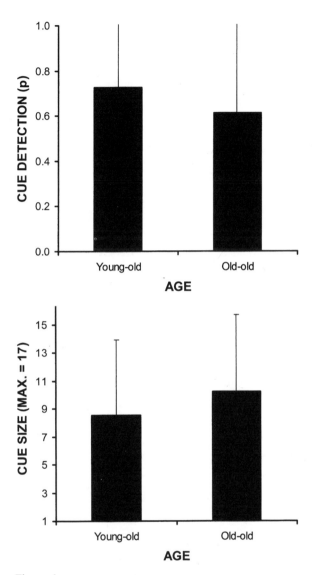

Figure 4
Average ProM test performance as a function of age group. (Bars are standard deviations.) The top panel shows the proportion of participants who detected the ProM cue; the bottom panel shows the size of the ProM cue when it was detected.

Table 4

The pattern of intercorrelations of age, RetM, ProM, and card sorting under different conditions

	Age	RetM	ProM	CS-ND	CS-D
Age		−0.26	0.28	0.35	0.23
RetM	−0.26		−0.21	−0.33	−0.27
ProM	0.28	−0.21		0.32	−0.24
CS-ND	0.35	−0.33	0.32		0.66
CS-D	0.23	−0.27	−0.24	0.66	

correlation for ProM and RetM with age. (The different signs of the coefficients reflect the manner in which ProM and RetM performance were scored.) Also noteworthy in table 4 is the low correlation between ProM proper and explicit episodic RetM.

These findings complement those of the preceding experiment by showing a different kind of performance dissociation between explicit episodic RetM and ProM proper. In the preceding experiment, the retention-interval manipulation influenced ProM-proper test performance but not RetM test performance. By contrast, the materials manipulation used for the present experiment affected RetM test performance but not ProM-proper test performance. The results from the present experiment also showed that another factor, age group, had a comparable influence on both test types. This combination of findings illustrates the complex relationship between ProM proper and explicit episodic RetM.

The correlation data from the second experiment do not support the view that aging has a more profound effect on ProM-proper test performance than on explicit-episodic-RetM test performance (see Craik, 1986). The results revealed similar age-related performance declines in ProM proper and explicit episodic RetM. The results also showed that a widely used index of processing resources—card-sorting task performance— was only weakly and similarly correlated with ProM and RetM test performance. This finding replicates and extends the results reported by Uttl et al. (2001), and together with the outcome from the present experiment, they undermine the proposal that ProM test performance is more dependent on attention resources than RetM test performance.

Notes

1. Like all analogies, the analogy between prospectors and ProM is not perfect. A prospector is likely to use a conscious strategy to search the environment for telltale signs. By contrast, an important and defining feature of some ProM tasks (e.g., getting groceries en route from work to home) is that the search for task-relevant cues (e.g., the supermarket) is not guided by a strategy that is maintained in conscious awareness. For such tasks, the cues appear as part of ongoing thoughts, actions, or situations (e.g., driving home), when attention is focused elsewhere (e.g., on driving or listening to the radio).

2. The critical difference between monitoring and ProM proper is not defined by the time interval between instructions and the ProM cue. Monitoring tasks are those where an intention is maintained in consciousness until it needs to be executed. In contrast, for ProM proper, intentions are not maintained in consciousness through the retention interval while performing an ongoing task (see James, 1890). A clear operational distinction between monitoring and ProM proper may be difficult to achieve in each case. However, ProM researchers might go forward, as did RetM researchers in the 1960s (when they struggled to find clear operational distinctions between short- and long-term memory), by avoiding boundary cases and instead focus research on clear examples of monitoring and ProM proper.

3. The pixel size of the pictures used as ProM cues and as distractors varied slightly among the experiments; the experiments also differed slightly in terms of the number of ProM cue-size increments that were used. (Precise method details are reported in Uttl, Graf & Dixon, in preparation, and in Graf & Uttl, in preparation.)

References

Baddeley, A. D., & Wilkins, A. J. (1984). Taking memory out of the laboratory. In J. E. Harris & P. E. Morris (Eds.), *Everyday memory, actions and absent-mindedness*. New York: Academic Press.

Brandimonte, M., Einstein, G. O., & McDaniels, M. A. (Eds.) (1996). *Prospective memory: Theory and applications*. Mahwah, N.J.: Erlbaum.

Ceci, S. J., & Bronfenbrenner, U. (1985). "Don't forget to take the cupcakes out of the oven": Prospective memory, strategic-time monitoring, and context. *Child Development, 56*, 152–164.

Craik, F. I. M. (1986). A functional account of age differences in memory. In F. Klix & H. Hagendorf (Eds.), *Human Memory and Cognitive Capabilities: Mechanisms and Performances* (pp. 409–422). New York: Elsevier Science.

Craik, F. I. M., & Kerr, S. A. (1996). Commentary: Prospective memory, aging, and lapse of intention. In M. Brandimonte, G. O. Einstein & M. A. McDaniel

(Eds.), *Prospective memory: Theory and application* (pp. 227–237). Mahwah, N.J.: Erlbaum.

Crowder, R. G. (1996). The trouble with prospective memory: A provocation. In M. Brandimonte, G. O. Einstein & M. A. McDaniel (Eds.), *Prospective memory: Theory and application* (pp. 143–147). Mahwah, N.J.: Erlbaum.

Dobbs, A. R., & Reeves, M. B. (1996). Prospective memory: More than memory. In M. Brandimonte, G. O. Einstein & M. A. McDaniel (Eds.), *Prospective memory: Theory and application* (pp. 199–225). Mahwah, N.J.: Erlbaum.

Dobbs, A. R., & Rule, B. G. (1987). Prospective memory and self-reports of memory abilities in older adults. *Canadian Journal of Psychology, 41,* 209–222.

Einstein, G. O., & McDaniel, M. A. (1990). Normal aging and prospective memory. *Journal of Experimental Psychology: Learning, Memory, and Cognition, 16,* 717–726.

Einstein, G. O., & McDaniel, M. A. (1996). Retrieval processes in prospective memory: Theoretical approaches and some new empirical findings. In M. Brandimonte, G. O. Einstein & M. A. McDaniel (Eds.), *Prospective memory: Theory and application* (pp. 115–141). Mahwah, N.J.: Erlbaum.

Einstein, G. O., McDaniel, M. A., Smith, R. E., & Shaw, P. (1998). Habitual prospective memory and aging: Remembering intentions and forgetting actions. *Psychological Science, 9,* 284–288.

Ellis, J. (1996). Prospective memory of the realization of delayed intentions: A conceptual framework for research. In M. Brandimonte, G. O. Einstein & M. A. McDaniel (Eds.), *Prospective memory: Theory and application* (pp. 1–22). Mahwah, N.J.: Erlbaum.

Goschke, T., & Kuhl, J. (1996). Remembering what to do: Explicit and implicit memory for intentions. In M. Brandimonte, G. O. Einstein & M. A. McDaniel (Eds.), *Prospective memory: Theory and application* (pp. 53–91). Mahwah, N.J.: Erlbaum.

Graf, P., & Birt, A. R. (1996). Explicit and implicit memory retrieval: Intentions and strategies. In L. M. Reder (Ed.), *Implicit memory and metacognition* (pp. 25–44). Mahwah, N.J.: Erlbaum.

Graf, P., & Mandler, G. (1984). Activation makes words more accessible, but not necessarily more retrievable. *Journal of Verbal Learning and Verbal Behavior, 23,* 553–568.

Graf, P., & Schacter, D. L. (1985). Implicit and explicit memory for new associations in normal and amnesic subjects. *Journal of Experimental Psychology: Learning, Memory, and Cognition, 11,* 501–518.

Graf, P., & Uttl, B. (2001). Prospective memory: A new focus for research. *Consciousness and Cognition, 10,* 437–450.

Harris, J. E. (1983). Remembering to do things: A forgotten topic. In J. E. Harris & P. E. Morris, *Everyday memory: Actions and absentmindedness* (pp. 71–92). London: Academic Press.

Harris, J. E., & Wilkins, A. J. (1982). Remembering to do things: A theoretical framework and an illustrated experiment. *Human Learning, 1*, 123–136.

Hasher, L., & Zacks, R. T. (1979). Automatic and effortful processes in memory. *Journal of Experimental Psychology: General, 108*, 356–388.

James, W. (1890). *Principles of psychology.* New York: Holt.

Kidder, D. P., Park, D. C., Hertzog, C., & Morrell, R. W. (1997). Prospective memory and aging: The effects of working memory and prospective memory task load. *Aging, Neuropsychology, and Cognition, 4*, 93–112.

Kvavilashvili, L. (1987). Remembering intention as a distinct form of memory. *British Journal of Psychology, 78*, 507–518.

Kvavilashvili, L. (1998). Remembering intentions: Testing a new method of investigation. *Applied Cognative Psychology, 12*, 533–554.

Kvavilashvili, L., & Ellis, J. (1996). Varieties of intentions: Some distinctions and classifications. In M. Brandimonte, G. O. Einstein & M. A. McDaniel (Eds.), *Prospective memory: Theory and application* (pp. 23–51). Mahwah, N.J.: Erlbaum.

Loftus, E. (1971). Memory for intentions: The effect of presence of a cue and interpolated activity. *Psychonomic Science, 23*, 315–316.

Mäntylä, T. (1996). Activating actions and interrupting intentions: Mechanisms of retrieval sensitization in prospective memory. In M. Brandimonte, G. O. Einstein & M. A. McDaniel (Eds.), *Prospective memory: Theory and application* (pp. 93–113). Mahwah, N.J.: Erlbaum.

Maylor, E. A. (1993). Aging and forgetting in prospective and retrospective memory tasks. *Psychology and Aging, 8*, 420–428.

Maylor, E. A. (1996b). Does prospective memory change with age? In M. Brandimonte, G. O. Einstein & M. A. McDaniel (Eds.), *Prospective memory: Theory and application* (pp. 173–197). Mahwah, N.J.: Erlbaum.

Meacham, J. A. (1982). A note on remembering to execute planned actions. *Journal of Applied Developmental Psychology, 3*, 121–133.

Meacham, J. A., & Leiman, B. (1982). Remembering to perform future actions. In U. Neisser (Ed.), *Memory observed: Remembering in natural contexts.* San Francisco: Freeman.

Meier, B., & Graf, P. (2000). Transfer-appropriate processing for prospective memory tests. *Applied Cognitive Psychology, 14*, S11–S27.

Park, D. C., & Kidder, D. P. (1996). Prospective memory and medication adherence. In M. Brandimonte, G. O. Einstein & M. A. McDaniel (Eds.), *Prospective memory: Theory and application* (pp. 369–390). Mahwah, N.J.: Erlbaum.

Rabbitt, P. M. A. (1965). An age decrement in the ability to ignore irrelevant information. *Journal of Gerontology, 20*, 233–238.

Roediger, H. L. (1996). Prospective memory and episodic memory. In M. Brandimonte, G. O. Einstein & M. A. McDaniel (Eds.), *Prospective memory: Theory and application* (pp. 149–155). Mahwah, N.J.: Erlbaum.

Salthouse, T. A. (1980). Age and memory: Strategies for localizing the loss. In L. W. Poon, J. L. Fozard, L. S. Cermak, D. Arenberg & L. W. Thompson (Eds). *New directions in memory and aging: Proceedings of the George A. Talland Memorial Conference.* Hillsdale, N.J.: Erlbaum.

Salthouse, T. A. (1985). *A theory of cognitive aging.* Amsterdam: North-Holland.

Schacter, D. L., & Graf, P. (1986). Effects of elaborative processing on implicit and explicit memory for new associations. *Journal of Experimental Psychology: Learning, Memory, and Cognition, 12,* 432–444.

Spreen, O., & Strauss, E. (1991). *A compendium of neuropsychological tests: Administration, norms, and commentary.* New York: Oxford University press.

Tulving, E. (1972). *Organization of memory.* New York: Academic Press.

Uttl, B., Graf, P., Miller, J., & Tuokko, H. (2001). Age-related changes in pro- and retrospective memory. *Consciousness and Cognition, 10,* 451–472.

Contributors

Rolf Adolfsson is Professor of General Psychiatry at Umeå University. His long-term research interest is dementia and aging and, during the last ten years, molecular biological mechanisms behind schizophrenia, bipolar and unipolar disorders, and memory in aging. In the Betula Study, he is responsible for the databank of blood products, storage of DNA and the final diagnosis of dementia.

Lars Bäckman is Professor of Cognitive Psychology at Uppsala University and Director at the Stockholm Gerontology Research Center. His primary research interest is cognitive functioning in normal aging and dementia, with a special focus on memory. The research activities range from epidemiological work through experimental behavioral studies to functional and receptor imaging of the young and older brain.

Barbara R. Bjorklund teaches psychology at Florida Atlantic University. She has conducted research on children's cognitive development, close relationships in adulthood, and children's eyewitness memory. She is coauthor of *Looking at children* (Brooks/Cole, 1992), *Parents' book of discipline* (Ballentine, 1992), and *Journey through adulthood* (4th edition, Prentice Hall, 2003), and has served as a contributing editor to *Parents Magazine*.

David F. Bjorklund is a Professor of Psychology at the Florida Atlantic University. He is the author of *Children's thinking* (3rd edition, Wadsworth, 2000), coauthor of *The origins of human nature: Evolutionary developmental psychology* (American Psychological Association, 2002), and editor of *False memory creation in children and adults* (Erlbaum, 2000). His primary research interests are in children's memory and strategy development and in evolutionary developmental psychology.

Rhonda Douglas Brown is an Assistant Professor of Educational Studies and Psychology at the University of Cincinnati. Her primary research interests include children's eyewitness memory and false-memory creation.

Nelson Cowan is Professor of Psychological Sciences at the University of Missouri. His research focuses on working memory, its relation to attention, and its development. He currently is trying to quantify limits in the capacity and speed of processing in working-memory tasks. He is the author of a 1995 book in the

Oxford Psychology Series, *Attention and memory: An integrated framework*, as well as various journal articles including a 2001 target article in the *Behavioral and Brain Sciences* on capacity limits. He is a former associate editor of the *Journal of Experimental Psychology: Learning, Memory, and Cognition* and a current associate editor of the *Quarterly Journal of Experimental Psychology*.

Marc Cruts is a postdoctoral researcher in the Molecular Genetics department of the University of Antwerp, Belgium, headed by Prof. Dr. Christine Van Broeckhoven. He has contributed to the latest advancements in the field of molecular genetics of Alzheimer dementia. His current research activities aim at the identification of novel genes involved in Alzheimer dementia.

Richard J. Darby conducted research into aging and prospective memory at the University of Warwick, England, and now teaches psychology at the University of Wolverhampton, England.

Sergio Della Sala is Professor of Neuropsychology in the Department of Psychology at the University of Aberdeen, Scotland. He is currently editor of the journal *Cortex*. Originally trained in medicine, he worked for several years as a consultant neurologist and as a research neuropsychologist in northern Italy, before moving to his current position in Aberdeen. His major interests are in the cognitive impairments following brain damage as a result of brain disease or focal lesions. He is editor of *Mind myths: Exploring popular assumptions about the mind and brain* (Wiley, 1999).

Anik de Ribaupierre teaches differential and developmental psychology at the University of Geneva, in the Faculty of Psychology and Educational Sciences. Much of her research work and publications have been devoted to the study of cognitive development during childhood within a neo-Piagetian perspective. She has more recently extended her work to a lifespan perspective, with a particular focus on working memory and executive functions.

Roger A. Dixon is Professor of Psychology at the University of Victoria and Director of the Victoria Longitudinal Study (VLS). The VLS is a long-term investigation of predictors and profiles of actual changes in cognitive functioning with aging. His research activities are presently supported by the U.S. National Institute on Aging and the Swedish STINT Foundation.

Håkan Edwardsson is a senior psychiatrist, specialized in Geriatric Psychiatry at Norrlands University Hospital. He is one of two responsible medical doctors in the Betula study. He has a research collaboration within the Betula Study the role of ApoE in dementia.

Robyn Fivush is professor of Psychology at Emory University. She is the co-author of *Gender development* and co-editor of *Knowing and Remembering in Young children, The remembering self: Accuracy and construction in the life-story*, and *Ecological approaches to cognition and perception: Essays in honor of Ulric Neisser*. Her research focuses on the early development of autobiographical memory in social context, and the accuracy and retention of early childhood memories.

Laura Fratiglioni is Professor of Medical Epidemiology at the Karolinska Institute and Director at the Stockholm Gerontology Research Center. She is specializing in aging and dementia. Her major research areas are detection of risk factors for aging-related diseases particularly dementing disorders and description of the natural history of disability in old age.

Peter Graf is Professor of Psychology at the University of British Columbia, in Vancouver, Canada. He has recently served as an associate editor for *Memory & Cognition*, and has coedited *Implicit memory: New directions in cognition, development, and neuropsychology* (Erlbaum, 1993). His research focuses on episodic retrospective and prospective memory, its development across the adult lifespan and its breakdown in dementia and other disorders.

Graham Hitch is Professor of Psychology at the University of York, England. He carries out research on human memory and cognition, in particular working memory in children and adults. He shared the 1993 British Psychological Society Award for Cognitive Psychology with Dr. Neil Burgess of University College London for their report of an early connectionist model of phonological working memory.

Robert H. Logie is Anderson Professor and Head of the Department of Psychology at the University of Aberdeen, Scotland. He is currently editor of the *Quarterly Journal of Experimental Psychology* (A), and previously worked at the Medical Research Council Applied Psychology Unit in Cambridge, England. His major interests are in human working memory, particularly visuospatial working memory, both in healthy adults and in brain damaged individuals suffering from impairments of working memory as a result of Alzheimer's Disease or focal lesions. He is author of *Visuo-spatial working memory* (Psychology Press, 1995).

Elizabeth A. Maylor has been a Research Fellow at the Age and Cognitive Performance Research Centre in Manchester, England, at the Medical Research Council Applied Psychology Unit in Cambridge, England, and at the University of Warwick, England, where she is currently a Reader in Psychology. She is co-editor with Timothy J. Perfect of *Models of cognitive aging* (Oxford University Press, 2000). Her research work principally concerns the effects of normal aging on memory and attention.

Lars-Göran Nilsson is the Olof Eneroth Professor of Psychology at Stockholm University. He is Head of the Department of Psychology at Stockholm. His research interests are psychology of memory, aging and cognitive neuroscience. He has been the Director of the Betula Study since its start in 1988.

Lars Nyberg is Professor of Psychology and a Researcher in Cognitive Neuroscience at Umeå University. His research interests are in the area of functional neuroimaging of cognitive processes, with a special focus on episodic memory. The neuroimaging studies involve younger as well as older adults and patients with brain damage.

Nobuo Ohta is Professor of Psychology at the University of Tsukuba in Japan. He received a Ph.D. in psychology from Nagoya University in 1976. He conducted research with Endel Tulving at the University of Toronto during 1980–1981. Since then, his research has been mainly on implicit memory. He was the editor of a special issue on implicit memory for the *Japanese Psychological Review* (vol. 42, 1999). Recently, his research interests have extended to lifespan memory, memory disorders, and social problems relating to human memory. He is a convener of the Tsukuba International Conference on Memory.

David C. Rubin is Professor of Psychological and Brain Sciences at Duke University. He is author of *Memory in oral traditions: The cognitive psychology of epic, ballads, and counting-out rhymes* (Oxford University Press, 1995) and editor of several books on autobiographical memory including *Autobiographical memory* (Cambridge, 1986) and *Remembering our past: Studies in autobiographical memory* (Cambridge, 1996). His research interests are in long-term memory for complex material and events.

Timothy Salthouse is the Brown-Forman Professor of Psychology at The University of Virginia. His research is concerned with the nature and causes of adult age differences in cognitive functioning, and with the role of experience as a potential moderator of the consequences of those differences. He is former editor of the journal *Psychology and Aging*, coeditor of the *Handbook of aging and cognition* (Erlbaum, 2000), and the author of *Theoretical perspectives on cognitive aging* (Erlbaum, 1991).

Brent J. Small is Assistant Professor of Gerontology at the University of South Florida in Tampa. His research focuses on cognition in aging, with a special emphasis on pre-clinical Alzheimer's disease (AD). Currently, he is pursuing hybrid prediction models that include both brain-based and behavioral markers of pre-clinical AD.

Geoff Smith was a Research Fellow at the University of Aberdeen, Scotland, investigating the effects of dementia on prospective memory.

Hidetsugu Tajika is Professor of Psychology at the Aichi University of Education in Japan. His research interests are in memory and problem solving processes. He is the author of *Studies of retrieval processes in episodic memory* (in Japanese, Kazama Shobo, 1989).

Bob Uttl is Assistant Professor of Psychology at the Oregon State University. His primary research interests are changes in perception, processing resources, memory, and other cognitive functions due to normal and pathological aging.

Christine Van Broeckhoven is Professor of Molecular Genetics at the University of Antwerp, Belgium. Her laboratory has a major interest in detecting genes and genetic risk factors for complex neurological and psychiatric diseases. Her major project is Alzheimer dementia, but she is also recently engaged in genetic work on memory per se.

Name Index

Subject Index